Beyond Selflessness

Beyond Selflessness

Reading Nietzsche's Genealogy

Christopher Janaway

OXFORD

UNIVERSITY PRESS

Great Clarendon Street, Oxford OX2 6DP

Oxford University Press is a department of the University of Oxford.
It furthers the University's objective of excellence in research, scholarship,
and education by publishing worldwide in

Oxford New York

Auckland Cape Town Dar es Salaam Hong Kong Karachi
Kuala Lumpur Madrid Melbourne Mexico City Nairobi
New Delhi Shanghai Taipei Toronto

With offices in

Argentina Austria Brazil Chile Czech Republic France Greece
Guatemala Hungary Italy Japan Poland Portugal Singapore
South Korea Switzerland Thailand Turkey Ukraine Vietnam

Oxford is a registered trade mark of Oxford University Press
in the UK and in certain other countries

Published in the United States
by Oxford University Press Inc., New York

British Library Cataloguing in Publication Data
Data available

Library of Congress Cataloging in Publication Data
Data available

Typeset by Laserwords Private Limited, Chennai, India
Printed in Great Britain
on acid-free paper by
Biddles Ltd., King's Lynn, Norfolk

ISBN 978–0–19–927969–2

10 9 8 7 6 5 4 3 2 1

For Christine,
Nick, Peter, Freddy,
and Mateus

Preface

I have been reading Nietzsche for over twenty-five years, but for a long time felt unable to start writing a book about him. My background included a training in analytical philosophy, and from that perspective Nietzsche was once so far from 'central' as to lie off the edge of the known world. Though happy with the no-nonsense virtues of analytical philosophy, I found myself on something of a centrifugal path. Given the main preoccupations from my time as a graduate student onwards—Schopenhauer, Plato, aesthetics, the philosophy of art—Nietzsche always hovered on the horizon. I felt a desire to do something about him, but he made me nervous and insecure. I would sometimes give a short series of lectures, musing over a sequence of extracts from his works, but they always sounded bizarre and disconnected as soon as one spoke them aloud, and suddenly seemed all too clearly designed to sabotage the kind of commentary a philosopher was supposed to give.

In recent years the reception of Nietzsche has certainly changed for the better. Philosophy itself in the English-speaking world seems a bigger, more pluralistic, and in healthy ways a less self-assured field than it used to be, and Nietzsche now falls within the circle of legitimate figures to study. There is a corpus of responsible and valuable philosophical work on Nietzsche, without which I could not have come near to writing this book. And yet, I am still not sure if I ever want to be comfortable with Nietzsche. We now see that it is eminently possible to search Nietzsche's works for some propositions, and occasionally even some arguments, that sound plausible and sensible to today's academic philosophers. But doing that *alone* does not mesh with my experience of reading Nietzsche, and surely cannot really mesh with anyone's. So in this book I am often to be found enquiring why Nietzsche writes poetically, metaphorically, provocatively, ambiguously, with misdirection and avoidance of straightforward argument, and reflecting not only on local portions of his texts, but on the kinds of responses we may have to reading them. Nietzsche's project in the *Genealogy* is to discover truths about why we hold our contemporary moral values and to persuade us that we could shift our allegiance to different, healthier values. But both diagnosis and cure demand, in Nietzsche's view, not merely the construction of philosophical arguments, but a personal confrontation with conflicting and uncomfortable feelings that stem from our drives. In fact, I believe, disrupting our confidence in philosophy is part and parcel for Nietzsche of questioning our deepest-seated values. I welcome his inclusion as a bona fide philosopher, provided we do not have to pretend that that is all he is.

The work towards what eventually became this book began more than ten years ago and for a while remained somewhat piecemeal. I would like to express my gratitude to the Arts and Humanities Research Board for the award of research leave grants in 2001 and 2004, without which the pieces might never have come together in the way they have. The following published articles and chapters contain material in common with parts of the book, sometimes substantially revised: 'Nietzsche's Illustration of the Art of Exegesis', *European Journal of Philosophy*, 5 (1997), 251–68; 'Schopenhauer as Nietzsche's Educator', in Christopher Janaway (ed.), *Willing and Nothingness: Schopenhauer as Nietzsche's Educator* (Oxford: Oxford University Press, 1998), 13–36; 'Nietzsche's Artistic Revaluation', in José Luis Bermúdez and Sebastian Gardner (eds), *Art and Morality* (London: Routledge, 2003), 260–76; 'Schopenhauer et la valeur du "non egoïste"', in Christian Bonnet and Jean Salem (eds), *La Raison dévoilé: Études Schopenhaueriennes* (Paris, J. Vrin, 2005), 81–94 (text in French); 'Naturalism and Genealogy', in Keith Ansell Pearson (ed.), *A Companion to Nietzsche* (Oxford: Blackwell, 2006), 337–52; 'Nietzsche on Free Will, Autonomy, and the Sovereign Individual', *Proceedings of the Aristotelian Society*, suppl. vol. 80 (2006), 339–57; 'Guilt, Bad Conscience, and Self-Punishment in Nietzsche's *Genealogy*', in Brian Leiter and Neil Sinhababu (eds), *Nietzsche and Morality* (Oxford: Oxford University Press, 2007), 138–54. I gratefully acknowledge permission to reprint in all cases.

Over the years I have benefited from numerous objections, questions, and suggestions on the part of students, colleagues, and audiences at talks and presentations, not to mention much encouragement from different quarters. I offer my to thanks to everyone concerned. Two readers for Oxford University Press gave acute comments that led to a number of late improvements. I would specifically like to thank Aaron Ridley (who read the whole book in a penultimate draft), Brian Leiter, Sebastian Gardner,

Simon May, David Owen, John Richardson, Maudemarie Clark, Robert Pippin, Mathias Risse, Lanier Anderson, Bernard Reginster, Gudrun von Tevenar, Daniel Came, Chris Sykes, Peter Poellner, John Wilcox, Robin Small, Keith Ansell Pearson, Paul Loeb, and Elijah Millgram. I owe a very special debt of gratitude to Ken Gemes for being with me throughout the book's genesis as collaborator, critic, host, and friend over countless cups of tea. And my greatest appreciation and love goes to Christine Lopes for her love and support, and for challenging me about Nietzsche. The book is dedicated to her and to my four great sons.

C.J.
Southampton, England
January 2007

Contents

A Note on Translations and Abbreviations

Unless otherwise stated, I have used the following translations of Nietzsche's works, referring to them with the following abbreviations.

A	*The Anti-Christ*, trans. R. J. Hollingdale (with *Twilight of the Idols*) (Harmondsworth: Penguin, 1968)
BGE	*Beyond Good and Evil*, ed. Rolf-Peter Horstmann and Judith Norman, trans. Judith Norman (Cambridge: Cambridge University Press, 2002)
BT	*The Birth of Tragedy*, ed. Michael Tanner, trans. Shaun Whiteside (Harmondsworth: Penguin, 1990)
D	*Daybreak*, ed. Maudemarie Clark and Brian Leiter, trans. R. J. Hollingdale (Cambridge: Cambridge University Press, 1997)
EH	*Ecce Homo*, ed. and trans. Walter Kaufmann (with *On the Genealogy of Morals*) (New York: Vintage Books, 1967)
GM	*On the Genealogy of Morality*, trans. Maudemarie Clark and Alan J. Swensen (Indianapolis: Hackett, 1998)
GS	*The Gay Science*, ed. Bernard Williams, trans. Josefine Nauckhoff and Adrian del Caro (Cambridge: Cambridge University Press, 2001)
HA	*Human, All Too Human*, trans. R. J. Hollingdale (Cambridge: Cambridge University Press, 1986)
NcW	*Nietzsche contra Wagner*, in *The Anti-Christ, Ecce Homo, Twilight of the Idols, and Other Writings*, ed. Aaron Ridley, trans. Judith Norman (Cambridge: Cambridge University Press, 2005)
TI	*Twilight of the Idols*, trans. R. J. Hollingdale (with *The Anti-Christ*) (Harmondsworth: Penguin, 1968)
UM	*Untimely Meditations*, trans. R. J. Hollingdale (Cambridge: Cambridge University Press, 1983)
WLN	*Writings from the Late Notebooks*, ed. Rüdiger Bittner, trans. Kate Sturge (Cambridge: Cambridge University Press, 2003)

WP   *The Will to Power*, ed. Walter Kaufmann, trans. Walter
          Kaufmann and R. J. Hollingdale (New York: Vintage Books,
          1968)
Z   *Thus Spoke Zarathustra*, trans. R. J. Hollingdale
          (Harmondsworth: Penguin, 1969)

References to Nietzsche's works are by *section* number, not page number, with the exception of *WLN*, where I refer to page numbers. The use of [...] in a quoted passage from Nietzsche indicates an editorial omission. Where ... occurs without brackets it is a punctuation device of Nietzsche's own.

   German texts of Nietzsche referred to are:

KSA   *Kritische Studienausgabe*, ed. Giorgio Colli and Mazzino
          Montinari, 15 vols (Munich: Deutscher Taschenbuch Verlag
          and Walter de Gruyter, 1988)
SB   *Sämtliche Briefe. Studienausgabe*, ed. Giorgio Colli and Mazzino
          Montinari, 8 vols (Munich: Deutscher Taschenbuch Verlag
          and Walter de Gruyter, 1986)

1

Nietzsche's Aims and Targets

1 Reading Nietzsche's *Genealogy*

This book offers a reading of Friedrich Nietzsche's *On the Genealogy of Morality*, the work which has come to be regarded, especially in the English-speaking world, as his most sustained philosophical achievement, his masterpiece, and the most vital of his writings for any student of Nietzsche, of ethics, or of the history of modern thought. I shall refer to other texts by Nietzsche, especially his earlier published works *Beyond Good and Evil*, *The Gay Science*, and *Daybreak*, for elucidations of what is at stake in the *Genealogy*. But the centre of gravity is always the interpretation of the *Genealogy* itself, and the questions a reading of it raises: the nature of those modern moral values that locate goodness in selflessness, in compassion towards others, and in guilty hostility towards one's own instincts; the psychology and history that generated these values; their contribution to sickness and health; the complexity of human feelings and drives; the nature of philosophical truth-seeking; the significance of suffering; and the call for the creation of new values that affirm rather than deny life. I begin with some remarks about the kind of reading offered in the following pages.

In the increasingly urgent concern with Nietzsche in recent times two extreme trends are apparent. One extreme has reflected to the point of obsession on the nature of reading itself, on masks, playfulness, arbitrariness, and the radical problematization of meaning. Nietzsche has been co-opted into an assemblage of very recent theory and hailed as its originating and exemplary figure, and sometimes it has been thought that his writings are not 'about' anything other than style, the nature of metaphor, the undecidability of meaning, or the instability of the 'author position'. At the other extreme it has become possible to adopt towards Nietzsche's extraordinary, perplexing, and emotive literary achievement an attitude that amounts to denial, as if he were just an ordinary philosopher with a programme of theories about knowledge and reality, the nature of the human mind, and the status of values, that differed only superficially from the contents of a contemporary journal article. Both extremes in Nietzsche interpretation, for all the admirable sophistication and insight they may have shown, have tended to over-polarize and oversimplify debate; worse, they have risked stretching Nietzsche's unique writings between two alien forms of dogmatism about method.

The idea that present-day assumptions about philosophy may be 'alien' to historical texts is vulnerable to the challenge that we cannot strip away all our prior assumptions and view the bare text for what it 'really' is. One point likely to be agreed upon wherever one stands on issues of philosophical method is that no one approaches any text without applying to it their own aims, interests, theories, assumptions, prejudices, anxieties, horizons, perspectives, or whatever else they may be called. Reading Nietzsche himself has taught us that much. But that we must construe the text from some angle or other does not mean that all angles are equally appropriate. So one aim and one anxiety behind the present book is that Nietzsche not be treated as though he were some determinate species of theorist from the latter half of the twentieth century, or as though, were he so, he would somehow be improved.

In general, then, I do not see the prime task as that of fitting Nietzsche into an independently existing theoretical programme. Rather I aim, somewhat naively no doubt, to transmit something of the richness and reward to be found in reading Nietzsche's texts themselves. Friends have accused me of very close reading, and indeed I have often tried to start with some stretch of the *Genealogy*—one of its treatises, sections, sentences, or prominent words—and work outwards to an interpretation of the assumptions and aims that might best make sense of it. The non-linearity and intricate construction of a text such as the *Genealogy* demand that it be read slowly, with care and imagination; its rhetorical power, provocativeness, and moodiness call for an open and self-conscious awareness of how it is affecting one and how it may be meant to affect one.

The *Genealogy* centres on the morality that has arisen from the Judaeo-Christian tradition, whose values, according to Nietzsche, give priority to selflessness, holding it good to be compassionate and self-sacrificing, to suppress one's natural self, to feel guilt about one's instincts, and to value a projected 'higher world' of absolute value of which one's imperfect human nature is unworthy. Nietzsche poses two large questions about this morality: How did we come to believe in it so firmly and with such powerful emotional attachments? and, Are these beliefs and attachments good, advantageous, or healthy for human beings? On my account Nietzsche is seeking truths in answer to both questions. The historical part of his enquiry relies on the idea that there are truths about the complex manner in which our values came into existence, became entrenched, and were subject to various elaborations and reinterpretations. The truths in question are psychological, concerning generic states of mind that, according to Nietzsche's hypotheses, explain the formation of affective and judgemental states at different stages of culture and leave their residue in today's concepts and feelings. For example, Nietzsche claims that the valuing of passive humility and harmlessness towards others arose from a feeling of resentful hatred in those who were subservient but lacked the power to retaliate against their masters. Again, he claims that guilt came to be valued positively because feelings of suffering inflicted internally upon ourselves by our natural instincts could thus become legitimate and meaningful to us.

The evaluative part of Nietzsche's project asks us to question the value of morality, and proclaims it true that morality is inimical to human flourishing and progress, in particular the prospering of higher types of human being. The self-hatred and emotional conflictedness promoted by morality are, in Nietzsche's eyes, forms of sickness that produce more suffering than they cure and lead us on a downward path towards nihilism and a total negation of our self-worth. Hence Nietzsche repeatedly moots the creation of new values that lie beyond the good and evil of the Christian inheritance, beyond selflessness, and in the direction of self-affirmation or self-satisfaction, states of which not everyone will be capable, and which may be attained, if at all, by different human beings in different ways.

While so far none of this departs in any large-scale manner from recent analytical readings, this book stands apart in its determination never to lose sight of the unique and powerful ways in which Nietzsche affects the reader as he pursues his philosophical aims. I give thematic prominence to questions about Nietzsche's method of writing, and seek to show why we should not succumb to the analytical habit of sidelining such questions. To treat Nietzsche's ways of writing—explicitly or implicitly—as mere modes of presentation, detachable in principle from some elusive set of propositions in which his philosophy might be thought to consist, is to miss a great part of Nietzsche's real importance to philosophy. Nietzsche simply does not behave as a conventional philosopher. He is not averse to putting forward hypotheses—candidates for acceptance as true—or even to presenting an argument sometimes where necessary. But more often than not he uses a wide range of rhetorical effects that appear to persuade, coax, or tempt the reader by quite other means, or to play with our attitudes to an extent that pushes us to the brink of bafflement. Nietzsche's way of writing addresses our affects, feelings, or emotions. It provokes sympathies, antipathies, and ambivalences that lie in the modern psyche below the level of rational decision and impersonal argument. I argue that this is not some gratuitous exercise in 'style' that could be edited out of Nietzsche's thought. Rather, for Nietzsche to have proceeded as the paradigmatic philosopher, excluding personal emotions from the investigation, seeking to persuade by impersonal rational considerations alone, would in his eyes have risked failure to grasp the true nature of our values and loss of an opportunity to call them into question. Without the rhetorical provocations, without the revelation of what we find gruesome, shaming, embarrassing, comforting, and heart-warming, we would neither comprehend nor be able to revalue our current values. On the one hand, feelings play a vital explanatory role in the genesis of our moral attitudes, and, on the other, the transition to new values that Nietzsche seeks can occur only through an alteration in our deepest-seated habits of feeling, a change of the same enormity as the shift that once led to the formation of Judaeo-Christian values.

For Nietzsche revising our views about the nature of our values goes together with revising our conceptions of self. Nietzsche's hypothesis is that each individual is a composite of drives and affective states, of which our conscious knowledge is never a complete or adequate reflection. We are not essentially rational or essentially unified or essentially known to ourselves. The drives that compose us compete and strive against one another and organize themselves hierarchically, giving rise to a multiplicity of feelings and attitudes within the individual. This view of the self, I would argue, has to be reflected back upon the self that is seeking knowledge of the history and value of our values. If we readers of Nietzsche are a plurality of drives and affects of the kind his texts suggest, do we not learn and understand best by engaging more of ourselves? Philosophers have tended to think that feelings and natural drives impede the search for knowledge, and that eliminating them in favour of the single viewpoint of the pure impersonal eye (or 'I') is to move closer to objectivity and an ideal form of knowing. Against this Nietzsche urges—and this is the core of his so-called 'perspectivism'—that engaging a multiplicity of feelings that better reflects the nature of our selves is both indispensable and beneficial for knowledge. So Nietzsche's emotive and pluralistic style can be seen as integral to a reorientation of our conception of enquiry away from that traditionally accepted by philosophy, and this reorientation can be seen as needed before we can comprehend and transcend the values of morality.

Nietzsche's challenge to philosophy's conception of itself is not just an instrumental means towards his critical investigation of morality. For he sees in philosophy's habitual self-understanding as an impersonal, objective enquiry into truth a mutation of the very same valuing of selflessness that underlies morality. Expunge one's feelings and prejudices, investigate the world as a 'pure subject', ideally from no particular point of view within it, fight against the influence of one's natural inclinations, be disinterested—why? Philosophers, Nietzsche claims, have conceived their task and themselves as if they were simply rational subjects, have tended to devalue their own feelings and subjectivity, the body, and even the entire empirical world of change, imperfection, and transience, and have sought something 'higher', more 'real' or 'objective', in subservience to which they must suppress their natural selves. He claims that they have conceived their task and themselves in these ways because of a persistent involvement with an ideal of asceticism whose origin is in Christian morality. The final six sections of the *Genealogy*, which I regard as its true culmination and one of Nietzsche's most profound passages, present the thought that the core of philosophy—what remains of it once God, the eternal, the absolute, and the transcendent are cast into oblivion by a rigorously scientific form of investigation—is a belief in the unconditional value of truth. This pure heart of philosophy is itself, he claims, the most resilient strain of the morality of selflessness. In setting up the pursuit of truth as an unconditional value, one is not only mimicking Christianity's ideal of self-denial in the face of a single absolutely valuable 'other', but enacting a value that is literally moral: that of being truthful at all costs. Nietzsche urges us to question whether truth at all costs is something we should be pursuing.

It is not that truth has no value for Nietzsche, let alone that he thinks we can have no knowledge of truths—on the contrary, he pursues truths about psychology and history throughout the book, and makes it clear that the drive to truthfulness is the most powerful instrument in the modern destruction of Christian religious doctrines and the morality of selflessness—rather that philosophy's assumption of the unconditional value of truth is questionable. Why (since Plato) does it not respect the creation of fictions, artistic beautifications of both world and self, as at least equally valuable for life? Why can it not leave life unexamined to some extent, refraining from the relentless scrutiny of beliefs, content not to enquire whether they are true or false, but rather to acquiesce in those that are helpful to us? Why should it matter absolutely whether they are true or not? The ending of the *Genealogy* is not so much a closing as an opening out: we must experiment with the idea that pursuing and holding true beliefs is not of unconditional value, and until we have questioned our own assumed status as pure seekers of knowledge, we will not fully have called into question the value of the morality of selflessness.

2 The Opposition

The Preface to the *Genealogy* makes it clear that Nietzsche seeks a critique of the values of morality, and plants the thought that these values are inimical to the highest potentials for humanity. Setting himself against a majority assumption of the Western culture that has inherited Judaeo-Christian values, he is not surprised to have found no followers of his own, and considers his book hard to read. (He later predicts that it will be 200 years before there is cultural change sufficient to eliminate what he is attacking; see *GM* III. 27.) He expects most of his readers to hold that denying one's own interests and desires for the benefit of others, refraining from expressing one's own will and aggressive instincts, being motivated by the well-being of others before one's own, is not only good, but *the* good. His task is to turn his reader to asking: What psychological explanations are there for the fact that human beings have thought it healthy to be unegoistic? Is it good to be unegoistic? What if we stopped thinking it good to be unegoistic, stopped assigning unqualified value to selflessness in its many manifestations? What if we even lost the habit of dividing acts and character types into 'egoistic' and 'unegoistic'?[1]

The *Genealogy*—subtitled *Eine Streitschrift*, 'A Polemic'—devotes much of its energy to a diagnosis of the origins of Christianity (Nietzsche describes it in these terms in his retrospective assessment in the section of *Ecce Homo* entitled 'Genealogy of Morals') and presents a many-sided critique of the influence of Christianity's values on contemporary European thought and culture. But is the *Genealogy* well calculated to persuade genuine Christians out of their faith? Are Christians its main target audience? There is a second-hand anecdote that tells of Nietzsche imploring an elderly believing Catholic of his acquaintance not to read his books because 'there was so much in them that was bound to hurt her feelings';[2] and he would have been right to think that some Christians might be more offended than persuaded by the *Genealogy*. Some might laugh or just turn away. But a *Streitschrift* should do more than insult or provoke rejection—and if Nietzsche had been solely or primarily concerned to influence Christian believers, his book might seem a miscalculation. Nietzsche's attack seems better addressed to the non-religious (or not especially religious) person who clings to a conception of morality inherited unthinkingly from Christianity. Nietzsche is then in the posture of the 'madman' from *The Gay Science*, section 125, addressing those around him in the marketplace who carry on as if not believing in God were a matter of little consequence; or of the section where he says 'God is dead; but given the way people are, there may still for millennia be caves in which they show his shadow' (*GS* 108).

The *Genealogy* also contains a strong strand of opposition to philosophers for the way they have attempted to account for morality. In his Preface, Nietzsche names just two thinkers as his antagonists: Arthur Schopenhauer and Paul Rée. I regard it as significant that no other thinker is assigned such a role, and, taking Nietzsche at his word on this matter, will use the

---

[1] For recent discussion of Nietzsche on egoism, altruism, and selfless motivation, see Reginster (2000*a*, *b*).

[2] From a memoir by Resa von Schirnhofer, in Gilman (1987: 195). The elderly acquaintance in question was an Englishwoman called Emily Fynn. Nietzsche delighted in the company of Fynn and her daughter, mentioning them often in correspondence. In 1887 Nietzsche asked his friend Overbeck to send him a copy of Tertullian, from which he wanted to extract passages showing the vitriolic vindictiveness of Christianity (this became *GM* I. 15), and in the same letters he mentions having a merry time with the Fynns at social occasions in the hotels of Sils-Maria (Letters to Overbeck, 17 July and 30 Aug. 1887, *SB* viii. 109–11, 138–41).

philosophies of Schopenhauer and Rée as starting points, returning to them with some frequency as points of orientation. At different stages both had inspired Nietzsche's earlier thought. The pessimism and elevated aesthetic theory of Schopenhauer's *The World as Will and Representation* had swept him off his feet as a young man and influenced his first book, *The Birth of Tragedy*.[3] Rée's naturalistic 'English' style of thinking had given his work a new direction somewhat later.[4] But by the time of the *Genealogy* both can be evoked as pasts he is happy to leave behind, embodying that which he had to 'struggle almost solely with' and that to which he 'emphatically said "no" [...] proposition by proposition' (*GM*, Preface, 5, 4). So part of what is meant by the book's label 'A Polemic' is, arguably, that Nietzsche is waging war against the explanations and evaluations of morality given by his 'great teacher' and his closest ever collaborator, and thereby fighting off elements in his own intellectual past. Nietzsche targets the values of morality for his critique, but is also in open conflict with specific modes of theorizing about morality that he regards as complicit with the values of morality itself.

Schopenhauer and Rée are very different thinkers, but they have features in common. Both reject the metaphysics of Christianity—God, immaterial souls, rewards in an afterlife, and any divine order or purpose to the world. Both deny that being moral leads to greater happiness, or that human beings can make any genuine or substantial moral progress. Both argue that human individuals lack free will and responsibility for their actions. Schopenhauer, unshackled from the dogmas and inherent optimism of Christianity, is able, as Nietzsche says, to pose the 'terrifying' question of the meaning of existence (*GS* 357), answering it by propounding a global metaphysics of the will, a blind striving force that underlies all beings and traps us in a hateful round of desire and suffering, unless we renounce our individuality and attachment to life. Rée similarly rejects all Christian explanations of values, but goes one step further by ousting Schopenhauer's transcendent metaphysics altogether in favour of a scrupulous empiricist naturalism. Rée is also a would-be genealogist, substituting an account

---

[3] For an account of Nietzsche's pro-Schopenhauerian period, see Janaway (1998*b*: 13–27).

[4] The best account of Nietzsche's intellectual relationship with Rée can be found in Small (2005). See also Donnellan (1982); Small (2001: 180–6; 2003). See Pfeiffer (1970) for a thorough collection of evidence, much of it bearing on personal relations between Nietzsche, Rée, and Lou Salomé. For more on Rée, see Chs. 2, 3, and 5 below.

of the origin and development of our moral feelings for Schopenhauer's deliberately ahistorical picture of human motivation.[5]

Yet both these hard-nosed opponents of the Christian world-view are in thrall to the assumption that selflessness, compassion, or what Rée continually calls 'the unegoistic' (*das Unegoistische*) is constitutive of morality. Both regard the unegoistic as 'value in itself' (*GM*, Preface, 4, 5). Indeed Rée appears to accept Schopenhauer's conception of what morality is—essentially selfless compassion, justice, and kindness—and seek to explain it without recourse to Schopenhauer's extreme metaphysical claims. Both thinkers take it for granted that selfless morality can be justified in some non-Christian manner, either within a pessimistic metaphysics of will or by a naturalist, evolutionary account. The importance to us of Nietzsche's named antagonists is not merely that they are the catalysts for the polemic of the *Genealogy*, but that they exemplify a widespread assumption that selflessness has positive *value*—they are representative of a more pervasive problem 'in present-day Europe [...] the prejudice that takes "moral", "unegoistic", "*désintéressé*" to be concepts of equal value' which 'already rules with the force of an "*idée fixe*" and sickness in the head' (*GM* I. 2). Yet it is this very prejudice that needs to be cured, according to Nietzsche, this very value that must be called into question. Read this way, Nietzsche's attack on moral values incorporates a polemic against the kind of anti-, or non-, or post-Christian theorist of morality who has not dispersed the 'shadows of God', who has inherited the conviction that, if genuine value is to be reached, it is the self that must in some way be suppressed, denied, levelled, or sacrificed. Nietzsche's book is both a critique of value conceived as selflessness and a battle with those of us who still conceive it thus despite disowning the theistic world-view.

3 Genealogy and the Value of Moral Values

Nietzsche introduces the task of genealogy by saying that 'we need a knowledge of the conditions and circumstances out of which [moral

---

[5] For Nietzsche, Rée falls into the category of those (albeit unsuccessful) 'English psychologists whom we [...] have to thank for the only attempts so far to produce a history of the genesis of morality' (*GM* I. 1), while Schopenhauer's total lack of a historical sense is 'un-German to the point of genius' (*BGE* 204). One fails in the attempt at history; the other fails even to attempt it.

values] have grown, under which they have developed and shifted' (*GM*, Preface, 6). But he juxtaposes this task of discovering origins with another, more emphatically expressed: 'we need a *critique* of moral values, *for once the value of these values must itself be called into question*'; '*what value do they themselves have?* Have they inhibited or furthered human flourishing up until now?' (*GM*, Preface, 6, 3). A prime methodological question facing the reader of the *Genealogy* is, therefore: How does the account of the *origins* of moral values relate to the task of *evaluating* them? Nietzsche more than once gives a succinct answer to that question. In *Ecce Homo* he calls the *Genealogy*'s essays psychological studies 'preliminary' to the revaluation of all values, and in the Preface to the *Genealogy* he describes 'hypothesizing about the origin of morality', his own included, as undertaken 'solely for the sake of an end to which it is one means among many', that of questioning 'the value of morality [...] in particular [...] the value of the unegoistic, of the instincts of compassion, self-denial, self-sacrifice' (*GM*, Preface, 5). This strongly suggests that genealogy, knowing or hypothesizing the conditions of the origin of our values, is distinct from, and instrumental towards, the critique or revaluation of values that Nietzsche hopes will take place. Genealogy does not itself complete the process of revaluation, but is a necessary start on the way to it.[6]

First, then, what is genealogy? Alexander Nehamas has written that for Nietzsche genealogy is 'history, correctly practiced', and more recent writers have echoed that statement.[7] But this formulation may run the risk of being uninformative: there are some notable differences between genealogy and other forms of history. Like ordinary family genealogy, Nietzsche's investigation of morality is restricted to those aspects of the past that causally terminate in our specific present-day states, and so is a highly selective exercise, ignoring vast tracts of history from which our current attitudes do not clearly descend. If I am pursuing my own genealogy, my being a descendant of *X* is decisive in *X*'s being a salient object of study for me. Only tangentially, if at all, do I care to discover who lived in the

---

[6] Loeb (2005) argues that because of Nietzsche's aristocratic conception of values he is able to regard the origin of moral values in slavish attitudes as already sufficient critique of their value. However, Nietzsche is not writing for readers who already subscribe to aristocratic values; hence his revaluative strategy does not, I suggest, rely solely on genealogy, but uses it in a 'preliminary' way as a means towards revaluation.

[7] Nehamas (1985: 246 n. 1); see also Geuss (2001: 336); Leiter (2002: 166 n. 1, 180).

neighbouring plot of land to my ancestors, how they fit into wider patterns of change in social attitudes or movements of labour, what were the most significant political events and personages of that age, and so on. Genealogy lacks the horizontal spread of interest characteristic of much historical work and is a vertical tree-shaped study, rooted in ourselves as the eventual outcome. So too with Nietzsche's genealogy: it is extremely selective of its past and always guided by the question, How did *we* come to feel and think in *these* ways of ours? Indeed, I shall argue that such enquiry is ultimately to be conducted in the first-person singular. The individual is the target for the kind of historical scrutiny Nietzsche describes: 'Your judgement, "that is right" has a prehistory in your drives, inclinations, aversions, experiences [...] you have to ask, "*how* did it emerge there?" and then also, "*what* is really impelling me to listen to it?"' (GS 335).

The history provided by Nietzschean genealogy is to a large extent psychological. It seeks truths about interpretations made in the past and explains their being made in terms of the psychological states of those who made them. For example, in the First Treatise of the *Genealogy* it claims truth for the proposition 'The slaves in ancient societies had a reactive feeling of *ressentiment* and attained an enhanced feeling of their own power by interpreting the exercising of power by the strong as something evil that no one ought to do and that all are free not to do'. Genealogy involves claims that psychological states such as *ressentiment* really existed in the past and that they gave rise to more ingrained feelings of inclination and aversion towards certain behaviours and character-types, which in turn issued in the concepts 'good' and 'evil' and many generally held beliefs such as 'It is evil to exercise one's power over someone weaker than oneself'.

Another notable feature of Nietzsche's procedure, however, is that it involves a projected or imagined generic psychology, not properly localized to times, places, or individuals. For example, when Nietzsche diagnoses the psychological origins of Christian values, we start in a Greek world reminiscent of the Homeric age, but are sometimes among early Christian sects and the Roman Empire, at other times somewhere vague in the history of Judaism, and so on.[8] What interests Nietzsche is the type of psychological state—especially in this case the undischarged reactive aggression of *ressentiment*—that can explain why a type of personality in a

---

[8] Discussion with Ken Gemes brought this to my attention.

type of predicament adopts a type of values. Types are not wholly ahistorical for him—one cannot have a 'masterly' or 'slavish' character without specific cultural structures in which such characters can form—but their influence can endure through history into very different cultures. In Western culture, for the most part, we do not have individuals standing in master–slave relationships, but, for Nietzsche, the residue of the psychological states that produced master-values and slave-values persists and informs our own evaluations.

Nietzsche's genealogy, then, is an attempt to explain our having those beliefs and feelings that constitute our moral values in the here and now, by tracing their causal origins to generic psychological states—typically drives, affects, inclinations, and aversions—that we can reconstruct as having existed in certain types of human being in the real past, and as having caused our present attitudes through the mediation of interpretations and conceptual innovations made by successive developments of culture. This enquiry into the prehistory of one's attitudes is not a dispassionate exercise for Nietzsche, but includes an engagement of one's own affects and prejudices. I have already remarked on the prominence of positive and negative feelings, inclinations, and aversions in Nietzsche's genealogical explanations. He has a related conviction that one can truly succeed in an investigation into one's values only by being emotionally involved in it: 'It makes the most telling difference whether a thinker has a personal relationship to his problems and finds in them his destiny, his distress, and his greatest happiness' (GS 345). Rée, as we shall see, exemplifies for Nietzsche the genealogist who fails partly because he is wedded to a conception of cool, detached scientific discovery and does not personalize his enquiry. I shall argue that Nietzsche's evident concern to provoke the affects of his own readers is intimately related to his genealogical project, and that in this way Nietzsche's conception of 'history, correctly practiced' is once again quite distinctive.

Recalling that such discovery of past psychological origins is in the aid of Nietzsche's more important aim for the present and the future, namely the critique, or 'calling into question', of moral values, we need now to ask how he conceives such a critique. In works later than the *Genealogy* Nietzsche describes his task, with increasing emphasis and shrillness, as the revaluation of all values (*Umwerthung aller Werthe*).[9] He spoke of the task under the same name in a passage of the earlier *Beyond Good and Evil*, hoping for '*new philosophers* [...] who are strong and original enough to give impetus to opposed valuations' (*BGE* 203). It is a surprise then to find in the *Genealogy* itself only three occurrences of the form of words 'revaluation of values'. One is in Nietzsche's mention of a book project still in progress entitled *The Will to Power: Attempt at a Re-valuation of All Values*.[10] This suggests that he regards the revaluation as happening, if at all, in a future beyond the *Genealogy*, an impression confirmed by his retrospective description of the *Genealogy* as 'three [...] preliminary studies by a psychologist for a revaluation of all values'.[11]

By contrast, the two further mentions of 'revaluation of values' in the text of the *Genealogy* apply to something that has already taken place: the invention by the Jews of the opposition 'good' and 'evil' which reigns supreme in morality today.[12] Nietzsche is hoping for a repeat or reversal of what has happened before in history: that behaviour and attitudes and types of human character that have been evaluated negatively should be evaluated positively and vice versa—indeed, *Umwerthung* carries a sense of values being reversed or turned on their head, not merely examined afresh, as may be connoted by the 'critique' or 'calling into question' of the *Genealogy*'s Preface.[13] Specifically, in calling for a revaluation, Nietzsche would be calling for the assignment of positive value to characteristics of human behaviour that have been decried as 'egoistic', and negative value to those that have been lauded as 'unegoistic' or selfless. So, for instance, strong

[9] See *TI*, Foreword; 'The Four Great Errors', 2; 'What I Owe to the Ancients', 5; *A* 13, 61, 62; *EH*, 'Why I Am So Wise', 1; 'Why I Am So Clever', 9; 'Human, All Too Human', 6; 'Daybreak', 1; 'Beyond Good and Evil', 1; 'Genealogy of Morals'; 'Twilight of the Idols', 3; 'The Case of Wagner', 4; 'Why I Am a Destiny', 1, 7.

[10] *GM* III. 27. Nietzsche never completed such a work, the eventual publication with this title after his death being, as is commonly known, a compilation by his sister Elisabeth Förster-Nietzsche and Heinrich Köselitz, known as Peter Gast. The evidence suggests, furthermore, that Nietzsche himself abandoned the attempt to publish such a book. See Magnus (1988*b*); Montinari (1982).

[11] *EH*, 'Genealogy of Morals'. Note, however, that he can also describe the revaluation of former values as having begun before the *Genealogy* in *BGE* (see *EH*, 'Beyond Good and Evil', 1).

[12] *GM* I. 7, 8. Ridley (2005*a*: 185) comments rightly that 'it is partly in proposing that, and in attempting to explain how, traditional morality *is* the product of such a re-evaluation that Nietzsche's own re-evaluation consists'.

[13] Ridley (2005*a*), by contrast, hears the connotation of an open-ended calling into question also in *Umwerthung*, hence preferring 're-evaluation' to the more common 'revaluation' (p. 171 n. 1).

self-expression or self-determination might become something positive in the eyes of someone who had made the new revaluation, and self-suppression, conformity, and putting others first would become something negative. This, I suggest, would mean more than just making judgements that attach value-terms to the respective traits, more than just a change in beliefs. In *Daybreak*, the work where he reports that his battle against the morality of selflessness began,[14] Nietzsche announced his programme with the words 'We have to *learn to think differently*—in order at last, perhaps very late on, to attain even more: *to feel differently*' (D 103). The person who has genuinely revalued the prevailing Judaeo-Christian values will, then, have his or her affective polarities altered, and will be horrified, ashamed, afraid, contented, admiring, or loving in ways that differ from the present norms—although, as Nietzsche says in the same passage, it does not follow that he or she will approve of all types of action that are now condemned, or vice versa, only that he or she will approve and condemn for 'other reasons than hitherto'.

That takes me to a final opening remark. For all his cataclysmic portrayal of the future revaluation as 'the tremendous task', 'the great war', 'the shattering lightning bolt',[15] Nietzsche envisages something in one respect more modest than the transformation that brought about Christianity and Western morality. That is, Nietzsche does not expect or even desire that *all* agents, *all* judging subjects, will share allegiance to the same new values. The expectation of common and even universal values is built into current morality, but is indeed, in Nietzsche's eyes, precisely one of the deleterious aspects of current morality that a revaluation could free us from. Nietzsche emphasizes how rare, few, and unique will be the 'new philosophers' who have qualities sufficient to transform their values,[16] how they will 'create tables of what is good that are new and all their own', how they will be ashamed if others share their judgements and taste, and 'nauseous about some people's moral chatter about others'.[17] If current moral values come to be seen as deleterious to human flourishing, it will not be the majority who see them thus—Nietzsche prides himself on not coinciding with the majority view. If a whole culture, or even humanity in general, is ever to receive the benefits of Nietzsche's critique

[14] See *EH*, 'Dawn' [i.e. 'Daybreak'], 2.
[15] *EH*, 'Twilight of the Idols', 3; 'Beyond Good and Evil', 1; 'The Case of Wagner', 4.
[16] See e.g. *BGE* 43, 203; and perhaps *GM* II. 24.   [17] See *GS* 335; *BGE* 43.

of moral values, the primary work will be for him to influence the attitudes of a small number of individuals, as yet unknown, who may read his book. It is here, on the project of persuading or realigning the individual reader's habits of evaluation, that I shall place the greatest stress in what follows.

2
Reading Nietzsche's Preface

1 Section 1

The Preface to *On the Genealogy of Morality* opens with a beautiful and evocative piece of writing that may be read as a self-contained 'prose-poem', for want of a better word. Most immediately striking in this first section is the image of the bleary-eyed daydreamer whose whole life was a chiming of bells heard too dimly and too late to be counted correctly. Self-knowledge, we read, is something 'we knowers' never attain, and necessarily so: 'we remain of necessity strangers to ourselves, we do not understand ourselves, we *must* mistake ourselves'. Why must we? We are simply left to speculate, clueless as yet at the very start of the book. This opening throws the reader off balance: we might be tempted to pass over it, seeking stability in what follows, a policy encouraged by Nietzsche's construction. For a glance ahead discloses section 2 as a more conventional beginning, where the author tells us what the book will be about—the origin of our moral prejudices—and divulges something of the route by which he reached his ideas. So section 1, with its whimsical–melancholy picture of self-elusiveness, remains detached and disconcerting.

Who are 'we' in this passage, 'we knowers' (*wir Erkennenden*)? One might understand this as 'we humans' or 'we subjects of knowledge'—perhaps then a Kantian 'we', perhaps a Schopenhauerian one. In early years Nietzsche was enthusiastic about Schopenhauer's thought and continued an intense debate with it, a fact soon to be acknowledged in section 5 of the Preface. Schopenhauer held that the epistemological subject, the subject of knowledge, was 'the knower never the known' (*das Erkennende, nie Erkannte*). According to Schopenhauer, 'everyone finds himself as this subject, yet only in so far as he knows, not in so far as he is object of knowledge...We never know it, but it is precisely that which knows wherever there is knowledge.'[1] Each conscious being is this subject of knowledge, but what this subject is is perpetually, necessarily, elusive to the one who 'finds himself' as it: an eye that cannot see itself.[2] Can the reader of Schopenhauer fail to hear an echo of this in Nietzsche's opening words?

However, Kaufmann and Hollingdale translate Nietzsche's *wir Erkennenden* here as 'we men of knowledge', suggesting a restricted group of researchers, scholars, thinkers, or philosophers. Nietzsche can then be felt to draw the reader into a kind of complicity: 'People like you and me, engaged as we are in intellectual enquiry, in the pursuit of knowledge...'. In this light we may see more vividly Nietzsche's contrast between the life of 'knowledge' and 'the rest of life' or 'so-called "experiences"'. The image of the daydreamer and the bell, though still poignant, becomes a variant of the age-old caricature of the out-of-touch, unworldly thinker (which dates back at least to the stargazing Thales falling into a ditch[3]). We cannot know ourselves, because, as Nietzsche says, we have never gone in search of ourselves.[4] Nietzsche appears to issue a warning to the kind of person who will read his book, and to include himself in its scope: the quest for knowledge demands a form of self-ignorance or self-neglect, necessitates our not understanding our own lives.[5]

On this reading the thought is not that self-knowledge is impossible as such, rather that a life of dedicated scholarship can be sustained only

---

[1] Schopenhauer (1969: i. 5).   [2] Schopenhauer (1974: ii. 46).

[3] See Barnes (2001: 15). In this anecdote reported by Diogenes Laertius an old woman taunts the philosopher: 'Do you think, Thales, that you'll learn what's in the heavens when you can't see what's in front of your feet?'

[4] In contrast with Nietzsche's beloved Heraclitus, whose fragment B101 is *edizēsamēn emeōuton*—'I went in search of myself' (Kahn 1979: 116), or 'I enquired into myself' (Barnes 2001: 69).

[5] Or is it a warning? Elsewhere we encounter Nietzsche's conviction that self-ignorance is a necessary condition of authentic creativity for artists and thinkers: 'To become what one is, one must not have the faintest notion *what* one is [...] *nosce te ipsum* [know yourself] would be the recipe for ruin [...] Meanwhile the organizing "idea" that is destined to rule keeps growing deep down—it begins to command' (*EH*, 'Why I Am So Clever', 9). In other words, the part of the self that will genuinely organize and shape one's work might have to remain free from tampering by conscious cognition in order to succeed. See also *BGE* 266; *GS* 335; and the discussions in May (1999, esp. 191–3) and Conway (2001: 121–2).

by leaving oneself unexamined.[6] This more focused reading gains support from the following part of section 1:

It has rightly been said: 'where your treasure is, there will your heart be also'; *our* treasure is where the beehives of our knowledge stand. We are forever underway toward them, as born winged animals and honey-gatherers of the spirit, concerned with all our heart about only one thing—'bringing home' something.

This reads best as a picture of dedicated enquirers flying out to seek knowledge for their 'home', a figurative place where precious knowledge accumulates. The preceding quotation is from the Christian Bible (Matt. 6: 19–21) where Christ in his sermon on the mount says: 'Lay not up for yourselves treasures upon earth, where moth and rust doth corrupt, and where thieves break through and steal: but lay up for yourselves treasures in heaven … For where your treasure is, there will your heart be also.' Nietzsche thus reinforces the idea that the life of knowledge is unworldly, even otherworldly. As the Christian's heart is in heaven, the truth-seeker's is in the sweet, nourishing stock of knowledge to which he or she contributes.

Towards the end of the *Genealogy*—in what I shall claim is the culmination of the book's argument—Nietzsche thematizes the rigorous self-denying pursuit of truth in science and scholarship and renders it questionable under the notion of the 'ascetic ideal'. Nietzsche there refers again to 'we knowers today, we godless ones and anti-metaphysicians',[7] and the sting in the tail of his book is that our modern, scientific, essentially atheistic conception of knowledge-seeking is akin to Christianity in that we remain wedded to an idealized vision in which the truth is a kind of holy grail, something of unquestionable unconditional worth to which our lives must be selflessly dedicated. 'We knowers today' are alienated from ourselves because we conceive ourselves as pure rational intellects in search of this precious truth, and have to suppress or deny the great bulk of the real self,

---

[6] The interpretation of 'we are strangers to ourselves' given by Gemes (2006*b*) agrees with mine in taking the necessity of self-ignorance as what is needed by a specific type of person for its own preservation (and in taking Nietzsche's task as a progression towards some kind of restorative self-knowledge). However, the 'we' for Gemes is narrowed only to modern human beings in general. I would agree that contemporary scholars and philosophers exemplify characteristics that Nietzsche diagnoses in all moderns. However, Nietzsche's description of the obsessive search for knowledge in section 1 of the Preface hardly locates a feature of all modern beings, and seems much more pointedly aimed, in a similar way to the discussions of 'we knowers today' in *GM* III. 24.

[7] *GM* III. 24. Note also the reference to 'we "knowers"' earlier in the same section.

which, for Nietzsche, is composed of many competing drives and feelings. The *Genealogy* diagnoses the origins of our attachment to selflessness and truthfulness and holds out some hope that we might understand and value ourselves in fuller and healthier ways that affirm and facilitate life. This provides an example of the many new resonances we may be able to catch on turning back to this first page—though nothing will fully dispel its air of enigma.

2 Section 2

Section 2 of the Preface springs the first-person singular upon us with 'My thoughts on the *origins* of our moral prejudices [...]'. It is now no longer a case of 'we', but of 'I' and 'you' in confrontation—a most explicit example of what Nehamas has called Nietzsche's 'effort always to insinuate himself between his readers and the world'.[8] (Nietzsche sustains this mode: every other section of the Preface uses the first-person singular in its opening sentence.) Nietzsche tells us that his polemical book will concern the origins of our moral prejudices (a wider 'we' thus providing the object of investigation), but he elucidates that idea no further yet, and concentrates this section on himself. The book now acquires a historical context, Nietzsche even indicating a date, a place, and a stretch of his life in which he produced his earlier polemic *Human, All Too Human*. The book is not going to be an impersonal enquiry, and is in some measure to be about Nietzsche himself. Nietzsche states that his ideas have not fundamentally changed in the ten years since *Human, All Too Human*. They may have ripened, he hopes, a thought picked up by the dominant simile of this section, that of a philosopher's products as fruits, the philosopher the tree on which they grow. What matters is that the philosopher's disparate thoughts are organically connected and grown from a single stock, not how they taste to anyone else.

Now Schopenhauer comes into view again. Schopenhauer holds that the central character of the human individual is unalterable, and writes that trying to reform someone's character by means of talk and moralizing 'is like trying through external influence to turn lead into gold, or by careful

---

[8] Nehamas (1985: 37).

cultivation to make an oak bear apricots'.[9] It could be a coincidence that Nietzsche repeats this Schopenhauerian tree image, but it seems unlikely. For Schopenhauer the fundamental unifying character of the individual is what he calls the *will*, an explanatorily primary and enduring essence, with the 'I' or knowing subject, by contrast, being merely an 'apparent' entity.[10] Nietzsche parallels this when he calls thoughts and values 'witnesses to one will' and emphatically describes his, the philosopher's, fundamental character as 'a common root [...] a basic will (*Grundwille*) of knowledge which commands from deep within'. These locutions make the allusion look deliberate.

The will for Schopenhauer is a metaphysical or trans-empirical essence, a self as it is in itself. We should not attribute *this* kind of view to Nietzsche, since by the time of writing the *Genealogy* he consistently opposes any transcendent metaphysics. (The recently written first chapter of *Beyond Good and Evil* and Fifth Book of *The Gay Science* are evidence of that.) Yet we might find in Nietzsche an analogous but different view of the self: that all human individuals have an unalterable core, constituted of certain organic states, which gives a unity to their character through the myriad acts and states of mind that are theirs. Think of his poetic words in the earlier *Thus Spoke Zarathustra*: 'You say "I" and are proud of this word. But greater than this [...] is your body and its great intelligence [...] Behind your thoughts and feelings, my brother, stands a mighty commander, an unknown sage—he is called Self. He lives in your body, he is your body' (*Z* I. 4). This Self, bodily grounded, could be an enduring, unchanging essence out of which Nietzsche's many thoughts grow organically, like fruit from a tree.[11]

Or might there be an altogether different way with this idea of unity in section 2? When Nietzsche explicates the image of tree and fruit, his remarks are limited to 'philosophers' of a kind to which he portrays himself as belonging. A philosopher's values, 'yes's and no's and if's and whether's' must have organic unity. And how are these values (or 'thoughts') manifested? In a series of texts. Nietzsche's fruits are the contents of *Human, All Too Human*, the *Genealogy* itself, and the several books in

---

    [9] Schopenhauer (1999: 46).   [10] See Schopenhauer (1969: ii. 278).
    [11] Leiter (2002: 8–10) presents a view broadly of this nature, stating that for Nietzsche each individual has 'a fixed, psycho-physical constitution', and invoking both the tree metaphor and Schopenhauer's use of it.

between. So what is the tree? Shall we opt for Friedrich Nietzsche, the human being causally responsible in the recognized way for the existence of these texts—in which case we must entertain the idea of some deep psychological unity over time, unqualified and unexplained as yet, residing in this human being? Or shall the tree be the authorial presence constructible from, or constituted by, the texts themselves? In apparent support of the latter reading, the Nietzsche text immediately prior to the *Genealogy* prefigures Barthes and Foucault with the thought that 'the "work", whether of the artist or of the philosopher, invents the person who has created it, who is supposed to have created it'.[12] But to read section 2 of Nietzsche's Preface in this way is to disorient its central metaphor—unless a fruit can 'invent' the tree from which it has grown. And section 2 easily permits the less contrived biographical reading—the reading which locates the 'one will', the 'one health', and the 'one soil' in the psychological–physiological individual, in Nietzsche the human being, whose thinking and writing were historical events. If Nietzsche did not mean the 'fundamental will' to have some such psychological reality, how can it make sense for him to say that it spoke ever more definitely from 'deep within'? Deep within what, unless Nietzsche's psyche? It is not made clear here what the 'one will', 'one health', and so on literally consist in. But Nietzsche believes—or so I shall argue—that there are psychological truths about human individuals, and that his method of enquiry is a way to uncover such truths. He develops models of psychological reality, among them a conception of multiple drives standing in differing relations of competition, integration, and hierarchy, and he must have taken any such general model to apply to himself.

3 Section 3

Nietzsche remains in autobiographical mode, and exploits another idea of a changeless underlying self, though this time holding it at a greater distance. There is, he says, a characteristic in him, a scruple or tendency

[12] *BGE* 269. Compare 'the modern scriptor is born simultaneously with the text, is in no way equipped with a being preceding or exceeding the writing' (Barthes 1977: 145); and 'It would be … wrong to equate the author [or author function] with the real writer' (Foucault 1986: 112). A good critical account of these views is given by Lamarque (1990).

towards scepticism, which appeared early (at least as early as 13) and did so inexplicably for someone in his surroundings (the son of a Lutheran pastor raised in the small towns of Röcken and Naumburg). It was a sceptical attitude towards morality, an attitude which he calls his own 'a priori'—supposedly a non-empirical, unchanging aspect of himself. Nietzsche refers to this as appearing 'spontaneously' and 'irrepressibly', as something which may have a will of its own: 'Was *this* what my "a priori" wished (*wollte*) of me?'—did 'it' will him, at the age of 13, to regard God as the origin of evil? Nietzsche merely poses the rhetorical question, playfully says he might *almost* have the right to call this trait his 'a priori', and refers to it always within quotation marks, carefully avoiding commitment to any metaphysical assertion about the self.

There is also clever irony in the thought that Nietzsche's 'a priori' character should be 'immoral', or 'immoralistic', and yet issue its own 'categorical imperative'. Kant's well-known doctrine of the categorical imperative posits an absolute 'ought' as the basis of morality, an 'ought' addressed not to the empirical self in the realm of nature, but to the will of a purely rational self residing in a supposed noumenal (non-empirical) realm of freedom, insulated from natural causes. The 'a priori' in Kant is the source of the absolute imperative of morality. Nietzsche imagines a contrary imperative: the (*ach! so anti-Kantische*) imperative to oppose and criticize morality, an imperative that arises—'almost', 'perhaps'—from the demands of an abiding transcendent source within himself. The rhetoric of this passage uses one of Nietzsche's most characteristic devices: the train of thought has coherence only if hung on a conceptual framework which he brings into play but never proposes for the reader's acceptance. It is rather that, by making sense of the framework he offers only ironically, we discern precisely what Nietzsche opposes.

In the second half of section 3 Nietzsche brings the narrative up to date, saying that he learned not to seek the origin of evil in any supernatural realm 'behind' the world. 'God' was not the source of either good or evil; both were human, all too human. And here for the first time we encounter an elucidation of the governing problems and methods of the *Genealogy*:

A little historical and philological schooling, combined with an innate sense of discrimination in all psychological questions, soon transformed my problem into a different one: under what conditions did man invent those value judgements good and evil? *and what value do they themselves have?* [...] In response I found and ventured a number of answers; I distinguished ages, peoples, degrees of rank among individuals; I divided up my problem; out of the answers came new questions, investigations, conjectures, probabilities.

The turn away from metaphysics (from what is posited as 'behind' the world) opens up an ever self-renewing form of empirical enquiry into the world ('this' world, as he calls it elsewhere), an enquiry which is psychological, historical, and philological; in other words, Nietzsche's chosen method is to ask questions about people's states of mind, about the usage and change of linguistic terms, and about the place of words, values, and beliefs in the development of cultures and of classes within cultures.

Finally, the most revealing sentences of this section for what is to come are these:

under what conditions did man invent those value judgements good and evil? *and what value do they themselves have?* Have they inhibited or furthered human flourishing up until now? Are they a sign of distress, of impoverishment, of the degeneration of life? Or, conversely, do they betray the fullness, the power, and will of life, its courage, its confidence, its future?

To evaluate the practice of making the moral judgements exemplified by ' ... is good' and ' ... is evil' requires asking what function the practice has for the persons, classes, or cultures who partake in it. But from the start Nietzsche plots moral discourses and beliefs on an axis running from decline to ascendancy, weakness to strength, psychological poverty to empowerment. These, though not moral notions, are evaluative ones. Under scrutiny are those of us who operate with moral values; to be evaluated is our health or well-being.

4 Section 4

Nietzsche next gives us more autobiography, partially fictionalized. He has told us that *Human, All Too Human* was begun in Sorrento in the winter of 1876–7. We now read that a stimulus for his work was *The Origin of the Moral Sensations* by Paul Rée. The text does not reveal that Rée was Nietzsche's close friend and associate at that time, nor that they spent five months together in Sorrento with another friend, Albert Brenner, engaged in shared intellectual enquiry. This intense collaboration, idealized as a kind of monastic 'college for free spirits', was unparalleled in Nietzsche's career. It issued in *Human, All Too Human* and Rée's aforementioned book, changed the direction of Nietzsche's philosophy, and lost him former friends, in particular the Wagners. Here Nietzsche manages to acknowledge a debt to Rée, but with carefully contrived dismissive rhetoric. The reader would not guess that Rée in his gratitude had referred to Nietzsche as the father of his own book (and to himself as its mother), nor that when both books appeared their publisher deemed it appropriate to describe *Human, All Too Human* as continuing the work begun by Rée,[13] nor that it was Rée who two years earlier had begun writing in an aphoristic style consciously influenced by that of La Rochefoucauld, not only in its tone, but also in its intent to debunk the pretensions of so-called moral behaviour—a tone and intent that Nietzsche had followed in *Human, All Too Human*, in clear contrast to his previous published writings.

Thinking back to the tree metaphor and the idea of an 'a priori' imperative, we can now see both as imparting a face-saving 'spin' on Nietzsche's career: as if it could not have been because of anyone's influence that Nietzsche started on his course of questioning the value of our moral values, because it was already deep in his character to do so. In the intervening years Nietzsche had fallen out with Rée both personally and intellectually, and is set on claiming every 'fruit' as uniquely his own. Rée is conceded worth only as the antipode, or opposite, on which Nietzsche's own energy can feed (the same kind of role in which he also cast his former heroes Schopenhauer and Wagner[14]). Rée's is an 'overly smart little book', for which Nietzsche fabricates an instrumental use: that he could negate everything it contained. Although such wholesale negation falsifies the initially fertile relationship between the two, Nietzsche concludes this section by documenting with some accuracy how his Sorrento-inspired book did indeed diverge from Rée's. Nietzsche's self-reference here becomes inter-textual, and quite demanding: to appreciate his points we must consult nine passages in *Human, All Too Human* (including its final part, here called simply the 'Wanderer'), and one in his next book,

---

[13] See Small (2001: 184; 2003, pp. xiii–xiv; 2005: 33; Donnellan (1982, esp. 595–601, 607–8); also Nietzsche's letters to Erwin Rohde, 16 June 1878 (*SB* v. 333), and to Rée, June 1877 (*SB* v. 246).   [14] See *NcW*, 'We Antipodes'; *EH*, 'The Birth of Tragedy', 1.

Daybreak. Nietzsche may disparage the habits of scholarship sometimes, but he still demands them in his reader.[15]

For Rée the judgement of actions as 'good' and 'bad', the feeling of conscience, and the institutions of punishment all had a single analysis, which went, briefly, as follows. In a distant human past there was utility-value in linking egoistic behaviour with disapproval and unegoistic behaviour with approval; natural selection favoured communities whose members made these associations and thereby attained internal peace. This situation persists more or less ahistorically, the only change being that, through the process of relentless repetition and the habitual formation of feeling-associations, we have forgotten the original link between approbation and utility. Once reminded of that link, however, we can demystify morality and see plainly what value our moral concepts and practices really have. Nietzsche was already doubting whether our moral feelings have any positive value at all. But this doubt was allied to an incipient suspicion about the naivety of the method of 'English genealogy' Rée practised. Nietzsche already realized that we are strangers to ourselves in ways that his colleague could not see. Rée did not suspect that there was a complex history of power-relations, reinterpretations, and ambivalent feelings packed into the words we use to describe our moral attitudes and into those attitudes themselves, or that deciphering them would be an intricate and taxing exercise requiring severe self-examination and a radical departure from established methods of enquiry.

---

[15] Following the scholarly trail Nietzsche lays for us (through *HA* I. 45, 96, 99, 136; II/1. 89, 92; II/2. 26; *D* 112) we find the following early divergences from Rée: (1) Rée treats human communities as if they were homogeneous and not characterized by different perspectives and internal power relations. But terms such as 'good' and 'bad' had a different significance in different sections or castes of ancient communities: the noble and powerful were 'good' by nature, while the oppressed classes understood the terms according to what was harmful to them. (2) The naturalistic approach to morality (of which Rée is self-consciously a proponent) has not begun to explain the phenomena of asceticism and saintliness which attach to Christian morality, and should do so. (3) Rée proceeds as if 'moral' *means* 'unegoistic'; he ignores a more ancient form of morality that consists simply in adherence to a community's established tradition or law. The attaching of 'good' and 'evil' to the egoistic and the unegoistic comes later, and is not fundamental to all conceptions of the moral. (4) The administering of justice is in origin not—contrary to Rée—a means of deterring people from future egoistic actions that are detrimental to social peace. It has little to do with egoism or altruism, and is rather a means of regulating power relations, as an exchange or equilibrium between roughly equal parties. (5) Punishment has a different and more complex origin than in Rée's account: 'terrorizing' agents out of their egoistic tendencies is 'neither essential nor present at the beginning' in the history of punishment. Punishing a transgression is originally restoring a power equilibrium. It enacts a form of regulated retribution, by treating the punished party as no longer equal or equivalent to others.

Nietzsche describes his early opposition to Rée not as 'refutation' but as 'putting in place of the improbable the more probable, sometimes in place of one error another one'. In isolation it is easy to read this as saying that whether or not his own genealogical claims were true, and whether or not Rée's were false, was of little or no importance to him. But then unless he were concerned with truth and falsehood, what could it mean to describe himself as 'emphatically saying "no"' to Rée's book, 'proposition by proposition, conclusion by conclusion'? This apparent contradiction is diminished by a close look at the German text. Kaufmann's translation serves us well here, with Nietzsche saying that he never encountered any other book 'to which I would have said *to myself* No'.[16] By contrast, he says that *in his book* (*Human, All Too Human*) he referred to Rée's propositions, not to show them false but in the spirit of increasing probability and perhaps committing his own errors. This contrivance forms another part of Nietzsche's retrospective face-saving strategy in the Preface. The posture is that, while his earlier book was not wholly free of Rée's influence and did not publicly engage in refuting Rée's claims, in his heart he already regarded them as false.[17]

5 Section 5

The focus here remains the intellectual struggle that Nietzsche claims issued in *Human, All Too Human*. But Nietzsche now distinguishes sharply between hypothesizing about the *origin* of morality and questioning its *value*. The former is only a means, and not the only means, towards the latter, which is 'something much more important'. Nietzsche may again appear to distance himself from the idea of truth-seeking when he says that the value of morality was more important to him than 'my own or anyone else's hypothesizing about the origin of morality'. But his more precise gloss—that hypothesizing about the origins of morality served as a *means* to evaluating it—suggests that such instrumental value attaches precisely to the *discovery of truths* about morality's origins. I shall assume from here on that Nietzsche's project includes the search for such truths.

---

[16] My emphasis; in *bei mir Nein gesagt hätte*, 'bei mir' is explicitly rendered in none of the translations by Clark and Swensen, Diethe, or Smith.

[17] Nietzsche's retrospective comments about the influence of Schopenhauer on *BT* are strikingly similar. (See *BT*, 'Attempt at a Self-Criticism', 6; *EH*, 'The Birth of Tragedy', 1.)

But how did Nietzsche address the question of the value of morality? By struggling or coming to terms (*sich auseinandersetzen*) with the figure who is here honoured (by contrast with Dr Rée and his tidy, smart, little book) as Nietzsche's 'great teacher': Arthur Schopenhauer. Schopenhauer had died when Nietzsche was 15 years old and it was exclusively his writings that taught Nietzsche, beginning with a rapturous early reading in Nietzsche's student years in Leipzig, an experience reflected in his first book, *The Birth of Tragedy*, his essay *Schopenhauer as Educator*, and his friendship with Richard and Cosima Wagner, who were also devotees of Schopenhauer.[18] Nietzsche's close association with Rée put an end to this phase of his life: the naturalism of Rée's approach to morality ended any willingness to applaud Schopenhauer's metaphysics,[19] and the fact that Rée was Jewish finished him off socially in the eyes of the Wagners.[20] But what was his 'struggle' with Schopenhauer's conception of morality? 'In particular the issue was the value of the unegoistic, of the instincts of compassion, self-denial, self-sacrifice, precisely the instincts that Schopenhauer had gilded, deified, and made otherworldly until finally they alone were left for him as the "values in themselves", on the basis of which he *said "no"* to life, also to himself.'

'The unegoistic' (*das Unegoistische*) is Rée's term, but it aptly describes Schopenhauer's conception of values so far as they are attainable in human life. Schopenhauer's axiology is marked by a repeated gravitation towards will-lessness and abandonment of individuality. The subject of aesthetic experience is a '*pure, timeless, will-less painless subject of knowledge*', an eye that passively mirrors the world rather than interacting with it via the embodied and willing individual of ordinary experience.[21] The ultimate salvation of what Schopenhauer calls 'denial of the will to life' is glossed as a prolongation of this same state of will-less objectivity.[22] And moral

---

[18] See Janaway (1998*b*: 13–27).

[19] Nietzsche was at best ambivalent about Schopenhauer's metaphysics from an early date. See Janaway (1998*a*: 18–19, 258–65).

[20] See Small (2005: 48–9): 'The sharp-eyed Wagners had taken an immediate dislike to Rée on the grounds of his perceived Jewishness.... Cosima Wagner saw his influence as the last stage in the decline of Nietzsche's allegiance to Bayreuth, which had been visibly wavering for some time: "Finally Israel intervened in the form of a Dr Rée, very sleek, very cool, at the same time as being wrapped up in Nietzsche and dominated by him, though actually outwitting him—the relationship between Judaea and Germany in miniature."' Cosima's diary for 1 November 1876 contains the words: 'In the evening we are visited by Dr Rée, whose cold and precise character does not appeal to us; on closer inspection we come to the conclusion that he must be an Israelite' (Wagner 1978: 931).

[21] See Schopenhauer (1969: i. 178–9, 186).

[22] See Schopenhauer, 390.   [23] Ibid. 370–4; also Schopenhauer (1995: 203–14).

value, for Schopenhauer, stems from the attitude in which one withdraws faith from one's individual will and identifies with the world of willing beings as a whole.[23] Schopenhauer finds value only in disengagement from willing, detachment from bodily individuality, and loss of self—at least where self is construed as anything other than a pure contemplative subject, an unmoved, impersonal eye with no direction or place in the world.[24] The key to the attainment of *any* genuine value for Schopenhauer is indeed 'saying "no" to life'.[25]

Dwelling on the aspect of Schopenhauer's thought of which he is especially sceptical (and fearful), Nietzsche pauses for an extended rhetorical display, repeatedly using his trademark stylistic effect of intensified listing ('compassion, self-denial, self-sacrifice'; 'gilded, deified, made otherworldly'; 'the beginning of the end, the standstill, the backward-glancing tiredness, the will turning *against* life'). The emotional temperature is dramatically raised by this passage. We sense that Nietzsche is scandalized by Schopenhauer's conception of value and that this feeling sustains a drive to find a manner in which to say 'yes' to life and to the world. The self-denial that is so prominent in Schopenhauer is no less than 'the *great* danger to humanity', and is so threatening because Nietzsche diagnoses Schopenhauer as symptomatic of 'the ever more widely spreading morality of compassion' and a nihilistic self-negation pervading European thought. In this highly charged passage we find the central preoccupation of the *Genealogy*: our current morality is one of selflessness, or of 'unselfing' (*Entselbstung*), as Nietzsche later put it.[26] We have come to attach value to denying, losing, or suppressing ourselves, in a way that threatens to leave us not valuing ourselves at all for what we are or might become. These themes carry over into section 6.

6 Section 6

The value of the morality of compassion has not been questioned hitherto, but once one regards it from the Nietzschean sceptical outlook—with mistrust, suspicion, fear—an 'immense new vista' is revealed for the

---

[24] See Nietzsche's pointed allusion to this notion in *GM* III. 12.

[25] See esp. Schopenhauer (1969: i. 324; ii. 571–7).

[26] *EH*, 'Dawn' [i.e. 'Daybreak'], 2. Here Nietzsche states that it was already in *Daybreak*, his next book after *Human, All Too Human*, that he took up the fight against this *Entselbstungs-Moral*.

investigator, in which all confidence in received wisdom about values collapses, setting for Nietzsche and his reader the challenge that

we need a *critique* of moral values, *for once the value of these values must itself be called into question*—and for this we need a knowledge of the conditions and circumstances out of which they have grown, under which they have developed and shifted [...] knowledge of a kind that has neither existed up until now nor even been desired.

The rhetoric of section 6 of the Preface continues in the impassioned tone of the previous section, assisting Nietzsche to present his task as enormous, original, and shocking. We have never doubted that 'good' was of higher value than 'evil', but could it be that what we habitually call 'good' and feel positively towards is precisely what is detrimental to human potential, 'so that precisely morality would be to blame if a *highest power and splendor* of the human type—in itself possible—were never attained? So that precisely morality were the danger of dangers?' Though Nietzsche puts all this in interrogative mode, he has already asserted that he regards the morality of selflessness as the great danger to humanity. Nietzsche's criterion of evaluation is, again, whether our moral values are beneficial or detrimental to the flourishing of human beings, or of certain future human beings who may exceed in power and splendour what humanity has thus far attained. Nietzsche is concerned with the healthy psychological functioning of human beings and their achievement of the fullest human potential—albeit that, as we read on, we find him caring little for humanity en masse, or at best seeing the furtherance of 'man in general' as happening through the achievements of a few exceptional individuals.[27]

Some time ago Philippa Foot suggested that in his quest for 'producing a stronger and more splendid type of man' Nietzsche proposes to judge morality by aesthetic or at least 'quasi-aesthetic' standards.[28] Nietzsche's term *Pracht* ('splendour') certainly has an aesthetic ring to it, connoting magnificent appearance or excellence on display. Here Nietzsche is very much thinking of a human being who is to be admired by onlookers. Elsewhere he speaks highly of individuals who attain stylistic unity or wholeness, at times explicitly comparing their value to that of a work of art.[29] But Foot in effect charges that, in opposing morality on the grounds of its

---

[27] See e.g. *GM* I. 11, 16; II. 12, 24; III. 14.   [28] Foot (1973: 163–6).
[29] See *GS* 290; *TI*, 'Expeditions of an Untimely Man', 49.

alleged obstruction of power and splendour, Nietzsche adopts a criterion of value that is quasi-aesthetic and therefore *not ethical*—and it this that we may question. Maudemarie Clark[30] has recently claimed that Foot 'did not seem to fully appreciate the possibility that [Nietzsche's] opposition to morality was coming from the viewpoint of an alternative ethical orientation' because 'she still basically equated "ethics" and "morality"'—whereas 'a distinction between ethics and morality ... is now widely accepted among philosophers'.[31] Nietzsche's concern can now be seen as ethical, in that he is interested in what it is to be the most excellent type of human being, to lead the best life a human being can lead. His persistent attention to the health of the psyche is also in some ways parallel with Plato's recognizably ethical concerns in the *Republic*. 'Morality' is a particular set of beliefs and attitudes, centred around selflessness, guilt, blame, and responsibility, that Nietzsche will strive to reveal, from an ethical standpoint, as not just ugly or distasteful, but as an inferior and harmful form for human beings to impress upon their lives.

7 Section 7

Nietzsche here abandons his style of high declamation and returns to the appraisal of Rée's work, though the personal tone continues. Nietzsche, as often, portrays himself as a lonely researcher seeking 'friends', and becoming disappointed in Rée. He criticizes Rée's methods as erroneous and as leading to absurd results, contrasting what he calls 'real history', which he himself is striving to practise, with Rée's project of 'English hypothesizing into the blue'. Real history of morality is glossed as concerning 'the

---

[30] Clark (2001). Clark addresses particularly the role of Bernard Williams in this shift. See esp. Williams (1985: 174–96)—though it should be noted that not everyone who distinguishes ethics and morality does so in the way Williams does.

[31] Clark (2001: 104). See also p. 103: 'in the 1970s, no such distinction even seemed to be on the horizon: Morality was morality, and "ethics" was used as an equivalent term'. Thus (in the 1970s) Foot is concerned whether Nietzsche is an immoralist or a moralist: 'in much of his work he can be seen as arguing about the way in which men must live in order to *live well*. It is the common ground between his system and that of traditional and particularly Greek morality that makes us inclined to think that he must be a moralist after all .... [He] was interested ... in the conditions in which men—at least some men—would flourish' (1973: 166–7). More recently Foot has written, 'his crucial idea was ... about what constituted a good life for a human being, that is, his idea of human good' (2001: 112). In both cases we might say that Foot portrays Nietzsche as occupying an ethical viewpoint, from which he criticizes morality.

morality which has really existed, really been lived', and as 'that which can be documented, which can really be ascertained, which has really existed, in short, the very long, difficult-to-decipher hieroglyphic writing of the human moral past'. Understanding this past as it was lived requires a highly differentiated study of cultures and psychologies, and of the way the products of different cultural and psychological circumstances interact and overlap. Rée, Nietzsche tells us, substitutes for this complex investigative project his reading of Darwin. Viewing human beings as homogeneous and more or less ahistorical 'Darwinian animals', Rée thinks to explain the development of the moral evaluation of selflessness simply through the selection for success of those communities that had a habit of associating feelings of approval with altruistic acts. Nietzsche jokes that in Rée's book we find 'the Darwinian beast politely joining hands with the most modern, unassuming moral milquetoast (*Moral-Zärtling*) who "no longer bites"', a pointed remark on Rée's claim that the worth of egoistic and unegoistic persons is literally the same as the utility-value that attaches to vicious and docile dogs.[32]

Nietzsche pictures this tender milquetoast's facial expression as good-natured, indolent, and weary, and then veers apparently in another direction—though one characteristic of much of his writing—to consider the *mood* in which we do philosophy or genealogical investigation. He implies that Rée's approach to morality does not take it seriously, presumably meaning that for Rée established morality is not something *troubling*: it neither demands any radical historical investigation nor poses any crisis of value for the investigator, but can be coolly accommodated in a neat explanation. Nietzsche, by contrast, urges us to become troubled, but also to regard morality in a state of 'cheerfulness'. Being serious and being cheerful are compatible for Nietzsche: invoking the title of another of his recent books, he talks of a 'gay science', an investigation at once disciplined and joyful. Eventually we shall see morality as one part of the comedy of our lives, perhaps enjoying some of its possibilities but not being overburdened by it. This glancing reference to comedy might represent an even greater affront to the modern conception of morality than the attack

[32] See Rée (2003: 123): 'Just as any other harmful animal, such as a vicious dog, is bad because he is bad for human beings, yet considered by himself is not bad but just an animal of a certain nature, so too the cruel person is bad because he is bad for human beings, yet considered by himself he is not bad but just a person of a certain nature.' The word for 'vicious' here is *bissig*: liable to bite.

on it as a great danger, for morality is generally regarded as placing on us paramount demands that trump those of other values. The section ends with an extravagant and unexplained reference to 'the Dionysian drama of the "Destiny of the Soul"' and 'the great old eternal comic poet of our existence'. Dionysus for Nietzsche is consistently the god of *tragedy*, but the Dionysian attitude to the hardness and destruction in human existence is, whether in early or later works, one of affirmation and rejoicing.[33] The 'great old eternal comic poet' recalls the Dionysian force of nature, the 'primordial artist of the world', from Nietzsche's first book, *The Birth of Tragedy* (*BT* 1, 5). There such a notion was whimsical, if seriously meant. Here it seems just whimsical.

8   Section 8

The final section of the *Genealogy*'s Preface looks forward to the work ahead, also in somewhat ambivalent spirit: there is advice about how to read the book, but considerable emphasis on its probably being unintelligible, hard on the ears, difficult, and not yet 'readable'. Three main difficulties apparently arise. First, to understand this book we need to have read Nietzsche's previous writings with effort and attention. Secondly, we need to experience his texts with especially heightened emotional involvement—with the work of fiction *Thus Spoke Zarathustra* one needs to have been 'deeply wounded and [...] deeply delighted by each of its words'. Thirdly, Nietzsche says that his reader must 'almost be a cow' in order to practise the art of rumination that his writings require for their proper interpretation or exegesis (*Auslegung*). Much has been written on Nietzsche's comment here that the whole of his Third Treatise, 'What Do Ascetic Ideals Mean?', serves as a demonstration of how to interpret or decipher an aphorism that is 'placed before the treatise' for that purpose. The assumption that the aphorism in question is the brief motto from *Thus Spoke Zarathustra* that appears beneath the title of the treatise gave a field day to certain interpreters who were enamoured of a total undecidability of meaning or reference and of the view that only a play of metaphors could result from any attempt to use language. The inclusion of 'woman'

---

[33] See *BT* 16; *TI*, 'What I Owe to the Ancients', 5.

as a metaphor for wisdom in that motto apparently made such a reading all but irresistible for that mixture of feminism and deconstructionism through which it was once fashionable to approach Nietzsche. In this case at least, such a reading was clearly over-radical, because built upon a mistake. As I argue in Chapter 10 below,[34] the aphorism upon which the Third Treatise is a commentary is in fact section 1 of the treatise itself, which like the remainder is about the meaning of ascetic ideals.

More on that particular issue below—but I should remark that even without that over-radical reading Nietzsche leaves us as readers of his Preface in a sufficiently challenging predicament. The task is one never before attempted or conceived. Huge personal effort is required. The future of humanity is at stake. Our trusted values must be unlearned, we will need to become emotionally involved with the subject matter to the extent of great elation and despair, and yet we start virtually in the dark, necessarily unknown to ourselves and guided only by a piece of writing that nobody yet knows how to read. Anyone approaching the *Genealogy* after its Preface should at the very least be warned to read slowly and closely, reflecting not only on what Nietzsche says but on how he says it, what moods and feelings he is out to foster in the reader, and what new self-exploration he may require of us.

[34] Previously published as Janaway (1997a). The line taken there, defended on internal evidence from the text, is independently supported by scholars who have argued (a) that evidence from the publishing history of the *Genealogy* shows that Nietzsche added this section 1 as an afterthought and did so before writing the relevant part of Preface, 8; (b) that recent interpreters have used poor methods of argumentation in support of the over-radical reading (see Clark 1997, Wilcox 1997, 1999; also Clark and Swensen 1998: 148).

3

Naturalism and Genealogy

Most commentators on Nietzsche would agree that he is in a broad sense a naturalist in his mature philosophy. He opposes transcendent metaphysics, whether that of Plato or of Christianity or of Schopenhauer. He rejects notions of the immaterial soul, the absolutely free controlling will, or the self-transparent pure intellect, instead emphasizing the body, talking of the animal nature of human beings, and attempting to explain numerous phenomena by invoking drives, instincts, and affects which he locates in our physical, bodily existence. Human beings are to be 'translated back into nature', since otherwise we falsify their history, their psychology, and the nature of their values—concerning all of which we must know truths, as a means to the all-important critique and eventual revaluation of values. This is Nietzsche's naturalism in the broad sense, which will not be contested here.

Brian Leiter has recently offered a more pointed characterization of Nietzsche's naturalism, however, that would give it specific links with the methods and results of science. For Leiter, if we look at 'Nietzsche's actual philosophical practice, i.e. what he spends most of his time doing in his books', we find a naturalism that is 'fundamentally *methodological*'.[1] Nietzsche is a naturalist, Leiter argues, in virtue of holding a view that 'philosophical inquiry ... should be continuous with empirical inquiry in the sciences',[2]—a naturalist who

aims to offer theories that explain various important human phenomena (especially the phenomenon of morality), and that do so in ways that both draw on actual scientific results, particularly in physiology ... but are also *modeled* on science in the sense that they seek to reveal the causal determinants of these phenomena, typically in various physiological and psychological facts about persons.[3]

---

[1] Leiter (2002: 6 and n.).   [2] Ibid. 3.   [3] Ibid. 8.

I want to suggest that if we pay attention to Nietzsche's artistic and rhetorical methods and a range of his methodological statements, we may find that this statement risks giving an exaggerated impression of the continuity with science that Nietzsche seeks and achieves.

1 Methodological Naturalism

Let us look at Leiter's claims, starting with the task of 'translating man back into nature' found in *Beyond Good and Evil*, 230. Leiter says that here Nietzsche 'calls for man to stand "hardened in the discipline of science"'.[4] This already involves a slight over-reading. Nietzsche states that as regards the rest of nature we stand before it hardened in the discipline of science; he calls for us in future to stand before ourselves in a similar way, blind and deaf to 'the siren songs of old metaphysical bird catchers' whose message is 'you are more, you are higher, you are of a different origin'.[5] Nietzsche's call urges us to reject the kind of metaphysics that invokes some realm other than the empirical to account for certain aspects of humanity. But it is not a call literally to investigate ourselves scientifically, rather a call to emulate the staunch discipline of scientists as we resist any temptation towards metaphysical theorizing about ourselves. A similar analogy is made in *The Gay Science* 319: 'we [...] want to face our experiences as sternly as we would a scientific experiment, hour by hour, day by day!' Then in *The Gay Science* 335 Nietzsche urges upon us a particular kind of enquiry into our evaluations: 'Your judgement, "that is right" has a prehistory in your drives, inclinations, aversions, experiences, and what you have failed to experience; you have to ask, "*how* did it emerge there?" and then also, "*what* is really impelling me to listen to it?"' Nietzsche describes this process of self-questioning with the words 'reflect more subtly', 'observe better', 'study more', and finally 'become the best students and discoverers of everything lawful and necessary in the world: we must become *physicists*'. But Nietzsche does not mean that we can achieve the requisite self-discovery literally by doing physics. Rather, there is a discipline and depth to the self-study which he finds it fruitful to see as *analogous to* a scientific approach.

[4] Ibid. 7.   [5] *BGE* 230; trans. Kaufmann.

That Nietzsche's method is not literally scientific does not matter for Leiter, however, given his fuller statements concerning methodological naturalism. To be methodologically naturalist, philosophical enquiry should either (*a*) be supported by, or justified by, the actual results of our best science in its different domains; or (*b*) employ or emulate successful, distinctively scientific ways of understanding and explaining things. Leiter refers to these as 'Results Continuity' and 'Methods Continuity' respectively.[6] But if Nietzsche were to satisfy the requirements for philosophical naturalism solely on the grounds of Methods Continuity, he would not have to employ specifically scientific methods, for instance scientific means of testing theories; it is sufficient that his methods *emulate* scientific ways of understanding the world. And this comes down to explaining various phenomena by locating their causal determinants.[7]

So, for Leiter, if one is a naturalist just on the grounds of a commitment to Methods Continuity, the continuity one advocates with science can in fact be relatively loose, consisting in the giving of explanations of phenomena through locating their causes. A worry here might be that this kind of continuity on its own does not rule out very much, given that belief systems such as Christianity, Satanism, and astrology all attempt to explain various phenomena by locating their causes. If what makes these theories beyond the pale for naturalism is that they do not *use* scientific methods, well and good. But if mere *emulation* of scientific method through the giving of causal explanations is sufficient for naturalism, as it must be to let in Nietzsche as a naturalist on these grounds, then naturalism on the grounds of Methods Continuity looks to be rather a broad church.

This problem can be obviated by invoking Results Continuity. If one is a naturalist by virtue of commitments to both Methods Continuity and Results Continuity, then one will seek to explain phenomena in terms of their causes, and require, in Leiter's words, 'that philosophical theories ... be supported or justified by the results of the sciences'—to which he adds that 'theories that do not enjoy the support of our best science are simply *bad* theories'.[8] The attribution of this requirement of 'support or justification' lends a much stronger sense to 'continuity' with science, but arguably gives rise to problems for Leiter's account, because no scientific support or justification is given—or readily imaginable—for the central

---

[6] Leiter (2002: 4–5).   [7] Ibid. 5 and 8 (quoted above).   [8] Ibid. 4.

explanatory hypotheses that Nietzsche gives for the origins of our moral beliefs and attitudes. For a prominent test case, take Nietzsche's hypothesis in the *Genealogy*'s First Treatise that the labelling of non-egoistic inaction, humility, and compassion as 'good' began because there were socially inferior classes of individuals in whom feelings of *ressentiment* against their masters motivated the creation of new value distinctions. This hypothesis explains moral phenomena in terms of their causes, but it is not clear how it is *justified* or *supported by* any kind of science, nor indeed what such a justification or support might be. Other cases fall into the same pattern. Nietzsche's crucial hypothesis about the origin of bad conscience (in the Second Treatise) is that instincts whose outward expression against others is blocked turn themselves inward and give rise to the infliction of pain on the self. What scientific results justify or support this claim is again obscure. If we are to regard the explanations of morality given by Nietzsche as supported or justified by the results of the sciences, the onus is on Leiter to show what that support or justification consists in.

At one point Leiter talks of the continuity between Nietzsche's philosophy and one particular 'result' that preoccupied mid-nineteenth-century Germans: 'that man is not of a "higher… [or] different origin" than the rest of nature'.[9] However, the status of this as a 'result' is perhaps debatable: it is hard to say whether the exclusively empirical nature of humanity was a conclusion or an assumption of scientific investigation in the nineteenth century or at any time. But let us allow that 'man is not of a different origin than the rest of nature' has—and that Nietzsche regards it as having—scientific justification. Then we still face the question whether Nietzsche's explanations of the origins of moral concepts, bad conscience, and so on are themselves supported or justified by 'man is not of a different origin than the rest of nature'. And rather than saying that this general programmatic claim provides the justificatory ground for Nietzsche's explanations, it is more plausible to say that it functions as a background assumption which constrains what will count as a good causal explanation. This suggests a weaker results continuity than Leiter's, namely one that requires simply that explanations in philosophy be compatible with our best science, or not be falsified by appeal to our best science. A theorist who held that any explanation given in philosophy must be continuous

---

[9] Ibid. 7.

with the results of science just to this extent might have some claim to the title of naturalist—at least as much claim as the Methods Continuity theorist who holds merely that philosophy must emulate science by giving casual explanations. I argue that a weaker 'naturalism' which requires of its hypotheses that they cite causes to explain the change in value distinctions, and are falsified by nothing from archaeology, history, philology, psychology, biology, or physics, represents Nietzsche's stance in the *Genealogy* better than that which Leiter attributes to him. In other words, Nietzsche is a naturalist to the extent that he is committed to a species of theorizing that explains X by locating Y and Z as its causes, where Y and Z's being the causes of X is not falsified by our best science.[10]

There is also a nagging worry about Results Continuity arising from some of Nietzsche's discussions of his central concept of will to power. The problem is that Nietzsche presents will to power as a *counter* to what he sees as the dominant paradigm in science, the 'democratic idiosyncrasy against everything that rules and desires to rule', a prejudice about method which has 'become lord over the whole of physiology and the doctrine of life—to its detriment [...] by removing through sleight of hand one of its basic concepts, that of true *activity*' (*GM* II. 12). Nietzsche says that the scientific explanation of organisms' behaviour in terms of reactive adaptation to the environment must be rejected in favour of the view that at all levels of the organic world there is spontaneity, active appropriation, interpretation, and the imposition of form and meaning. His statements earlier in the same passage clearly imply that all happening in the organic world is a form of interpretation of one thing by another.[11] On a straightforward reading, Nietzsche goes out of his way to reject Results Continuity with scientific biology.

---

[10] Nietzsche sometimes voices what sounds like scepticism about causation, *BGE* 21 being an example: 'we should use "cause" and effect" only as pure *concepts*, which is to say as conventional fictions for the purpose of description and communication, *not* explanation. [...] *We* are the ones who invented causation, succession, for-each-other, relativity, compulsion, numbers, law, freedom, grounds, purpose.' A strong line with such passages (see Leiter 2002: 22–3; Clark 1990: 103–5) is to read them as merely a neo-Kantian denial that there are causal connections in the realm of the 'in itself' (and the passage just quoted explicitly says as much). In that case, there is no serious Nietzschean scepticism about causal explanation as such. But even if one takes Nietzsche's talk of 'fictions' as presenting the claim that our beliefs in causes and effects are falsifications *tout court*, it has to be said that his genealogical *practice* consists largely in explaining moral attitudes in terms of circumstances—historical, cultural, psychological—that gave rise to them, i.e. in giving causal explanations. (And any psychological story he tells about why we came to believe in causes and effects will presumably also be a causal explanation.)

[11] Since 'all happening in the organic world is an *over-powering*' and 'all over-powering [...] is a new interpreting' (*GM* II. 12).

To pursue this issue further requires careful attention to some much discussed questions concerning the notion of will to power—is it a criterion of value, an explanatory principle, a metaphysics, a cosmological theory, a merely psychological theory, or no real theory at all, just a self-conscious projection onto nature of Nietzsche's own preferred values?—a task of some magnitude that I reserve for a later chapter.[12] But the case raises a pointed question about Nietzsche's attitude to Results Continuity: if science persists in spurning concepts of will-like activity and competition in its descriptions of nature, will continuity with the results of science be an overriding desideratum for Nietzsche? If so, he should be prepared to fall in line and abandon his notion of will to power as unconfirmed. It is hard to be confident, however, that Nietzsche would not rather continue to blame scientists for consistently misreading reality in this respect, however well established their results might become. Possibly he believes that a perfected scientific enquiry would find that relations of overpowering and interpretation were indeed the best models for biological process. But in that case more recent science does not display Results Continuity with Nietzsche.

For now I want to move on to some other, and I think deeper, questions about Nietzsche's methods, methods which in many respects are indeed discontinuous with those of empirical scientific enquiry. Any page of Nietzsche looks starkly unlike scientific literature. He usually does little systematic marshalling of evidence, does not locate the phenomena that compose his explanations precisely in space or time, presents neither clear linear arguments nor unambiguous conclusions, and seems unconcerned about the repeatability of results. Instead he champions a literary, personal, affectively engaged style of enquiry that deliberately stands in opposition to science as he thinks it tends to conceive itself: as disinterested, impersonal, and affectively detached. We might wonder how happy Nietzsche would be to claim methodological continuity with science, given some of his remarks to the effect that failure of affective engagement, failure to personalize one's enquiry into the origin of values, leads to failure to unearth the truth about them. Such a line of thought arises out of explicit contrasts Nietzsche draws between his methods and those of his former close friend the naturalist and would-be genealogist of morality Paul Rée.

---

[12] See Ch. 9 below on will to power in the *Genealogy*.

2 Rée, Selflessness, and Real History

The Preface of the *Genealogy* makes plain Nietzsche's preoccupation with Rée as an opponent. In his book *The Origin of the Moral Sensations* Rée gives an account of our practice of judging egoistic actions and attitudes 'bad' and unegoistic actions and attitudes 'good', presenting an unadorned naturalistic picture influenced by Darwin and utilitarian thought, and employing mental processes such as association and habitual conditioning to explain the origin of our beliefs and other attitudes. Nietzsche calls all this 'English psychology'; and in fact his uses of the terms 'English psychologists' and 'English genealogists' in the *Genealogy* demonstrably refer to Rée in particular.[13] Rée's mission statement is reminiscent of Nietzsche's: 'Today, since Lamarck and Darwin have written, moral phenomena can be traced back to natural causes just as much as physical phenomena: moral man stands no closer to the intelligible world than physical man.'[14] So what goes wrong? On what grounds does Nietzsche object to Rée's results and methods? His most fundamental point of disagreement with Rée, as we saw in previous chapters, is over the assumption Rée shares with Schopenhauer: that 'the unegoistic' is constitutive of morality and is something of positive value. Rée is paradigmatic for Nietzsche of a type of modern thinker who has rejected Christianity, transcendent metaphysics, and even free will, yet still clings to selflessness as the prime moral value. But—most importantly in the context of our discussion of method—Nietzsche charges such thinkers with allowing their inherited conception of value to govern their conception of method and their own self-understanding as enquirers. The well-known ending of the *Genealogy* charges that the scientific 'disinterested pursuit of truth' is but a subtle and disguised manifestation of Christian, ascetic valuation. I shall suggest that Rée is a target for particular criticism on this score as well: he fails because he approaches his subject matter with a cold, impersonal detachment.

A relevant passage is *The Gay Science* 345. Nietzsche there alludes to Rée[15] in a covert way as the only person he has attempted to convert from a method of selflessness to one of personal involvement:

The lack of personality always takes its revenge: a weakened, thin, extinguished personality, one that denies itself and its own existence, is no longer good for

---

[13] See argument for this in Ch. 5 below. [14] Rée (2003: 87).
[15] The allusion is noted in an editorial footnote to *GS* 345 (p. 202 n. 3).

anything good—least of all for philosophy. 'Selflessness' has no value in heaven or on earth; all great problems demand *great love*, and only strong, round, secure minds who have a firm grip on themselves are capable of that. It makes the most telling difference whether a thinker has a personal relationship to his problems and finds in them his destiny, his distress, and his greatest happiness, or an 'impersonal' one, meaning he is only able to touch and grasp them with the antennae of cold, curious thought. In the latter case nothing will come of it, that much can be promised; for even if great problems should let themselves be *grasped* by them, they would not allow frogs and weaklings to *hold on* to them; such has been their taste from time immemorial—a taste, incidentally, that they share with all doughty females. [...] in one single case I did everything to encourage a sympathy and talent for this kind of history—in vain, as it seems to me today. These historians of morality (particularly, the Englishmen) do not amount to much: usually they themselves unsuspectingly stand under the command of a particular morality and, without knowing it, serve as its shield-bearers and followers, for example, by sharing that popular superstition of Christian Europe which people keep repeating so naively to this day, that what is characteristic of morality is selflessness, self-denial, self-sacrifice, or sympathy and compassion.

The allegation is that adherence to the conception of morality as selflessness left Rée, unwittingly, trapped in a sterile mode of investigation that could bring only philosophical failure.

Two metaphors with parallels in the *Genealogy* leap out of this passage. The description 'old, cold, boring frogs' is applied at the opening of *GM* I to so-called 'English psychologists', the term there a playful reference to Rée in particular, given that the theory up for criticism is transparently his.[16] Secondly, in the epigram of *GM* III wisdom is a woman who loves only someone 'carefree, mocking, violent', the opposite of the 'weakened, thin, extinguished' type evoked here.[17] That epigram introduces Nietzsche's essay on the meanings of the ascetic ideal, and points forward to the essay's challenging claim that contemporary objective, scientific method, which prides itself on leaving behind Christianity, theism, and the transcendent altogether, is but another version of an originally Christian, metaphysical

---

[16] As I argue in Ch. 5 below.

[17] See Ch. 10 on the role of this epigram, including its parallel with *GS* 345. It is no doubt unworthily 'personal' to remark that Nietzsche's friendship with Rée ended because of a disastrous rivalry for the attentions of a real woman, Lou Salomé, who in the end favoured Rée. But Nietzsche's metaphors about what women prefer can begin to take on an unpleasant tone if one keeps this fact in mind for too long.

faith in ascetic self-denial before something absolute and quasi-divine, namely truth. Rée's empiricist, atheist, Darwinian approach is problematic because it exemplifies the contemporary method of enquiry that Nietzsche embroils in his complaint against the ascetic ideal.

Confirmation comes from Rée's own words, in a passage towards the end of *The Origin of the Moral Sensations* where he pronounces that 'Nothing can be sacred to the philosopher but truth,' and continues:

if disinterested knowledge does not make someone better or more non-egoistic directly, nevertheless a certain utility [*Nutzen*] is indirectly linked with it. That is, knowledge is peaceable by its nature: everyone can devote themselves to knowledge of the same thing without feeling rivalry or hostility. But desire is always warlike: two people cannot desire the same thing without feeling mutual hostility. Hence, the writings and works of art that inspire one to knowledge of the true and beautiful, although otherwise useless, have the utility of leading people away from activities arousing hostility (owing to desire) to peaceable activities.[18]

Rée is then the paradigm, or at least the most intimately known example, of the cold, froglike type who errs not just in adopting selflessness as definitive of morality, but in aspiring to make it definitive of himself as investigator. Nietzsche is simultaneously opposing morality as selflessness and opposing selflessness as a mode of enquiry.

The impersonality of scientific enquiry was not an uncommon theme, as in this description by William James a few years later:

When one turns to the magnificent edifice of the physical sciences, and sees how it was reared; what thousands of disinterested moral lives of men lie buried in its mere foundations; what patience and postponement, what choking down of preference, what submission to the icy laws of outer fact are wrought into its very stones and mortar; how absolutely impersonal it stands in its vast augustness,—then how besotted and contemptible seems every little sentimentalist who comes blowing his voluntary smoke-wreaths, and pretending to decide things from out of his private dream![19]

To the extent that scientific enquiry is committed to a vision of itself as affect-free, disinterested, and impersonal, it is, for Nietzsche, an offshoot of the values of selflessness that so urgently need revaluing. If we subject ourselves to the style of rigorous self-scrutiny he advocates, we will seek to

---

[18] Rée (2003: 164–5).   [19] James (1967: 720), from an essay first published in 1896.

expose and undermine the affective and historical foundations also of our predilection for impersonality in enquiry. So each of us should be asking, 'How did my attachment to the ideal of an impersonal, affect-free search for truth emerge?' and 'What impels me to follow that ideal?', and be looking for the answers in our inclinations and aversions and their cultural prehistory. Hence to say that Nietzsche wants continuity of method with the empirical sciences is at least over-simple. Given his views about the conception of truth-seeking that predominates in science, his preferred form of truth-seeking will interrogate our weddedness to that conception. Hence he can scarcely, without further questions asked, assume scientific enquiry as his model.

In the same year as the above passage from *The Gay Science* Nietzsche published the Preface to the *Genealogy*, including in section 7 some further methodological criticisms of Paul Rée. In both passages Nietzsche says that he vainly hoped to persuade Rée to abandon a poor conception of history for a better one. But it may look as though Rée would have been pulled in two incompatible directions if he had tried to follow both sets of advice. For according to the *Genealogy*'s Preface he was to stop his 'hypothesizing *into the blue*' in favour of a 'real *history of morality*', seeing 'that which can be documented, which can really be ascertained, which has really existed' (*GM*, Preface, 7). How could he have pursued 'real history', investigating what really existed, and at the same time have abandoned his cold and clammy objectivity for a personal approach to problems, in which they became 'his destiny, his distress and his greatest happiness'? (*GS* 345).

I want to argue that, for Nietzsche, Rée's failure to open himself in the right way to a deep examination of his personal affective states disabled him from doing 'real history', and that there are not two methods advocated as preferable to Rée's, but only one. As a first step, we must realize what is meant by 'real history' and by 'what really existed'. Consider an explicit example in the *Genealogy* of something that for Nietzsche 'actually happened':

One will already have guessed *what* actually happened with all of this and *under* all of this: that will to self-torment, that suppressed cruelty of the animal-human who had been made inward, scared back into himself [...] who invented the bad conscience in order to cause himself pain after the *more natural* outlet for this *desire to cause pain* was blocked—this man of bad conscience has taken over the religious presupposition in order to drive his self-torture to its most gruesome severity and sharpness.

(*GM* II. 22)

To do 'real history', judging by this example, is to explain the origins of our present-day attitudes by reconstructing the operation of a multiplicity of mental states, acts, drives, and mechanisms located in past human beings—though not specific datable human beings, but rather human beings conceived in generic fashion by a kind of projective reconstruction of how a certain psychological type would act and feel in a certain dynamic of power-relations and cultural inheritances.

Note especially the emphasis on the affects here: fear, delight in making-suffer, severe and sharp pain of self-torture; and at the end of the same passage, the emphasis on the affects awakened in the enquirer or reader: 'There is so much in man that is horrifying!' and 'All of this is [...] of such black gloomy unnerving sadness that one must forcibly forbid oneself to look too long into these abysses.' Nietzsche is exemplifying and encouraging the personal relationship to problems that he found lacking in Rée. And so I reach my central question: Might 'real history', as Nietzsche conceives it, demand a personal, affective responsiveness in the investigator?

3 Rhetorical Method and the Affects

In 1888, the year after the *Genealogy* appeared, Nietzsche composed his supposed autobiography, *Ecce Homo*. Although in general this work is approached with some degree of caution by many writers on Nietzsche, it is worth risking the thought that the single page of description entitled '*Genealogy of Morals. A Polemic*', which purports to be a résumé of the intentions informing the rhetoric of the *Genealogy*'s three treatises and an assessment of their achievement, can be taken at face value as a cogent summary analysis. Nietzsche here uses the vocabulary of discovering psychological truths, but equally strongly presents the achievement of the three treatises in artistic and rhetorical terms, pointing out their overall musical shape and mood, their ironic deceptions, and the powerful disorienting emotional effects they are calculated to have upon the unsuspecting reader. Thus:

Regarding expression, intention, and the art of surprise, the three inquiries which constitute this *Genealogy* are perhaps uncannier than anything else written so far. [...]

Every time a beginning that is *calculated* to mislead: cool, scientific (*wissenschaftlich*), even ironic, deliberately foreground, deliberately holding off. Gradually more unrest; sporadic lightning; very disagreeable truths are heard grumbling in the distance—until eventually a *tempo feroce* is attained in which everything rushes ahead in a tremendous tension. In the end, in the midst of perfectly gruesome detonations, a *new* truth becomes visible every time among thick clouds.

(*EH*, 'On the Genealogy of Morals')

I suggest that a rhetoric that arouses the affects is an appropriate part of Nietzsche's intended critique of morality because of the central role he assigns to the affects in his view of how we came to be attached to morality. His view of the latter is perhaps at its clearest in some passages from *Daybreak*:

It is clear that moral feelings are transmitted in this way: children observe in adults inclinations for and aversions to certain actions and, as born apes, *imitate* these inclinations and aversions; in later life they find themselves full of these acquired and well-exercised affects and consider it only decent to try to account for and justify them. [In] [t]his 'accounting', however, [...] all one is doing is complying with the rule that, as a rational being, one has to have reasons for one's For and Against, and that they have to be adducible and acceptable reasons. To this extent the history of moral feelings is quite different from the history of moral concepts. The former are powerful *before* the action, the latter especially after the action in face of the need to pronounce upon it.

(*D* 34)

'Only feelings, not thoughts, are inherited,'[20] says Nietzsche, and (in *The Gay Science*), 'You still carry around the valuations of things that originate in the passions and loves of former centuries!' (*GS* 57).

Other passages from *Daybreak* complicate the picture in certain ways, notably in that, while judgements originate in feelings, feelings also originate in past judgements:

Feelings and their origination in judgments.—'Trust your feelings!'—But feelings are nothing final or original; behind feelings there stand judgments and evaluations which we inherit in the form of feelings (inclinations, aversions). The inspiration born of a feeling is the grandchild of a judgment—and often of a false judgment!—and in any event not a child of your own! To trust one's

---

[20] My trans. of *nur Gefühle, aber keine Gedanken erben sich fort* (*D* 30).

feelings—means to give more obedience to one's grandfather and grandmother and their grandparents than to the gods which are in *us*: our reason and our experience.[21]

And finally, feelings and judgements are related in Nietzsche's conception of a future change in values:

I do not deny—unless I am a fool—that many actions called immoral ought to be avoided and resisted, or that many called moral ought to be done and encouraged—but I think the one should be encouraged and the other avoided *for other reasons than hitherto*. We have to *learn to think differently*—in order at last, perhaps very late on, to attain even more: *to feel differently*.

(D 103)

There are a number of relations pertaining between reason and the emotions in these passages. At the most fundamental level we inherit not moral concepts, but moral feelings, or aversions and inclinations, feelings 'for' and feelings 'against', acquired through unthinking cultural imitation. Our current moral concepts are *ex post facto* rationalizations of our relatively more basic inherited feelings, but our feelings themselves are, as Nietzsche says, 'nothing final or original'—just *these* positive and negative feelings were around to be inherited because they had fitted former moral judgements, which themselves were the rationalization of the feelings of earlier human beings. Affects enter at two stages in the account. In the *Genealogy*'s First Treatise, Nietzsche talks of a slave morality as the origin of Christian and post-Christian values. We, his readers, are not slaves, but we have inherited an affective allegiance to what counted as good in the conceptual scheme of slave morality. And in turn that conceptual scheme (including the thoughts that it is good not to express strength, good to suppress natural instincts, that all agents ought to feel responsibility and guilt for acting in certain ways, that all are equally capable of acting in the same way, and so on) arose because it resolved certain affects and drives for its inventors: in brief, it enabled them to resolve their feelings of powerlessness and resentment into a feeling of superiority over their masters.

We saw that to discover the prehistory of our values we require a stern self-examination in which the questions 'How did it emerge there?' and

---

[21] D 35. Cf. also D 99: 'We still draw the conclusions of judgments we consider false, of teachings in which we no longer believe—our feelings make us do it.'

'What is really impelling me to listen to it?' must be asked of any value judgement we are inclined to make. Now we see that on Nietzsche's view a large amount of inherited affect is packed into our current attitudes. From this we may conclude that the process of self-examination he urges upon us cannot succeed unless it takes on the task of separating out these many affective strands, in order to discover truths about which inclinations and aversions cause me to hold certain beliefs, what cultural institutions and conventions cause me to have those inclinations and aversions, what drives and affects brought about and sustained those cultural institutions, and so on.

In Leiter's naturalist account of Nietzsche central place is given to the explanation of moral beliefs in terms of a fixed set of psychophysical characteristics of the individual, which Leiter refers to as 'type-facts'.[22] Leiter suggests the following as a 'typical Nietzschean form of argument': 'a person's theoretical beliefs are best explained in terms of his moral beliefs: and his moral beliefs are best explained in terms of natural facts about the type of person he is'.[23] But if the schematic account I have offered here is somewhere near correct, we can suggest a more articulated interpretation of Nietzsche's naturalist position. It is not simply that my value beliefs are explained by my psychophysical constitution: rather that my value beliefs are rationalizations of my inclinations and aversions, that my inclinations and aversions are acquired habits inculcated by means of the specific culture I find myself in, that this culture inculcates just these habits because it has a guiding structure of value beliefs, and that this structure of value beliefs became dominant through answering to certain affective needs of individuals in earlier cultural stages. This yields two points that are not brought out in Leiter's account:[24] (1) the explanatory facts about me, even if located somehow in my psychophysiology, are essentially shaped by *culture*: I could not have the specific inclinations and aversions (and perhaps even drives) that give rise to my beliefs except by having learned them culturally; (2) the psychophysical element in the explanation of my beliefs cannot be given solely in terms of *my* psychology and physiology, but must encompass a huge host of affects, drives, and rationalizations located in human beings *other* than myself.

---

[22] Leiter (2002, esp. 8–9).   [23] Ibid. 9.
[24] Though he may not wish to deny them, as was implied in an earlier version of this chapter; Janaway (2006: 346–7).

Let us return to the question of Nietzsche's emotive rhetoric and his demand for personal attachment in one's enquiries into morality. Given that he sets himself to arouse the reader's feelings, is there any principled reason internal to Nietzsche's enterprise why he should do so? Does calling the reader into a personal affective engagement have a deeper justification, or is it nothing more than a vivid shock tactic that could be eliminated without real loss to the fundamental enterprise? It seems clear that the revaluation of values Nietzsche ultimately seeks is not just a change in judgements but a revision at the level of affects too. After we have learned not to make judgements using the standard moral vocabulary of 'good', 'evil', 'compassionate', and 'egoistic', we finally may come, says Nietzsche, *to feel differently*—an even more important attainment, it seems. It is plausible that this therapeutic or educative aim of bringing about revised affective habits has the arousal of affects as a prerequisite: it is likely, in other words, that only a certain training through experiencing feelings will fundamentally alter my dispositions to feel positively or negatively in specific ways. If my understanding of the origins of my moral prejudices is to be genuinely *transformative* of my attitudes, it must proceed from and work upon my feelings, not consist in my merely holding as true certain hypotheses about myself. But the arousal of affects could be even more deeply embedded than this in Nietzsche's philosophical project. It could be, I want to argue, that the very task of arriving at truths about the origin of my values demands the activation of my own feelings.

Understanding our values properly will, given Nietzsche's picture of their genesis, require *understanding* the roles of our affects in producing and sustaining them—but the question is whether such understanding is itself conditional upon our *feeling* the affects Nietzsche is bent upon arousing in us. Let us suppose that revaluation will involve both thinking differently and feeling differently, and that it has among its instrumental conditions both an engagement of the affects and an understanding of truths concerning the history of our values: can the second of these conditions be fulfilled for Nietzsche independently of the first? If not, Nietzsche appears to depart even more strongly from standard scientific and scholarly methods, as he conceives them, and to follow the implicit principle 'Unless one becomes affectively engaged, one cannot attain truths about the causal history of one's moral evaluations'. Does Nietzsche believe something like that? If so, then his typical rhetoric is not extraneous to his central aims, but, in arousing the reader's emotions, functions as an indispensable means towards the task of discovering the affective causal origins of one's moral evaluations.

How happy should we be to attribute such a view to Nietzsche? Suppose someone reads the *Genealogy* and remains stalwartly unresponsive to the rhetoric. Could we stipulate that he or she could have reached no understanding of any of Nietzsche's hypotheses about the origin of values? Must someone who never felt the slightest twinge of compassion or thrill of hero-worship or shame at their own reactions fail to grasp the explanation offered for the transition from master-values to slave-values? It is not a plausible position. But there is a less extreme view that would take the relevant understanding to be a matter of degree: that the more we allow ourselves to feel, the better we unlock the causal truth about ourselves, or as Nietzsche himself puts it, '*the more* affects we allow to speak about a matter [...] that much more complete will our "concept" of this matter, our "objectivity" be'.[25] In support of such a view one can argue that arousing feelings helps our capacity to identify the true subject matter of the self-scrutinizing genealogical investigation. If the target explananda are my own moral values, and my personal affects are an essential rung on the explanatory ladder, then in order to understand the origin of my values I must recognize that these affects are explanatory, and that they have a cultural–psychological prehistory; and in order to recognize this about my affects I must recognize what my affects are, to do which, arguably, I would first have to feel them consciously. The argument would be that unless we *feel* specific affects we will be unable to identify them as ours, and hence unable to assign them any role in explaining the origin of our own moral evaluations.

A related consideration is as follows: when one is investigating the nature and origin of morality, acknowledgement of the role of one's own affects may be blocked by rationalization. This is especially likely given the conception of impersonal, dispassionate objectivity that dominates philosophical enquiry, but which Nietzsche opposes and diagnoses as an outgrowth from the very evaluative attitudes of selflessness that he is out to expose in Christian and post-Christian morality. As inheritors of the values of selflessness, philosophers 'all act as if they had discovered and arrived at their genuine convictions through the self-development of a cold, pure,

---

[25] *GM* III. 12. See Ch. 12 below for a full discussion of this passage.

divinely insouciant dialectic' (*BGE* 5). So from Nietzsche's point of view entering into conventional theorizing about our values already stacks the odds against discovering the huge affective dimension to them. Without Nietzsche's provocations our temptation might be to rest upon our learned attitudes and concepts, listening to the voice within us that tells us that compassion, equality, humility, and so on are 'right', regarding these values by default as unique and canonical, and justifying them by argument that we tell ourselves is rational, impersonal, and detached—nothing to do with the affects. If, as Nietzsche often reminds us, it is easy for the investigator to be complicit in ignoring the explanatory role of his or her own affects, the self-scrutinizing investigation Nietzsche advocates will be likely to succeed better to the extent that I feel and engage with the inherited affects which are at the basis of my attachment to morality.

4 Perils of Present Concepts: *Causa Fiendi* and False Unity

Further contrasts between Nietzsche's genealogical method and Rée's emerge from the methodological remarks in *GM* II, sections 12 and 13, surrounding the history of punishment. Nietzsche includes in the scope of his criticism here 'previous genealogists of morality' who 'discover some "purpose" or other in punishment, for example revenge or deterrence, then innocently place this purpose at the beginning as *causa fiendi* of punishment'.[26] The genealogist who makes deterrence the cause of punishment's coming into being is Rée.[27] His mistake, for Nietzsche, is to discover a single contemporary purpose or meaning in some human institution and assume it as *causa fiendi*, the cause of the institution's coming into being. Rée proceeds under the false assumption that punishment, useful as a deterrent today, must have originated as a deterrent, indeed as a deterrent to egoism, even though (as Nietzsche would argue) the question whether an action is egoistic arrives in human history much later than the institutions of punishment. Rée exemplifies a tendency to place present uses of moral concepts—'punishment' for what deters the egoistic, and 'good'

---

[26] *GM* II. 12, on which, see also Leiter (2002: 168, 198).
[27] On Rée's account of punishment, see Ch. 5 below.

used as praising the unegoistic—at the origin of morality. By offering an explanation in which selflessness features as *the* morality once and for all, Rée's origin story, a glum, deflationary story about why the unegoistic is associated with praise and the egoistic with blame, reinforces the present dominant conception of moral values, and the opportunity to *evaluate* the practices of praising the unegoistic and deterring the egoistic vanishes.

Related to this *causa fiendi* error is that of supposing that there is a single, readily available meaning for our own present concepts. Nietzsche offers instead the thought that 'use', 'purpose', or 'meaning' are fluid, and can be assigned anew to the same type of punitive act in any number of reinterpretations over time. This history of diverse uses and purposes remains incorporated in the concept that we have inherited, making it rich but problematic. 'Today it is impossible to say for sure why we actually punish,' says Nietzsche profoundly: 'all concepts in which an entire process is semiotically summarized elude definition' (*GM* II. 13). Because so much history is compacted into our present concepts, they do not really have a single reliable meaning or definition, merely a 'kind of unity' brought about by historical crystallization: and, like a crystal, a concept has now hardened so that its once fluid elements are 'difficult to dissolve'.

To grasp the real history of our values we require, then, some process that dissolves or explodes our apparently unified present-day concepts into their more primitive psychological components. This, I believe, is where the personal affects, and Nietzsche's deliberate rhetorical evocation of them, enter the picture. To overcome our reliance on received moral thinking we must understand it as a result of the diverse affective psychology of past human beings, and realize how much it retains vestiges of that psychology compacted within it. But for Nietzsche—I have argued—this understanding proceeds best by way of personal affective engagement. Because our moral concepts are *ex post facto* rationalizations of inherited affects, to whose explanatory role we may be blind, our own feelings 'for and against' need to be aroused and questioned, if we are to grasp the variegated psychological truth behind our concepts.

Note that when Nietzsche accuses previous genealogists of relying on their limited acquaintance with present-day concepts—'their own five-span-long, merely "modern" experience'—and says that in consequence they 'aren't good for anything' and 'stand in a relation to truth that is not even flirtatious' (*GM* II. 4), he twice replicates the terminology he used to castigate Rée's methodological selflessness in *The Gay Science*. The two faults—selfless approach to problems and lack of instinct for history—are linked. If they are linked in the way I have suggested, then we can see why it is that Paul Rée could not turn to 'real history'. He thought of his task as a cold, impersonal enquiry and did not allow his own affective responses, his gut allegiances, fears, admirations, and ambivalences, to inform him about the nature of his own values. Thus he missed the enormous psychological complexity behind the concepts 'good', 'conscience', 'punishment', and so on, and assumed that their current commerce with the morality of selflessness was a safe guide to their coming into being. In other words, complicity with the dominant self-image of *enquiry* as disinterested and impersonal leads to blindness to the truth about the role of one's multiple personal affects in the formation of one's concepts, to a false trust in the unity and serviceability of those concepts for history, and to the error of positing present functions and meanings as causally explanatory when they are not.

5 Conclusion

We began this chapter with some issues surrounding naturalism. For brevity's sake, I shall itemize some points that have emerged explicitly or implicitly from the above discussion:

1. Nietzsche can be read as a naturalist in that he seeks explanations that cite causes in ways that do not conflict with science.

2. Nietzsche's commitment to continuity of results with the sciences is put in some doubt by some of his statements about the fundamental explanatory notion of will to power, which may essentially import notions of overpowering and interpretation into the biological realm.

3. Nietzsche's methods, on the evidence of 'what he spends most of his time doing in his books', are characterized by artistic devices, rhetoric, provocation of the affects, and exploration of the reader's personal reactions, and show little concern for methods that could informatively be called scientific. His 'Methods Continuity' with the sciences is thus minimal, amounting merely to a concern to explain morality in terms of causes.

4. If Nietzsche's causal explanations of our moral values are naturalistic, they are so in a sense which includes within the 'natural' not merely

the psychophysical constitution of the individual whose values are up for explanation, but also many complex cultural phenomena and the psychophysical states of past individuals and projected types of individual.[28]

5. To the extent that scientific method is conceived as an impersonal, affect-free search for truth, Nietzsche is critical of it, because he holds that it disables the identification of one's affects through feeling them, and so obstructs the transformative grasp of the truth about the causal role of affects in the production of one's values.

6. Nietzsche's method of self-scrutiny, in questioning the enquirer's attachment to the values of selflessness, must also question his or her allegiance to the methodology of cool, detached enquiry that tends to characterize science, since this for Nietzsche is a version of selflessness. Nietzsche cannot simply assume scientific practice as a fixed and unproblematic paradigm for his enquiry into values, since he regards scientific practice as imbued with the very values he spends most of his time calling into question.

[28] See Williams (1994: 239) on the question of the scope of 'naturalistic' moral psychology.

4

Selflessness: The Struggle with Schopenhauer

The issue for me was the *value* of morality—and over this I had to struggle almost solely with my great teacher Schopenhauer [...] In particular the issue was the value of the unegoistic, of the instincts of compassion, self-denial, self-sacrifice, precisely the instincts that Schopenhauer had gilded, deified, and made otherworldly until finally they alone were left for him as the 'values in themselves', on the basis of which he *said 'no'* to life, also to himself.

(*GM*, Preface, 5)

Nietzsche here writes in the past tense because he is describing the underlying motive ('the passion and the secret contradiction') of his earlier book *Human, All Too Human*. But how much is the aftermath of that struggle visible in the *Genealogy* and how much is the struggle still being fought? Schopenhauer makes an appearance in the Third Treatise of the *Genealogy* as a psychological case study, the paradigmatic philosophical exponent of the ascetic ideal whose advocacy of asceticism is driven by a powerful will to escape his own sexual desires (*GM* III. 6), and later in the same treatise his theory of an extreme objectivity attained in will-less experience is set up to be superseded by Nietzsche's perspectivism.[1] Schopenhauer has no explicit presence in the other two treatises on 'good and evil' and 'guilt and bad conscience', but if we pause to examine Schopenhauer's own treatment of these ethical topics in *On the Basis of Morality* and the Fourth Book of *The World as Will and Representation*, we may stand to deepen our understanding of the equation of morality

---

[1] *GM* III. 12: the 'pure will-less, painless, timeless subject of knowledge'—on which, see Chs. 11 and 12 below.

with the 'unegoistic' or selflessness that defines Nietzsche's central target throughout the *Genealogy*.[2]

1 Beyond the Individual

According to Schopenhauer each individual is an expression of will, and as such naturally strives to fulfil its ultimate drive towards life. Each individual gravitates towards survival and sexual reproduction and is constantly full of desires (supposedly all reducible to these basic drives) that press him or her forward into action. We are egoistic by nature and the untutored evaluative outlook of each human being is to identify with the bodily manifestation of will he or she is. One of Schopenhauer's most fundamental ideas is that this identification is really a mistake, because we all at bottom share the same nature. The multiplicity of willing beings leads to conflict, destruction, and suffering, since one manifestation of will frequently has to encroach upon another. But multiplicity itself is only a surface phenomenon, and all individuals are ultimately manifestations of the same will.

The only true basis for morality, according to Schopenhauer, is compassion (*Mitleid*), that which prompts us to seek the well-being of another or to alleviate their woe. Every human being, he thinks, has some element of compassion in their character, but it has to compete against other incentives (*Triebfeder*), namely egoism, the incentive to seek one's own well-being, and malice, the incentive to seek the woe of another.[3] It is the egoistic force that compassion most has to contend with. Egoism makes up the bulk of the human character because it is identical, in humans as in all animals, to 'the craving for existence and well-being'.[4] The individual is a material organism in which will to life expresses itself: hence striving for one's own ends is fundamental to each individual. Indeed, so fundamental is it on Schopenhauer's theory that one must wonder how compassionate action is possible at all. His solution is to argue that non-egoistic action is possible

---

[2] Reginster (2006) contains a substantial study of the influence of Schopenhauer on many aspects of Nietzsche's philosophy of value (see esp. chs. 3 and 4).

[3] See esp. Schopenhauer (1995: 192).

[4] Ibid. 131. Schopenhauer says that egoism is 'colossal' and 'natural': it 'towers above the world' (p. 132).

because it actually occurs—it happens that people refrain from harming others with no obvious gain to themselves, sacrifice themselves for others in battle, surrender their livelihoods to alleviate the pain of those they do not know—and that if it occurs it must be because a basic anti-egoistic trait is present in us. Following this incentive one will act morally, in conformity with the single moral principle 'Injure no one; on the contrary, help everyone as much as you can', and perform actions of pure or voluntary justice (justice unconstrained by fear of law or punishment) or love of humanity (*Menschenliebe*), which we could also call philanthropy or loving-kindness. Only such non-egoistic actions can count as having true moral worth.[5]

Schopenhauer seeks to ground his account of compassion in ambitious metaphysical claims about the individual. My feeling compassion or (as the German *Mitleid* literally suggests) 'suffering with' another has as its condition that 'to a certain extent I have identified myself with the other person, and in consequence the barrier between the I and the non-I is for the moment abolished'.[6] To be compassionate, someone must make 'less of a distinction than do the rest between himself and others'.[7] Thus,

The *bad* man everywhere feels a thick partition between himself and everything outside him. The world to him is an *absolute non-I* and his relation to it is primarily hostile .... The good character, on the other hand, lives in an external world that is homogeneous with his own true being. The others are not non-I for him, but an 'I once more'. His fundamental relation to everyone is, therefore, friendly; he feels himself intimately akin to all beings, takes an immediate interest in their weal and woe, and confidently assumes the same sympathy in them.[8]

Thus selflessness takes on a deeper meaning for Schopenhauer. It is not just that in order to be good, each individual should refrain from selfish, egoistic action and be motivated by the compassionate impulse that places others' suffering and well-being above one's own. Rather, it is *being* an individual self as such that obstructs the attainment of genuine value. To look out on the world from the viewpoint of a self that prides itself on its distinction from the rest of reality—though our embodied nature dictates that we are condemned so to do—already produces a skewing of values because it is ultimately a falsification. Schopenhauer operates with a two-level picture of nature, and a fortiori of human nature. On the one

---

[5] See esp. Schopenhauer, 138–9. [6] Ibid. 166; trans. slightly modified. [7] Ibid. 204.
[8] Ibid. 211; trans. slightly modified.

hand there are empirically real individuals who inhabit the spatio-temporal world of phenomena, on the other, the supposedly ultimate reality beyond experience, the undivided thing in itself—undivided because space and time constitute the principle of individuation (*principium individuationis*) and space and time are, following Kant, a priori forms of the subject's experience only, not properties or relations existing in the world in itself. Therefore, the world in itself contains no individuals. Individuals are real in our experience, but to put one's faith in them as ultimately real is an error.

In illustration of Schopenhauer's view the following powerful passage is perhaps worth quoting at length (a passage, incidentally, well known to Nietzsche, who had included it in support of his position in section 1 of his first book, *The Birth of Tragedy*):

The eyes of the uncultured individual are clouded, as the Indians say, by the veil of Maya. To him is revealed not the thing in itself, but only the phenomenon in time and space, in the *principium individuationis*... In this form of his limited knowledge he sees not the inner nature of things, which is one, but its phenomena as separated, detached, innumerable, very different, and indeed opposed .... Just as the boatman sits in his small boat, trusting his frail craft in a stormy sea that is boundless in every direction, rising and falling with the howling mountainous waves, so in the midst of a world full of suffering and misery the individual man calmly sits, supported by and trusting the *principium individuationis*, or the way in which the individual knows things as phenomenon. The boundless world, everywhere full of suffering in the infinite past, in the infinite future, is strange to him, is indeed a fiction. His vanishing person, his extensionless present, his momentary gratification, these alone have reality for him; and he does everything to maintain them, so long as his eyes are not opened by a better knowledge .... For the knowledge that sees through the *principium individuationis*, a happy life in time, given by chance or won from it by shrewdness, amid the sufferings of innumerable others, is only a beggar's dream, in which he is a king, but from which he must awake, in order to realize that only a fleeting illusion had separated him from the suffering of his life.[9]

Schopenhauer thinks that in order not to 'confine reality to one's own person', in order to see the other as 'I once more', one has to regard, or at least glimpse, reality from a viewpoint other that of individuality. The moral knowledge that 'sees through the *principium individuationis*' requires 'complete elevation above individuality',[10] 'complete reform of

---

[9] Schopenhauer (1969: i. 352–3).   [10] Ibid. 355.

man's nature', or 'denial of one's own self'.[11] Thus Schopenhauer carries 'unselfing' to an extreme metaphysical pitch, where the self becomes both an illusion and an obstacle to true value.

2 Good, Bad, and Conscience

For Schopenhauer we do not will an object because it is good—it is good because we will it. The concepts *good* and *bad* are essentially relative and denote the suitableness or unsuitableness of an object 'to any definite effort of the will'.[12] A good person is someone whose lasting character and mode of conduct make them benevolent and friendly to the will of others in general.[13] A person is bad (*schlecht*) or evil (*böse, méchant*)[14] when their character makes them act against the will of others generally. Schopenhauer's analysis encompasses not merely the person's external effects, however, but the inner state of their character and knowledge. In the case of the bad character, its two fundamental elements are (1) the failure of knowledge that leads to a misplaced confidence in the reality of the individual and a vision of the rest of the world as 'absolute non-I'; and (2) an excessively vehement will to life. The latter manifests itself in action that is *wrong*, namely when one individual 'breaks through the boundary of another's affirmation of will', 'affirms his own will beyond his own body by denying the will that appears in the body of another', and 'destroys or injures this other body itself, or compels the powers of that other body to serve *his* will'.[15]

For Schopenhauer, certain *feelings* naturally arise in agents and patients who are party to right and wrong actions. First, the feeling of having been wronged. This is distinguishable from the pain or disadvantage one suffers at someone's hands. For example, one's house might be destroyed by a hurricane just as effectively as by an act of terrorism: in both cases, one feels the pain of losing one's property and shelter. But the feeling of having the space of one's will transgressed upon by the affirmation of another individual's will is 'an immediate and mental pain ... entirely separate and

---

[11] Schopenhauer ii. 625.   [12] Ibid. i. 360.   [13] Ibid. 360–1.

[14] Schopenhauer, unlike Nietzsche, makes no distinction between *schlecht* and *böse*, except that the latter term is expressly reserved for describing 'beings with knowledge (animals and human beings)' (ibid. 361).   [15] Ibid. 334.

different from the physical suffering through the deed or annoyance at the loss, which is felt simultaneously with it'.[16] This feeling appears to be instinctive: each living creature is the expression of will to life and registers negatively the impingement of another on its sphere of self-affirmation.

Secondly, there is a natural feeling towards subsequent suffering to be endured by the wrongdoer:

it affords satisfaction not only to the injured party, who is often filled with a desire for revenge, but also to the completely indifferent spectator, to see that the person who caused pain to another suffers in turn exactly the same measure of pain ... [The mind] longs to see again the pain in the same individual to whom the guilt belongs.[17]

Natural though this pleasure in the transgressor's pain might be, it has, for Schopenhauer, nothing to do with the genuine purpose of punishment. Rather, 'Seneca perfectly expresses ... the theory of all punishment in the short sentence: "*Nemo prudens punit, quia peccatum est, sed ne peccetur*".'[18] Punishment, in other words, is deterrence (*Abschreckung*) rather than retribution (*Vergeltung*). It deters the affirmation of the will by individuals from overstepping its bounds.[19] Punishment should not be confounded with revenge, which seeks consolation by repaying past evil with more evil, and indeed Schopenhauer classifies pure backward-looking retribution, with no further deterrent purpose, as wickedness and cruelty—a case of inflicting pain for the sake of one's own satisfaction.[20]

A third feeling that arises in the case of wrongdoing is felt by the transgressor: Schopenhauer calls it the feeling of having done wrong, also *Gewissensbiß* or *Gewissensangst*—the distress, pain, or pang of *conscience*.[21] Conscience is an 'obscurely felt but inconsolable misery' that is inseparable from bad or evil action (*Bosheit*).[22] His (or her) self-affirmation as a willing being must disturb the individual, because there is 'roused in the innermost depths of his consciousness the secret presentiment' that he is no different from the beings on whom his self-affirmation has inflicted the suffering:

---

[16] Ibid. 335. [17] Ibid. 357.

[18] Ibid. 349: 'No sensible person punishes because a wrong has been done, but in order that a wrong may not be done.'

[19] Ibid. 347–8. [20] Ibid. 348. [21] Ibid. 335, 364–5.

[22] Ibid. 366, 364 (Payne translates *Bosheit* as wickedness).

The wicked man's inward alarm at his own deed, which he tries to conceal from himself, contains that presentiment of the nothingness and mere delusiveness of the *principium individuationis*, and of the distinction established by this principle between him and others. At the same time it contains the knowledge of the vehemence of his own will, of the strength with which he has grasped life and attached himself firmly to it, this very life whose terrible side he sees before him in the misery of those he oppresses.[23]

It is as if, in hurting something that is not really distinct from me, I also feel the hurt, while at the same time not being able to escape the knowledge that it is my very essence—and that of my victim—that is at fault. Bernard Williams has recently written that the feeling of guilt is one in which we internalize the victim, or identify with an idealized figure whom we have wronged and on whose behalf we experience pain.[24] Schopenhauer takes *identification* with one's victim extremely literally:

the difference between the inflicter of suffering and he who must endure it is only phenomenon, and does not concern the thing in itself which is the will that lives in both … in the fierceness and intensity of its desire it buries its teeth in its own flesh … tormentor and tormented are one. The former is mistaken in thinking he does not share the torment, the latter in thinking he does not share the guilt.[25]

To act unselfishly, on the other hand, is already to feel oneself serenely at one with things: 'The good person lives in a world of friendly phenomena; the well-being of any of these is his own well-being'[26] and there is a corresponding 'satisfaction we feel after every disinterested deed',[27] to feel which is to have a good conscience.

Of these naturally arising feelings it is only conscience, both good and bad, that has a deep justification, according to Schopenhauer. The pain of being transgressed against and the joy felt at the transgressor's pain, though natural to individuated beings, mark a failure to see beyond the illusion of individuation. But the sting of bad conscience arises because agents who do wrong have an intuitive grasp both of their own nature as vehement will and of their connectedness with all other agents because of the illusoriness of the individual.

---

[23] Schopenhauer, 366.   [24] See Williams (1993: 219–23).
[25] Schopenhauer (1969: i. 354).   [26] Ibid. 374.   [27] Ibid. 373.

3 Nonsense about Compassion?

In *The Gay Science*, well after his disillusionment with all of Schopenhauer's doctrines,[28] Nietzsche complains that what impresses some of his
contemporaries in Schopenhauer are not his virtues as a philosopher, but
his 'excesses and vices', among which he lists

> the indemonstrable doctrine of *One Will* ('all causes are merely occasional causes
> of the appearance of the will at this time and this place'; 'the will to life is present
> wholly and undividedly in every being, even the least, as completely as in all
> beings that have ever been, are, and shall be, taken together'), the *denial of the
> individual* ('all lions are at bottom only one lion'; 'the plurality of individuals is an
> illusion' [...]) the nonsense about *compassion* and how, as the source of all morality,
> it enables one to make the break through the *principium individuationis*.
>
> (GS 99)

Nietzsche regards Schopenhauer as a rigorous-minded thinker who inhabits
a 'higher culture' than his crude followers; in *Human, All Too Human* (the
great polemic against Schopenhauer) he had even found him a 'real moralist
genius' beneath 'the motley leopard-skin of his metaphysics' (*HA* II/1. 33).
But the doctrines listed here are, for Nietzsche, 'mystical embarrassments
and evasions' where 'the factual thinker let himself be seduced and corrupted
by the vain urge to be the unriddler of the world'.

Why, in the first place, would an ethics of compassion such as Schopenhauer's need the metaphysical thesis that individuality is illusory? Why, in
order for me to view the world selflessly, does my self have to be lost
from reality altogether? Supposing we cast Schopenhauer's transcendent
metaphysics aside as an embarrassment, might there not be a Schopenhauerian basis for unegoistic morality in the idea of the essential parity of all
beings who strive and suffer? There are arguably two distinct thoughts in
play in Schopenhauer's ethics, both of which he uses but without always
distinguishing them:

(1) All individuals that appear as phenomena share a single common
essence or inner nature, in that they are all manifestations of will.

---

[28] A disillusionment that had already occurred by December 1876, eight years earlier, if we are to
believe Nietzsche's confessional letter to Cosima Wagner on the subject (*SB* v. 210). See also Janaway
(1998*b*: 13).

(2) The thing in itself beyond all phenomena is non-individuated, and individuality is illusory.

Most often Schopenhauer combines the two thoughts by saying that

(3) The single undivided thing in itself is the will, of which the many individuals are phenomenal, and ultimately illusory, manifestations.

This last claim faces a number of problems, not least that the thing in itself ought to remain wholly unknowable, as Schopenhauer himself sometimes recognizes.[29] He could consistently hold both (1) and (2): that will is the common essence shared by all phenomenal individuals and that the unknowable thing in itself is outside the principle of individuation. But for the purposes of his ethics we might suggest that (1) is sufficient.

It is unnecessary to think that the ethically good person must lack belief in distinct individuals (a lack which might anyway threaten to make morality impossible or redundant). Instead, what might ground compassionate actions is the idea that, though individuals are separate, there is nothing of any fundamental importance about the individual that I am, that I and another suffering person are equally expressions of will to life, so that from the point of view of the world as a whole, it is a matter of indifference whether my ends are promoted and the other's thwarted, or vice versa. The thought would be that ethics requires an impersonal 'universal standpoint'[30] from which all individuals can be treated as prima facie of equal worth, and that one attains this standpoint on seeing that we are all equally organic sentient beings that must strive to satisfy the same ineliminable ends and desires and must suffer from not fulfilling them. To attain this insight is to move beyond the 'boatman's' position of granting 'reality' only to his 'vanishing person, his extensionless present, his momentary gratification'. It is perhaps, in some attenuated sense, to cease to trust the *principium individuationis*, and to 'make less of a distinction than do the rest between himself and others'—although these insights need not be given a strictly metaphysical interpretation. To be compassionate, I need

---

[29] Compare a notable passage in the second volume of *The World as Will and Representation*: 'the question may still be raised what that will, which manifests itself in the world and as the world, is ultimately and absolutely in itself; in other words, what it is, quite apart from the fact that it manifests itself as *will*, or in general *appears*, that is to say, *is known* in general. This question can *never* be answered, because, as I have said, being-known of itself contradicts being-in-itself' (Schopenhauer 1969: ii. 198).

[30] Ibid. 599–600.

only make no distinction in *value* between myself and others, so I need lose 'trust' in the 'reality' of individuals only in the sense of not considering my own individuality a source of real value. How even this kind of universal standpoint is to be attained by beings whose essentially willing nature inclines them to egoism remains a potential problem for Schopenhauer. But, that aside, the universal standpoint would provide sufficient ground for treating all individuals justly and lovingly and for the feelings of conscience. Many will agree with Nietzsche that the doctrines about the One Will and the illusoriness of the individual are an excess and a mystical embarrassment—but to dismiss them does not automatically dispense with an ethics founded upon the non-egoistic virtues. So Nietzsche's resistance to the morality of compassion, if it is to be effective, must not limit itself to a critique of Schopenhauer's metaphysics.

In sections 5 and 6 of the *Genealogy*'s Preface, Nietzsche refers repeatedly to *Mitleid* and *Mitleids-Moral* (compassion and the morality of compassion) as something 'deified' by Schopenhauer, but opposed by himself as worthless and detrimental. Even before asking why and how Nietzsche opposes *Mitleid*, we should pause to ask *what* it is for him, since the word *Mitleid* can be translated either as 'compassion' or as 'pity', and it has been suggested that Schopenhauer and Nietzsche tend to use the term with these two different connotations respectively.[31] This leaves the potential to argue that the single German word masks an *ignoratio elenchi* on Nietzsche's part: that the *Mitleid* he opposes is not the *Mitleid* that Schopenhauer honours as the basis of all morality. On the other hand, if 'compassion' is the better translation for Nietzsche's uses of *Mitleid*, then his negative picture of it may lack conviction because of inaccuracy about the nature of compassion.

A sustained and penetrating dissection of the states of mind involved in *Mitleid* occurs in *Daybreak*, sections 132–8, where *Mitleid* is a 'polyphonous being', a state with many complexities and subtleties (*D* 133). Schopenhauer misobserved and misdescribed *Mitleid*, Nietzsche claims: it is not a feeling of the same kind as is felt by the suffering other, and does not embody any profound understanding of the nature of suffering. Sometimes we regard the suffering of others as offensive, demeaning, or threatening to ourselves, and acting upon *Mitleid* occurs while we are thinking 'very strongly unconsciously' of ourselves, as Nietzsche puts it. We act upon

---

[31] See Cartwright (1988); von Tevenar (2001); also Foot (2001: 108–10); Salaquarda (1996: 98).

Mitleid if we see a chance to gain an advantage, to 'present ourselves as the more powerful and as a helper, if we are certain of applause, if we want to feel how fortunate we are in contrast, or hope that the sight will relieve our boredom' (*D* 133). Beneath our helping behaviour towards those who are suffering lies a complex of different kinds of pleasure and ways to rid ourselves of our own suffering. The gist of this line of thought is that there is a range of subtly self-serving motives behind helping someone who is suffering. Schopenhauer's reply, however, might be that of course helping others is often motivated by self-interest—we are, after all, dominated by egoism and, furthermore, what we will is not always fully transparent to our consciousness[32]—but that is just to say that our motives are often complex and hard to fathom, and that helping others in need is not always motivated by compassion. Even if what Nietzsche here analyses is something called *Mitleid*, it does not seem to be a case of acting out of compassion, and does not show that there exists no pure drive towards identifying with and alleviating the pain of others.

Nietzsche claims also that feeling *Mitleid* is harmful to the person for whom we feel it, in that it amounts to their being despised, and being exposed to shame and humiliation (*D* 135). Here it certainly makes sense to think that Nietzsche is objecting to *pity*.[33] We do not want to be the objects of pity, because it reveals us before the witnessing gaze of the pitier as passive and powerless, as victims, and, as Nietzsche says in *The Gay Science*,[34] pity is felt as a diminution of 'our worth and our will' because it threatens to rob us of our individuality. The sheer external fact of our suffering places us in the category 'to be pitied', without concern for the particularities of 'the whole inner sequence and interconnection that spells misfortune for *me* or for *you*'. Pitying someone can rob them of their dignity and describe them in a depersonalizing way. This is much less clearly true of feeling genuine compassion towards someone—assuming there is such a feeling. Schopenhauer could argue (and there is perhaps a hint of this, albeit unexplored, in his 'I once more' formula), that a genuinely moral compassion would involve precisely what is lacking in pity, namely a concern for the dignity and particularity of the other.

[32] See Schopenhauer (1969: ii. 208–11).
[33] I am here indebted to the work of von Tevenar (2001, 2007).
[34] *GS* 338. Here the Nauckhoff translation opts for 'compassion', however.

Next there is Nietzsche's thought that *Mitleid* harms those who feel it. To the extent that feeling *Mitleid* is genuinely painful, it is an increase in the amount of suffering in the world, and to take sufferings of this kind upon oneself in a habitual manner would leave one 'sick and melancholic', harming one's strength and self-purpose and as a consequence making one less effective as a helper or healer. If one thinks in the first place of the medical profession, Nietzsche has a plausible point here: a doctor worn down by boundless painful identification with the ills of his or her patients would be ineffective. Nietzsche extends the thought to all forms of benefit to human beings: 'He [...] whose desire it is to serve mankind as a physician *in any sense whatever* will have to be very much on his guard against that sensation—it will paralyse him at every decisive moment and apply a ligature to his knowledge and his subtle helpful hand.' Too much pain felt at the pain around one is weakening, and 'supposing it was dominant even for a single day, mankind would immediately perish of it' (*D* 134).

In a poignant passage in *The Gay Science* 338, the feeling of *Mitleid* becomes harmful to the one who feels it because it exerts an all but irresistible pull away from his or her own life and sense of purpose:

I know, there are a hundred decent and praiseworthy ways of losing myself *from my path*, and, verily, highly 'moral' ways! Yes, the moral teacher of *Mitleid* even goes so far as to hold that precisely this and only this is moral—to lose *one's own* way like this in order to help a neighbour. I, too, know with certainty that I need only to expose myself to the sight of real distress and I, too, *am* lost! If a suffering friend said to me, 'Look, I am about to die; please promise to die with me,' I would promise it; likewise, the sight of a small mountain tribe fighting for its freedom would make me offer my hand and my life.

Here the relevant feeling sounds more like compassion. There is no element of superiority, contempt, or depersonalization in the attitudes Nietzsche describes towards the dying friend or the mountain tribe. There is a self-serving element in one's attitude, in that it lures one away from an 'own path' whose imperious burden one can wish to shed. But the issue appears to concern self-sacrifice through a drive that identifies intimately with the other's suffering. Nietzsche, moreover, agrees with Schopenhauer that such genuine compassion is the core of morality, and that it constitutes a kind of 'unselfing', a diminution or loss of importance in the self. So here

Nietzsche is on target to question the value of the central operative concept in Schopenhauer's morality of compassion.

By the time of the *Genealogy* Nietzsche has developed further thoughts concerning the harm of feeling compassion. He warns that the well-being of the strong among human beings depends upon their being kept safe from the sick who threaten not just to distract and decentre the healthy, but to undermine, contaminate, or poison them. 'The sick are the greatest danger to the healthy', he says (*GM* III. 14)—but by what means do they pose a threat? By inducing 'the great *disgust* at man' but also 'the great *compassion* for man'. What Nietzsche fears is that the sick

walk about among us as bodily reproaches, as warnings to us—as if health, being well-formed, strength, pride, a feeling of power were depraved things in themselves [...] so that the happy would one day begin to be ashamed of their happiness and perhaps say among themselves: 'It is a disgrace to be happy! *there is too much misery!*' ...But there could not be any greater and more doomful misunderstanding than when the happy, the well-formed, the powerful of body and soul begin to doubt their *right to happiness*.

(*GM* III. 14)

The self-confidence of the happy would arguably be attacked in this way only by their feeling genuine compassion for the mass of sufferers around them. If the strong merely *pitied* the sick, then there would not be the same danger. Pity despises, distinguishes, and reinforces the superiority of the pitier, thus employing the sight of the other's suffering as a means of protection against the other. But compassion brings the other's suffering into a more intimate relation with oneself. Rather than lowering the other to a position beneath oneself, it has the capacity to put the sufferer and the compassionate one on a par. For Nietzsche the risk in allowing oneself habitual and widespread compassion is that one's own well-being becomes devalued. Hence his rather brutal idea that for their own sake the healthy must at all costs be segregated from the sick. We might say again that Nietzsche agrees broadly with Schopenhauer that compassion weakens the boundaries and importance of the individual self—but that in this there lies a danger for those few whom he considers capable of having worthwhile selves.

Nietzsche pushes his anti-egalitarianism to a shocking pitch, saying that the 'right to exist' of the healthy and strong is 'a thousandfold greater' than that of the weak and sick (*GM* III. 14). And here we encounter a more fundamental objection to Schopenhauer's morality of compassion. We asked what might be the ground for such a morality if the metaphysical embarrassments about the One Will and so on were cast aside, and we answered that it lay in establishing the legitimacy of some 'universal standpoint' from which the well-being and suffering of all willing individuals rated equal in value. But Nietzsche has a firm stance on this issue: that the well-being and suffering of all does not matter equally, and that the notion of its mattering equally is a specific historical invention of the slave revolt in morality, founded upon the need for the *ressentiment* of the weak to discharge itself by forming an overpowering interpretation of the nature and causes of their sufferings. They had to believe that their suffering could matter to their oppressors, and that whoever suffers at the hands of the stronger ought not to suffer. Once more Schopenhauer was right that selfless compassion is the foundation of morality, but wrong to see this morality as the only set of ethical values or as self-evidently the best.

So we have found two Nietzschean objections to Schopenhauer's morality of compassion that do not depend upon criticism of his metaphysics and cannot obviously be deflected by the charge that they attack only a non-Schopenhauerian attitude of pity. The two objections are: (1) that the morality of compassion is founded upon a questionable notion of a universal equality in value between individuals; (2) that feeling compassion is not of itself a good and beneficial attitude, because it can divert one from attending to one's own life and rob one of the sense of a right to one's own well-being.

4 Suffering and Saying No

There is one more powerful criticism of Schopenhauer's morality of compassion in Nietzsche's armoury: that it is wrong to regard suffering itself as an *objection to life*:

To consider distress of all kinds as an objection, as something that must be abolished, is the *niaiserie par excellence* and, on a large scale, a veritable disaster in its consequences, a nemesis of stupidity—almost as stupid as would be the desire to abolish bad weather.

(*EH*, 'Why I Am a Destiny', 4)

In fastening upon compassion for suffering as the prime value, morality gives preference to what is passive and vulnerable in humanity, rather than to its strength and creativity. This is well expressed in *Beyond Good and Evil*:

You want, if possible (and no 'if possible' is crazier) *to abolish suffering*. And us?—it looks as though *we* would prefer it to be heightened and made even worse than it has ever been! [...] The discipline of suffering, of *great* suffering—don't you know that *this* discipline has been the sole cause of every enhancement in humanity so far? [...] In human beings, *creature* and *creator* are combined: in humans there is material, fragments, abundance, clay, dirt, nonsense, chaos; but in humans there is also creator, maker, hammer-hardness, spectator-divinity and seventh day:—do you understand this contrast? And that *your Mitleid* is aimed at the 'creature in humans', at what needs to be molded, broken, forged, torn, burnt, seared and purified,—at what necessarily needs to *suffer* and *should* suffer?

(*BGE* 225)

While for Schopenhauer suffering is as such something lamentable about life, and life itself is a wrong path from which we require redirection and redemption, for Nietzsche life—for those who are strong enough and creative enough—is to be thoroughly affirmed. Suffering should not count against life, but be valued as something that breeds strength, inventiveness, courage, and greatness, at least in those in whom the 'creator' has not been stifled already by their weak natures or destructive circumstances.

Suffering indeed looms large in Schopenhauer's philosophy. He sees it as ubiquitous in human existence—'constant suffering is essential to all life'[35]—and as robbing that existence of any true value. To affirm life is natural for us because will to life is what we essentially are, for Schopenhauer. But a different outlook arises when the will to life is quietened or sedated by the realization that willing is as such a painful condition for all willing creatures. One then sees that the world devours itself to no avail, that it is of no consequence whether at any moment the particular portion of the world one is identical to is devouring or being devoured, and that nothing that one desires, hopes for, or succeeds in doing as an individual subject of willing constitutes a good sufficient to compensate for the burden of existing with all its suffering. This state of

---

[35] Schopenhauer (1969: i. 283).

knowledge is superior to the affirmation of life, for Schopenhauer, and is redemptive: 'true salvation (*Heil*), deliverance (*Erlösung*) from life and suffering, cannot even be imagined without complete denial of the will'.[36] Denial of the will occurs when knowledge acts as 'the quieter of the will', instead of motivating it as usual.[37] Rather than giving one *reason* to take an attitude of denial, knowledge seems to act causally here, knocking out the impulse to do, strive, or desire on one's own behalf as an individual: as a result 'the will ... turns away from life'.[38] Though the details of how this happens are obscure,[39] Schopenhauer seems to envisage that a deep insight into the ubiquity of suffering brings about in my consciousness a detachment of identification from the individual embodiment of the will that I am. 'Till then', he says, 'everyone is nothing but this will itself.'[40] What is denied is therefore nothing less than my essence, myself as such. After knowledge has quietened the will, the subject continues existing, but merely as if it were a will-less subject of knowledge, a disembodied point of view on the world.[41]

Schopenhauer thus advocates a selflessness that stretches way beyond morality. Morality is but a step on the road of total self-abnegation: 'from the same source from which all goodness, affection, virtue, and nobility of character spring, there ultimately arises also what I call denial of the will to life'.[42] As Nietzsche saw, Schopenhauer's moral selflessness is symptomatic of a tendency to negate the self altogether, a 'sublime lure and temptation [...] into nothingness', and the key to the attainment of value for Schopenhauer is saying no to life and to himself (*GM*, Preface, 5). Willing, living, existing as an individual human being are, if correctly understood, the occasion for lamentation, and anyone who sees things aright will not want even a single repetition of his or her life, and 'will much prefer to choose complete non-existence'.[43]

Denial of the will to life—or the threat of it, the need to oppose it—is prominent in the polemic of Nietzsche's mature works. After the

---

[36] Ibid. 397.　　　[37] Ibid. 285, 334, 379, 397.　　　[38] Ibid. 379.

[39] We are supposed to think that, while the individual has no freedom at all, the will in itself, existing beyond space, time, and causality, is 'absolutely free and entirely self-determining'—so much so that it can reverse direction and annul its own self-expression (see Schopenhauer 1969: i. 285, 286–8, 300–1, 386, 402). But then how can it be that knowledge *acts* (causally) upon the will so as to reverse its direction?

[40] Ibid. i. 397.　　　[41] Ibid. 390.

[42] Ibid. 378. I consistently use 'will to life' for *Wille zum Leben* instead of Payne's 'will-to-live'.

[43] Ibid. 324.

Genealogy he claims that he was the first to see the opposition between 'the degenerating instinct that turns against life with subterranean vengefulness (Christianity, the philosophy of Schopenhauer)' and 'a formula for the highest affirmation [...] a Yes-saying without reservation, even to suffering, even to guilt, even to everything that is questionable and strange in existence' (*EH*, 'The Birth of Tragedy', 2). He describes Christianity itself in Schopenhauerian terms as a 'denial of the will to life become religion', which sets itself against 'a higher order of values [...] that say Yes to life' (*EH*, 'The Case of Wagner', 2). Thus Nietzsche's reaction to Schopenhauer's conception of value sustains his drive to find a manner in which to affirm life as absolutely as Schopenhauer says no to it, an antidote, or antipode, designed to consist in the avoidance of self-denial or self-rejection in any degree whatever. While the *Genealogy* concentrates on undermining the negative ideals of selflessness and makes only veiled mention of affirmative ideals, Nietzsche had already made the connection explicit in *Beyond Good and Evil:*

Anyone like me, who has tried for a long time and with some enigmatic desire, to think pessimism through to its depths and to deliver it from the half-Christian, half-German narrowness and naiveté with which it has finally presented itself to this century, namely in the form of the Schopenhauerian philosophy; anyone who has ever really looked with an Asiatic and supra-Asiatic eye into and down at the most world-negating of all possible ways of thinking—beyond good and evil, and no longer, like Schopenhauer and the Buddha, under the spell and delusion of morality—; anyone who has done these things (and perhaps precisely *by* doing these things) will have inadvertently opened his eyes to the inverse ideal: to the ideal of the most high-spirited, vital, world-affirming individual, who has learned not just to accept and go along with what was and what is, but who wants it again *just as it was and is* through all eternity.

(*BGE* 56)

Nietzsche here alludes to his own idea of the eternal return (or eternal recurrence) of the same, which was set out by the character Zarathustra in Nietzsche's earlier book[44] and in *The Gay Science*, where he asks us to imagine a demon appearing and announcing that 'This life as you now live it and have lived it you will have to live once again and innumerable times

---

[44] See *Z* III, 'On the Vision and the Riddle'.

again'[45] and to consider whether we would rejoice or despair at the thought. Commentators have sometimes found it perplexing that the Nietzschean affirmer must apparently affirm an *absolutely identical* repetition of life, rather than a closely similar one. Why is no thought given to the choice of a mostly similar, but lightly edited life? But if Nietzsche's search for a 'highest formula of affirmation' is seen in the context of Schopenhauer's pessimism, he gains a motivation for attaining the maximum distance between his ideal and Schopenhauer's. Once one starts assessing life in terms of its pluses and minuses, setting all suffering per se down as a minus, as Schopenhauer does, one might imagine oneself on the slippery slope to Schopenhauer's *Nichtigkeit*, the 'nothingness' or worthlessness of life, if one tends, as Nietzsche does, to think of suffering as inevitable and pervasive. Finding a 'highest formula of affirmation', in which nothing of one's life can be set aside as unwanted, would be the surest way to stop the slide. In that case it becomes intelligible that Nietzsche should regard any hint of wanting or wishing that life be different as a negation of what is one's own, and most inalienably one's own—oneself.

Towards the end of this book we shall return to consider the positive values or ideals that Nietzsche might be able to substitute for those of selflessness. In closing, however, let us remark two more significant and perturbing features of Schopenhauer's treatment of suffering. First, that suffering is deserved; secondly, that, should it become severe enough, it is welcome for its capacity to break the will to life and deliver us into will-less resignation. Schopenhauer holds that 'every great pain, whether bodily or mental, states what we deserve; for it could not come to us if we did not deserve it'.[46] His reasoning towards this conclusion begins with the idea of eternal justice pertaining on a cosmic scale. In the world, he holds, there can never be more suffering than there is transgression:

If we want to know what human beings, morally considered, are worth as a whole and in general, let us consider their fate as a whole and in general. This fate is want, wretchedness, misery, lamentation, and death. Eternal justice prevails; if they were

[45] GS 341. The idea of eternal return is discussed at some length in the retrospective *Ecce Homo*; see *EH*, 'Why I Am So Wise', 3 (though not in Kaufmann's version); 'The Birth of Tragedy', 3; 'Thus Spoke Zarathustra', 1, 6. It also figures in *Twilight of the Idols*; see *TI*, 'What I Owe to the Ancients', 4, 5. See also the notes on 'European Nihilism' from 1887 (*KSA* xii. 211–17); trans. in Ansell Pearson and Large (2006: 385–9). [46] Schopenhauer (1969: ii. 580).

not as a whole contemptible, their fate as a whole would not be so melancholy .... If we could lay all the misery of the world in one pan of the scales, and all its guilt in the other, the pointer would certainly show them to be in equilibrium.[47]

However, even from such a cosmic equilibrium between guilt and misery it does not follow that *I* deserve all *my* misery.[48] For one thing, much suffering is not caused by wrongdoing or even by human action at all. And even if the argument is restricted to harm for which someone is to blame, it does not follow that *I* am to blame when I suffer.[49] The reader of the *Genealogy* must be reminded of the perversity of Nietzsche's ascetic priest in the Third Treatise, who says to his flock: 'That's right, my sheep! someone must be to blame for it [your suffering]: but you yourself are this someone, you alone are to blame for it—*you alone are to blame for yourself*!' (*GM* III. 15).

Schopenhauer also holds that we deserve to suffer because existence itself is a kind of hubris that must be requited:

Christianity is the doctrine of the deep guilt of the human race by reason of its very existence, and of the heart's intense longing for salvation therefrom. That salvation, however, can be attained only by the heaviest sacrifices and by the denial of one's own self, hence by a complete reform of man's nature.[50]

Again a comparison with Nietzsche's deconstruction of guilt and bad conscience in the Second Treatise of the *Genealogy* is inescapable. Nietzsche diagnoses

the *will* of man to find himself guilty and reprehensible to the point that it cannot be atoned for; his *will* to imagine himself punished without the possibility of the punishment ever becoming equivalent to the guilt; his *will* to infect and make poisonous the deepest ground of things with the problem of punishment and guilt.

(*GM* II. 22)

Nietzsche is also accurate about the relation between Schopenhauer's position and a tendency towards Buddhism, for, while he often gives

---

[47] Schopenhauer, i. 352.

[48] As David Hamlyn has pointed out; see Hamlyn (1988: 283).

[49] The strangeness of Schopenhauer's logic is particularly striking here. It is 'what I am in myself' that both transgresses and suffers. But 'what I am in myself' is the undivided will that is no more me than anything else. So the argument would have to go something like this: The world suffers as much as it transgresses. I am the world. So I suffer as much as I transgress. And a further dubious premiss is needed: that to suffer *as much as* one transgresses is the same as to *deserve* one's suffering.

[50] Schopenhauer (1969: ii. 625).

priority to Christianity, Schopenhauer advocates synthesizing East and West:

Christianity taught only what the whole of Asia knew already long before and even better ... that great fundamental truth contained in Christianity as well as in Brahmanism and Buddhism, the need for salvation from an existence given up to suffering and death, and its attainability through the denial of the will, hence by a decided opposition to nature, is beyond all comparison the most important truth there can be.[51]

Finally, Schopenhauer thinks that suffering is not valueless in the end: its worth lies in its potential to make one realize that no value can be found in *living*. The common route to attaining knowledge of the significance of suffering (for those who are not saints) is the undergoing of suffering sufficient to break the will to life[52]—'Suffering is the fleetest animal that bears you to perfection.'[53] In such a case suffering can be redeemed, for Schopenhauer, by its power to generate the knowledge that I, as much as every other living manifestation of will, am *nichtig*—worth nothing, in vain.[54] So from an allegedly higher point of view suffering can be accepted as a kind of good. But that higher standpoint finds *suffering* a good by denying that *life* as such can ever be. To speak the diagnostic language Nietzsche adopts in the Third Essay of the *Genealogy*, Schopenhauer hereby assigns an ascetic 'meaning' to suffering: that it can reveal the individual human being who lives, strives, and procreates as lacking genuine value. As Nietzsche puts it, he 'wills his own nothingness' so as to give a redeeming interpretation to his existing at all.[55]

---

[51] Ibid. 627–8.   [52] Ibid. i. 392, 397.

[53] A quotation from Meister Eckhart, which Schopenhauer uses at Schopenhauer (1969: ii. 633).

[54] Ibid. i. 397. In translation Schopenhauer here seems to talk of the 'essential vanity' of the will to life—but Payne uses 'vanity' to translate the word *Nichtigkeit*, or nothingness. Cf. the title of *The World as Will and Representation*, vol. ii, ch. 46, 'Von der Nichtigkeit und dem Leiden des Lebens', where Payne also uses 'vanity' for *Nichtigkeit*. This translation mutes the bleakness of Schopenhauer's message, and makes it harder to discern the connection with Nietzsche's conception of *das Nichts wollen* in *GM* III. 1 and 28.   [55] See *GM* III. 28, and Ch. 13 below.

5

Nietzsche and Paul Rée
on the Origins of Moral Feelings

In reading the *Genealogy*'s Preface we became aware of Nietzsche's pre-occupation with Paul Rée as an opponent, and have discussed some of the methodological differences at stake between Nietzsche's genealogy of morality and that which Rée purports to give. Rée is a closer opponent than Schopenhauer, not only because of his acquaintance and collaboration with Nietzsche, but because, while Schopenhauer's account is firmly ahistorical and supported by a transcendent metaphysics, Rée attempts a proper history of morality in naturalistic terms. A first glance at the organization of Rée's book sparks the hypothesis that the *Genealogy* may be designed as (among many other things) a kind of riposte to his former friend. Rée's first two chapters have titles strikingly similar to Nietzsche's, 'The Origin of the Concepts Good and Evil' and 'The Origin of Con-science' ('Der Ursprung der Begriffe gut und böse', 'Der Ursprung des Gewissens'), and the next two chapters deal with other issues central to Nietzsche's discussion, notably free will (or the absence of), responsibility (or the absence of), punishment, deterrence, and retribution. The dialogue between the *Genealogy* and Rée's *Origin of the Moral Sensations* is therefore worth exploring a little further.

1 Rée's Account of 'Good and Bad'

Rée's book is dominated by his account of the distinction between good and bad (the latter not distinguished by him from 'evil'—of which more later). In outline Rée argues as follows. Human beings have natural, inborn drives, of which the dominant and most ancient is an egoistic drive, directed towards self-preservation, sexual fulfilment, and the satisfaction of vanity. While egoism gives rise to hard-heartedness, envy, hatred, vengefulness, cruelty, and malicious pleasure,[1] there is an opposing 'unegoistic' or 'non-egoistic' drive, which is said to be the source of unselfishness, compassion, benevolence, sacrifice, selflessness, and love of one's neighbour.[2] Egoism is dominant in us, for if it were not, then the morality that values the unegoistic, which Rée takes to be morality as such, would not have arisen: this morality 'requires the existence of the bad (egoism): it is just in opposition to this undesirable behavior that non-egoistic behavior is what is desirable, praiseworthy, and good'.[3] Rée faces the same fundamental question as Schopenhauer: if egoism is dominant, how is it possible to act in the interests of others or to have the unegoistic feelings or traits of character? His answer, though eschewing anything remotely like the Schopenhauerian metaphysics, is similar: there simply exists an unegoistic or altruistic drive, which, though weaker than the egoistic, is also inborn in human beings. So unegoistic attitudes and behaviour naturally occur in human beings; and morality arises because positive feelings come to be associated with this part of our natural behaviour, and negative feelings with the more prevalent egoistic parts.

Rée shows his naturalistic credentials early on by rejecting the transcendental accounts of altruism offered by Schopenhauer and Kant: such accounts admittedly give a deeper significance to the good and the bad (and to their depictions in art), but 'a significance that is…too deep: for the explanation of those philosophers is deeper than the object to be explained'[4]—worse, for Rée, than giving no explanation at all. The right explanation is, he maintains, that of Darwin: an inborn social drive, an instinct to care for one's group, develops as a broadening of an original parental instinct in humans and other animals, and is preserved and strengthened by natural selection because more socially cohesive groups succeed at the expense of others. Rée's view is expressed with characteristic terseness in the following passage:

---

[1] *Hartherzigkeit, Neid, Hass, Rachsucht, Grausamkeit, Schadenfreude*, Rée (1877: 21, 45, 64). In the translation, see Rée (2003: 100, 113, 122–3).

[2] *Uneigennützigkeit, Mitleid, Wohlwollen, Aufopferung, Selbstlosigkeit, Nächstenliebe*, Rée (1877: 21, 45). In the translation, see Rée (2003: 100, 113).

[3] Rée (2003: 97). Small translates *das Unegoistische* with the perhaps more felicitous 'non-egoistic' and 'non-egoism'. [4] Ibid. 98–9.

Everyone cares partly for himself, partly for others.

Anyone who cares for himself at the expense of others is called bad (*schlecht*) and blamed; anyone who cares for others for their own sake is called good and praised. Such good actions are possible only because we have already inherited from our animal ancestors the drive to care for others.[5]

For Rée the original attaching of praise and blame to the two kinds of action is explained by way of utility and disutility: 'Egoistic actions that occur at the expense of others were originally condemned on account of their harmfulness; non-egoistic actions were originally praised on account of their usefulness (*Nutzen*).'[6] If negative feelings had not generally been felt towards egoism, and positive feelings towards the unegoistic, the familiar 'war of all against all' would have obtained. But a group in whose members the association of positive feelings with the unegoistic becomes habitual attains a state of greater 'peace' and prospers in comparison with others. In an early phase of development—still represented for Rée by the practice of *Wilden*, or 'savages'—for someone to be called good it was sufficient that they had useful *effects* for the community. But as the capacity for knowledge developed, it was realized that the usefulness of an individual's behaviour to the community was affected also by the individual's *motivation*. So, in morality proper, a shift has been made to praising or blaming individuals in the light of their *motives*. For example, a doctor who performs ordinary medical tasks benefits others, but, being also motivated by self-interest, is not praised as morally good. Nor is someone who never harms fellow human beings, but whose restraint is motivated merely by fear of being punished. The practice of moral praise attaches to actions that are purely unegoistic in their motivation, i.e. that aim at fostering the well-being of others or preventing harm to them *for their own sake*. And Rée argues that the peace of the community as a whole is enhanced by the arrival of such a practice: 'When people refrain from harming others not out of fear but for their own sake, peace is not imposed artificially from outside but comes from inside. Not only hostile acts but also hostile feelings such as envy and hate disappear; the mind itself is peaceable and peace extends throughout.'[7] In other words, the instrumental value of promoting peace in the group is best achieved if its members regard following the unegoistic instinct as valuable in itself.

---

[5] Rée 99.   [6] Ibid. Small translates *Nutzen* as 'utility'.   [7] Ibid. 96–7.

Rée carefully distinguishes the *original value* of these blamings and praisings from the value thought to obtain in current moral practice:

Egoistic actions ... were originally condemned on account of their harmfulness; non-egoistic actions were originally praised on account of their usefulness. Later, the former were condemned in their own right, and the latter praised in their own right.[8]

Rée equates goodness with utility: 'good and useful are used as synonyms ... for example, foods, utensils, soldiers are called good when they are useful'.[9] So if nowadays we praise and blame thinking that there is some intrinsic, non-utility-related goodness or badness in different types of action, we have fallen into an error, which Rée explains as arising through conditioning. Repeated conjunction of unegoistic actions with feelings of approbation has produced an unbreakable involuntary connection between the two in our minds, and likewise in the case of egoism and feelings of blame. We now praise the unegoistic actions and feelings *tout court*, unmindful that we came to do so because of their social usefulness.

Though the egoistic and unegoistic drives are inborn, there is, for Rée, nothing inborn or necessary in the relationship between the feelings of praise or blame and the two types of action. It is simply that from childhood, in the culture we happen to inhabit, we constantly see the unegoistic praised, the egoistic blamed, both in real life and in fictions, and then cannot help associating actions and feelings in this way. A human being in the state of nature (*Naturmensch*) might feel an antipathy towards someone acting cruelly, but the association of blame with cruelty is a culturally learned habit. A reverse conditioning could have given rise to habitual feelings of approbation towards expressions of egoism. Thus, for Rée, unegoistic behaviour has only utility value and no intrinsic value:

The good person is a useful animal (*ein nützliches Thier*), the bad person is a harmful animal ... just as the dog that bites considered in itself is not bad but just an animal of a certain nature, so too the cruel person considered in himself is not bad but just an animal of a certain nature. It is senseless to call cruelty considered in itself bad, just as it is senseless to describe as bad in itself an extreme temperature or anything else that is bad just for human beings.

---

[8] Ibid. 99.   [9] Ibid. 98; see also 120–1.

So if cruelty and egoistic behavior in general, considered in themselves, are not bad but just behavior of a certain nature, then this behavior considered in itself cannot be liable to blame, punishment, or retribution.[10]

2 How Rée Goes Wrong 'Right at the Beginning'

One can immediately see why Nietzsche says of Rée that 'in his hypoth-esizing we have [...] the Darwinian beast politely joining hands with the most modern, unassuming moral milquetoast who "no longer bites" ' (*GM*, Preface, 7), and that he 'sees [the altruistic manner of valuation] as the moral manner of valuation *in itself*' (*GM*, Preface, 4). However, something else deserves comment. In Rée's title for chapter 1 the topic is the concepts good and evil (*böse*). But throughout the chapter, and indeed right through the book as a whole, he refers to good and bad (*schlecht*), without ever addressing the question whether evil is the same concept as bad. Nietzsche's First Treatise capitalizes on this telling piece of inattention by making the opposition 'good and evil' both distinct from 'good and bad' and distinctive of a certain psychology underlying Judaeo-Christian morality. This is the first clue to the complexity of morality's origins to be discovered by Nietzsche's alternative form of genealogy.

In the Preface to the *Genealogy* we saw Rée singled out for his genealog-ical hypotheses of 'the specifically *English* sort', for thinking 'like all English genealogists of morality', and for 'English hypothesizing *into the blue*' (*GM*, Preface, 4, 7). When the First Treatise opens with its famous casual reference to 'these English psychologists', also known as 'these historians of morality', only a reader who has forgotten the immediately preceding Preface will fail to see Rée as at least included in the description, as typical of the species referred to. However, I shall contend that Rée is *the* referent of the playful phrase 'these English psychologists'. *The Origin of the Moral Sensations* is still the only book, apart from his own works, that Nietzsche has named up to this point. And, most importantly, the theory deftly presented and dissected in *GM* I. 1–3 is demonstrably that contained in Rée's book.

According to Clark and Swensen, 'it has been suggested that this phrase ["English psychologists"] refers to the British philosophers of the utilitar-ian—associationist school, perhaps especially Hume, Hartley, Hutcheson,

---

[10] Rée 123; trans. slightly amended.

Bentham, and Mill'.[11] But, although Rée adopts from this tradition the notions of utility, association of ideas, and feelings of approbation and blame, he augments these with the later (though still 'English') notions of natural selection and instinctive drives, and adds the idea that utility is now forgotten in moral judgements—so that for him they are not straightforwardly *judgements of* utility—and produces out of these materials a somewhat distinctive theory. And this is the theory Nietzsche in fact addresses in *GM* I. 1–3. That Rée is under discussion is apparent even at the level of vocabulary. Clark and Swensen note that Nietzsche uses the term 'usefulness' (*Nützlichkeit*), rather than 'utility' (*Utilität*), 'although Nietzsche is discussing utilitarianism here'.[12] But if Nietzsche is discussing Rée, then Rée's words *Nützlichkeit* or *Nutzen* are just right. The rather inelegant central term 'the unegoistic' (*das Unegoistische*) is also a straight lift from Rée, though Nietzsche has at his disposal *altruistisch*—a word Rée does not use.[13] Clark and Swensen are right when they say that 'the only thinker specifically associated with an "English" account of morality in GM is ... Paul Rée'. But arguably they should have left it there: if we are looking for Nietzsche's immediate target, there is no need for any further specu- lative listing of candidate Englishmen or indeed Scots. Herbert Spencer is mentioned in *GM* I. 3, but Nietzsche explicitly *contrasts* Spencer's theory with the one under discussion, as making more sense, though also wrong.[14] The theory under discussion in *GM* I. 1–3 is Rée's, pure and simple.[15]

To establish this claim we need only realize that the following statement of the theory by Nietzsche is an accurate paraphrase of Rée, occasionally verging on quotation:

The ineptitude of their moral genealogy is exposed right at the beginning, where it is a matter of determining the origins of the concept and judgment 'good'.

---

[11] Clark and Swensen (1998: 129). Their source is Thatcher (1989: 588).

[12] Clark and Swensen (1998: 129).   [13] Nietzsche uses *altruistisch* in *GM*, Preface, 4.

[14] On Rée and Spencer, see Small (2003, pp. xxii–xxv, xliii–xliv).

[15] See Small (2003, p. xli). Leiter (2002: 198) and Thatcher (1989: 588) note that Rée's theory is the one criticized and half-quoted here. Leiter states (p. 197) that Nietzsche uses the term 'English psychologists' 'extremely loosely' in *GM* I. 1, since the primary example discussed is Rée. Thatcher takes 'English psychologists' literally, and speculates that in *GM* I. 1 Nietzsche refers to W. E. H. Lecky's *History of European Morals* (1869), of which he possessed a much annotated copy, and of which he wrote in a letter, 'such Englishmen lack "the historical sense" and some other things too' (Letter to Overbeck, 24 Mar. 1887, *SB* viii. 49). Even if we read *GM* I. 1 more literally as making this general reference, it seems inadequate to say merely that to the list of British thinkers covered by Lecky 'the name of Paul Rée should be added'—for Rée is the chief target for criticism.

'Originally'—so they decree—'unegoistic actions were praised and called good from the perspective of those to whom they were rendered, hence for whom they were *useful*; later one *forgot* this origin of the praise and, simply because unegoistic actions were *as a matter of habit* always praised as good, one also felt them to be good—as if they were something good in themselves.'[16]

There is also a significant detail here: Nietzsche says 'they' go wrong 'right at the beginning'. At the beginning of what? The passage in quotation marks supplies the answer by giving the gist of Rée's *opening chapter* accurately in Rée's own vocabulary. The 'beginning' is that of Rée's book. The 'they' is Rée.

Nietzsche raises two argumentative objections against Rée's theory. The second, to which section 3 is devoted, is a crisp internal objection that charges Rée with 'inherent psychological absurdity'. A theory such as Spencer's, which Nietzsche says equates 'good' and 'useful' straight-forwardly, so that to judge something good is to make a judgement of its utility, is 'in itself reasonable and psychologically tenable', though still wrong by Nietzsche's lights. Rée, by contrast, thinks the origin of the concept 'good' in social usefulness is forgotten. But for this to be right, Nietzsche replies, either the actions labelled 'good' would have to have ceased to be useful, which is false, or we would have to have forgotten a usefulness that is constantly reinforced by experience, which is impossible (or at least utterly unexplained by Rée).

The other objection against Rée's theory of the origins of 'good and bad' leads straight into Nietzsche's own account in the remainder of *GM* I. It is that Rée is wrong about the origins of judgements of 'good' because of a false assumption about *who* originally made such judgements. Rée regards his original human community as a group of homogeneous individuals with a single potential benefit in cooperation. He ignores any form of cultural differentiation or power-relation within the community, concentrating

---

[16] *GM* I. 2. Compare Nietzsche's text with Rée's. Nietzsche: 'Man hat ursprünglich [...] unegoistis-che Handlungen von Seiten Derer gelobt und gut genannt, denen sie erwiesen wurden, also denen sie *nützlich* waren; später hat man diesen Ursprung des Lobes *vergessen* und die unegoistischen Handlungen einfach, weil sie *gewohnheitsmässig* immer als gut gelobt wurden, auch als gut empfunden—wie also ob sie an sich etwas Gutes wären.' Rée (1877: 17): 'Das Gute (Unegoistiche) [ist] wegen seines Nutzens, nämlich darum gelobt worden, weil es uns einem Zustande der Glückseligkeit näher bringt. Jetzt aber loben wir die Güte nicht wegen ihrer nützenden Folgen, vielmehr erschient sie uns an und für sich, unabhängig von allen Folgen, lobenswerth. Trotzdem kann sie ursprünglich wegen ihres Nutzens gelobt worden sein, wenn man auch später, nachdem man sich einmal daran gewöhnt hatte, sie zu loben, vergass, dass dieses Lob sich anfangs auf den Nutzen der Gemeinschaft gründete.'

only on survival advantages for the group as a whole vis-à-vis other competitor groups. Nietzsche's fundamental shift is towards differentiating concepts according to the individuals or classes who use them, and who thereby control and create values. So Nietzsche alleges that 'the judgement "good" does *not* stem from those to whom "goodness" is rendered'. Rather 'the noble, powerful, higher-ranking, and high-minded' laid claim to the description of themselves as good, and by virtue of the 'pathos of distance' regarded as bad 'everything base, low-minded, common, and vulgar' (*GM* I. 2). This has two fatal consequences for Rée's theory. First, that the concept of *usefulness* is out of place in explaining the origins of 'good'; secondly, that there is no original connection between 'good' and the *unegoistic* at all.

Part of Nietzsche's attack on the present-day *idée fixe* that associates the unegoistic with the concept 'good' is to untangle the two at the level of origins. So on Nietzsche's account, long before the unegoistic was marked out as especially valuable, and even before there were the concepts *egoistic* and *unegoistic*, 'good' and similar evaluations connoted nobility, prowess, and inclusion within a self-confident aristocratic class as someone with the appropriate manners and nature. The aristocrats were *aristoi*: the best.[17] The central narrative of *GM* I tells how those excluded from this conception of goodness—the slaves, Jews, and early Christians—fuelled by the reactive feeling of *ressentiment* at the sufferings that the more powerful inflicted upon them with blithe disdain, invented a competitor conception: that to be 'good' was to fail to act as the aristocrats did. 'Good' did indeed come, in Judaeo-Christian morality, to attach to the unegoistic, but only once the notion of being egoistic or selfish was coined as a creative redescription of the powerful.

It is crucial for Nietzsche that that attachment of 'good' to the unegoistic occurred at a certain time in history to serve the needs of a certain group who are defined by a reactive psychology because of the power-relation in which they stood to the noble class. The lesson is that 'good' is fixed to the unegoistic neither by nature or essence, nor by empirical universality, nor by first origin. That we think of it this way stems from a particular historical invention of those with a 'slavish' psychology, together with our

---

[17] Nietzsche's etymology of Greek value-words in *GM* I does not include *aristos*. Perhaps it seemed too obvious to mention, or perhaps it is implicitly included since it functions as the superlative of *agathos* (good).

living in a culture that inherited and embellished their mode of evaluation. What Nietzsche calls the 'herd instinct' (*GM* I. 2) forges the very concept of egoism and propagates the new notion that its opposite is good. When the herd instinct dominates, 'peace' becomes a premium, the individual's ability to harm others must be curbed, and Rée's kind of usefulness becomes plausible as the criterion of value for the human group. But this kind of calculation of utility, where, as Nietzsche says, feelings must be kept at a 'low degree of warmth', simply has nothing to do with the ebullient, creative self-definition Nietzsche attributes to the inventors of the earlier concept of 'good'.

Now we can see some justification behind Nietzsche's hyperbolical remark that he could say no to Rée's theory proposition by proposition (*GM*, Preface, 4). 'Good' did not attach originally to the unegoistic, it was not usefulness that marked out the good from the bad, and usefulness (if it had been relevant) could not anyway have been forgotten. But Nietzsche's shift in method is also significant. 'I distinguished ages, peoples, degrees of rank among individuals; I divided up my problem,' he says in the Preface, accurately. Instead of treating human beings as an undifferentiated and more or less ahistorical biological species, whose values bottom out in mere adaptation and survival (and for whom a 'herd morality' might indeed be appropriate), Nietzsche recognizes that values arise to fulfil psychological functions that are impossible to describe independently of the cultural position occupied by their inventors.

3 Conscience, Blame, and Punishment

Conscience, for Rée, is a reflexive version of the moral feeling of disapprobation. Having the contingent, habitual association of feelings of blame with egoistic actions, we come involuntarily to associate the same feelings with our own actions, so that 'a man who appears bad and blameworthy to himself because he has inflicted suffering on another feels what is called pangs of conscience (*Gewissensbisse*)'.[18] When we act egoistically, we automatically feel an unpleasant feeling of blameworthiness. When we act so

---

[18] Rée (2003: 102). Small translates *Gewissensbisse* as 'remorse', which gives more elegant English, but loses the connection with *Gewissen*, conscience. Rée incidentally disagrees with Darwin about conscience. The latter suggests that conscience is a dissatisfaction at failing to exercise one's altruistic drive and that something akin may be felt by other animals. Rée points out that this dissatisfaction

as to benefit others, we involuntarily have a pleasant feeling of having done something good and praiseworthy. (Pleasant feelings are supposedly concurrent with acting unegoistically, while unpleasant pangs of conscience are felt only after the event: egoistic motivation must dominate in such a way that it blocks out the feeling of blameworthiness until too late, as it were.)

Now, generally speaking, people assume that they feel pangs of conscience in situations where they could have acted otherwise. But Rée rejects this, because he believes it simply false that one ever could have acted otherwise, if that is taken to mean that someone had a capacity to do *B* that could have been realized in the very same circumstances in which they in fact did *A*.[19] It is permitted to think, 'It was in my nature to have done otherwise if circumstances had been in some way different'. But in any other sense 'I could have acted otherwise' is an illusion. Conscience will be felt differently depending what assumptions one makes about responsibility, and to illustrate the point Rée presents a series of cases.[20] The normal attitude embraces an unreflective acceptance of freedom to act otherwise: but pangs of conscience felt under this assumption rest on an illusion. Secondly, someone who accepts that there is no responsibility for actions, but who cannot relinquish the sense that there is responsibility, might (as Schopenhauer does[21])posit responsibility for one's character or essence. Conscience would then be felt differently, directed not to the *operari* but to the *esse* (not to the acting but to the being—Rée rehearses Schopenhauer's terms here[22]). Someone with this attitude would still be subject to the habitual association of blameworthiness with egoism and would still blame him- or herself, feeling disturbed that his or her character was such as to issue in an egoistic action.

Thirdly, someone whose beliefs coincide with the position Rée himself defends will still feel pangs of conscience, but will feel them more weakly. He or she will believe that it was impossible to have done otherwise, and that no action is in and of itself blameworthy, but because of the power of habitual associations to outweigh rational reflection, will still be conditioned

---

is not sufficient for pangs of conscience, because it contains no feeling of blameworthiness (see Rée 2003: 102–3). However, Small (2003, pp. xxviii–xxix) argues that Rée is objecting to what is merely a simplification Darwin makes of his own theory for illustrative purposes.

[19] Rée (2003: 106).   [20] Ibid. 107–10.   [21] Schopenhauer (1999: 83–8).
[22] Ibid. 65, 87.

to associate bad feelings with his or her own egoistic actions. (Rée rather tellingly compares this to the case of a convinced atheist who persists in feeling that it is prohibited to deny or defame God.) So it is merely error and conditioning that make pangs of conscience possible, and even correcting the error of belief in free will would not liberate us from our conditioning. On the other hand (fourthly), if the conditioning had been entirely absent, we would not feel conscience at all; and (finally) someone successfully subjected to reverse conditioning would feel unegoistic actions as blame-worthy (a thought perhaps echoed by Nietzsche's suggestion (*GM* II. 24) that we could learn to attach bad conscience to those of our inclinations which oppose the natural, instinctive, and animal sides of ourselves).

Two years before the publication of the *Genealogy*, Rée returned to the same topic with a book entitled *The Development of Conscience*[23]—a longer volume which commentators agree adds little philosophically to *The Origin of the Moral Sensations* and on which Nietzsche comments disparagingly in correspondence.[24] One point that emerges clearly from this later treat-ment, however, is the connection between conscience and punishment. Rée asserts that to blame ourselves for what we have done is to consider ourselves worthy of punishment (*strafwürdig*), and speaks interchangeably of 'punishing conscience, pang of conscience, or consciousness of guilt'.[25] In his earlier book the discussion of punishment certainly parallels that of conscience: both allegedly arose because of their utility in deterring egoism, but both are now misunderstood because of the mistaken belief in free will. Rée takes a very clear line on the question whether punishment is deterrence (*Abschreckung*) or retribution (*Vergeltung*): we are under the illusion that punishment is a backward-looking retribution, but in reality it functions only as a means of minimizing future wrongdoing. Punishment originates in its usefulness as a deterrent to egoistic behaviour in a com-munity, which is thereby able to maintain its peace. If punishment did not exist, or if the practice fell away now, then, says Rée, people would act on egoistic impulses such as hate and revenge and 'each person would snatch as much of the property of others as could be acquired by force, without concern for their happiness or indeed life'.[26] He uses metaphor very little, but the one that follows is bleak and unforgiving: 'Every state or society

---

[23] Rée (1885).   [24] See Donnellan (1982: 608–9); Small (2003, pp. xxxix–xl, xlv–xlvii).
[25] Rée (1885: 211–12).   [26] Rée (2003: 113).

is a great menagerie in which fear of punishment and fear of shame are the bars that prevent the beasts from tearing one another to pieces. And sometimes these bars break apart.' Nietzsche recycled the metaphor in his wholly different theory of the internalizing of instincts brought about by civilization (*GM* II. 16). In Nietzsche's account the human animals endure the bars of civilization as a curtailment and oppression of their natural selves, and become more complicated self-tormenting creatures.

According to Rée we habitually experience a 'feeling of justice' (*Gerechtigkeitsgefühl*), which links egoistic action with the idea of its deserving retribution. But such a link is founded upon the two false beliefs that there is free will, and that the practice of punishment by the state exists in order to enact retribution.[27] Seeing egoistic action and punishment constantly conjoined, and falsely believing that egoistic agents could have acted otherwise, we cannot help feeling that punishment is backward-looking in its significance, and that it is a deserved repayment or retribution for freely chosen egoistic behaviour. But on retribution Rée replicates Schopenhauer's view (minus the metaphysical underpinnings), even resting weight on the passage from Seneca that Schopenhauer had quoted: 'Nemo prudens punit, quia peccatum est, sed ne peccetur'[28] ('No sensible person punishes because a wrong has been done, but in order that a wrong may not be done'). In truth, for Rée, 'nobody deserves blame or punishment because of his bad actions'.[29] It is, consequently, important for Rée that we distinguish both justice and punishment from revenge. Revenge too is what Schopenhauer said it was: the fulfilment of a wish to deny another's superiority over us. It is always personal and has its origin in our natural propensity to vanity. The 'feeling of justice', by contrast, is parasitical upon the institution of punishment, which, as we saw, arises as a deterrence for the overall benefit of the community. The 'feeling of justice' is impersonal: we feel it in reaction to all egoistic actions, whoever commits them and whoever suffers from them.

Conscience and retributive punishment share the following characteristic on Rée's account: they rest on an assumption that someone should suffer because of an already committed egoistic action. But neither conscience nor retribution has any basis in reality, because no one is responsible for,

---

[27] Ibid. 115–16.   [28] Ibid. 116. Cf. Schopenhauer (1969: i. 349).
[29] Rée (2003: 120).

and no one deserves to suffer because of, any action they have done. The feeling of conscience and the retributive feeling of justice would cease if it were possible to unlearn our habits of association, but the effect of long conditioning is so hard to break that it is unlikely we will ever escape these moral illusions.

4 Conscience and Punishment: Replies to Rée in the *Genealogy*

Nietzsche did not initially say no to everything in Rée's account. Nietzsche's earlier treatment of freedom and responsibility in *Human, All Too Human* follows Rée closely, stating that the will is totally unfree[30] and that fear of the consequences prevents us from facing the thought that responsibility is an illusion. It is perhaps Rée, in the medium of his blunt prose, who manages to sound even more merciless than Nietzsche in his presentation of their common position: 'Holding others responsible is thus based ... on the error of supposing that the human will is free ... When we have understood the necessity of all human actions, we will no longer hold anyone responsible.'[31] Responsibility is a plain illusion for Rée and for the Nietzsche of *Human, All Too Human*, but fear of this truth and its consequences has greatly hindered understanding of moral phenomena.[32]

However, in the Second Treatise of the *Genealogy* Nietzsche disagrees with Rée over the role of the belief that agents 'could have acted otherwise' in the generation of the feeling of justice. Leading into his discussion of bad conscience and guilt, Nietzsche invokes 'our genealogists of morality' in familiar fashion:

Have these previous genealogists of morality even remotely dreamt [...] that punishment as *retribution* developed completely apart from any presupposition concerning freedom or lack of freedom of the will? [...] The thought, now so cheap and apparently so natural, so unavoidable, a thought that has even had to serve as an explanation of how the feeling of justice (*Gerechtigkeitsgefühl*) came into being at all on earth—'the criminal has earned his punishment *because* he could

---

[30] See *HA* I. 18, 39, 99, 102, 106; II/1. 33, 50; II/2. 12.   [31] Rée (2003: 111).
[32] Nietzsche's use of the notion of free will has changed somewhat by the time of the *Genealogy*, or so I shall argue in Ch. 7 below.

have acted otherwise'[33]—is in fact a sophisticated form of human judging and inferring that was attained extremely late; whoever shifts it to the beginnings lays a hand on the psychology of older humanity in particularly crude manner.

(*GM* II. 4)

Rée is the target once again, for the 'cheap' theory of the *Gerechtigkeitsgefühl* is the one that says, 'The feeling of justice … arises out of two errors, namely, because the punishments inflicted by authorities and educators appear as acts of retribution, and because people believe in the freedom of the will.'[34] For Nietzsche, by contrast, punishment originated as a transaction of debt repayment, restoring a balance by granting the injured party a legitimate excess of power over the transgressor. This institution meshes with a deep human satisfaction in inflicting cruelty, rooted ultimately in a fundamental drive to discharge power. All of this greatly pre-dates the notion that human agents 'could have done otherwise', which notion Nietzsche relates to a specifically moralized or Christianized version of punishment that seized upon and reinterpreted pre-existing practices.

To explain the origin of what he calls 'bad conscience' Nietzsche invokes basic drives, a process of internalization of the instincts, the pre-moral relationship of debtor to creditor, and the idea of the absolute God developed by Christianity. Nietzsche's explanatory drives, the will to power and its manifestation as a need to inflict cruelty, are, unlike Rée's, neither 'egoistic' nor 'unegoistic'—though he is aware that we will find it irresistible to impose our recent attitudes and classify them as selfish, bad, and wrong. Nietzsche flushes out as reactions to his own text the very attitudes which are obstacles to proper genealogy. He knows, and hopes, that his descriptions of earlier human joy in inflicting suffering will be 'repugnant to the delicacy, even more to the Tartuffery of tame domestic animals (which is to say modern humans, which is to say us)' (*GM* II. 6). In the process we learn to recognize the error of assuming, with Rée, that values originated simply as a means to taming the human animal. Nietzsche's complex and challenging history of 'bad conscience' (on which, see Chapter 8 below) is in a different league of theorizing altogether from Rée's account of 'pangs of conscience'. Nietzsche's explanation exceeds Rée's in seeing

---

[33] Thatcher (1989: 591) annotates the last six words of this quoted passage (*weil er hätte anders handeln können*) as a direct citation from Rée, in view of a similar explicit citation in the notebooks; *KSA* xi. 616 n. 38 [18] (1885).   [34] Rée (2003: 115).

our moral inheritance as containing an enormous complexity of originally independent elements, and in removing the preoccupations and valuations of post-Christian morality from the description of its origins.

In Nietzsche's important methodological remarks surrounding the history of punishment in *GM* II. 12 Rée's position in which usefulness provides the genetic explanation of moral values is particularly under pressure from Nietzsche's historiographical principle that 'the cause of the genesis of a thing and its final usefulness (*Nützlichkeit*), its actual employment and integration into a system of purposes, lie *toto caelo* apart'.[35] When Nietzsche includes in his scope 'previous genealogists of morality' who 'discover some "purpose" or other in punishment, for example revenge or deterrence, then innocently place this purpose at the beginning as *causa fiendi* of punishment', Rée is undoubtedly the genealogist who places deterrence as the cause of punishment's coming into being.[36] As commentators have noted,[37] it is ironic that Nietzsche's sharp critique of the methodological error involved here, which he diagnoses as akin to the error in regarding 'the eye as made to see, the hand as made to grasp', is more in line with Darwin than the would-be Darwinian Rée.[38] Nietzsche's position still parallels Rée's in one respect—for both, justice is an impersonal institution whose aim is to supersede revenge:

Considered historically, justice on earth represents [...] precisely the battle *against* reactive feelings, the war against them on the part of active and aggressive powers [...] Everywhere justice is practiced and upheld one sees a stronger power seeking means to put an end to the senseless raging of *ressentiment* among weaker parties subordinated to it [...] thus achieving in the long run the opposite of what all

---

[35] *Nützlichkeit* and its cognates recur a further five times in section 12.

[36] The genealogist who places revenge at the beginning is Eugen Dühring, whom Nietzsche explicitly criticizes for this very view in the preceding section 11. It was Dühring who introduced into German philosophy the notion of *ressentiment* that Nietzsche uses so prominently in the *Genealogy*'s First Treatise. But Nietzsche rejects Dühring's claims that the feeling of justice (*Rechtsgefühl*) 'is essentially a *ressentiment*, a reactive sentiment', and that it belongs in the same category of feeling as revenge, from which stem 'the whole system of moral and juridical concepts of right'. (See Dühring 1865: 219–34; on Dühring and Nietzsche, see Small 2001, esp. 171–80, and Venturelli 1986.) Rée and Dühring, whatever their differences, make the same mistake in their genealogizing. They discover a single contemporary purpose or meaning in some human institution and assume it as *causa fiendi*, the cause of the institution's coming into being.   [37] Leiter (2002: 168); Small (2003, p. xli).

[38] But later in the same passage Nietzsche criticizes the modern 'idiosyncrasy' that makes scientists 'place "adaptation" in the foreground' at the expense of the 'activity' that for Nietzsche must permeate nature: the criticism is aimed expressly at Herbert Spencer, but is of course against Darwin too. See Moore (2002: 45–55) on Nietzsche's anti-Darwinian conception of physiology and its sources in 19th-century theorists.

revenge wants [...]—from now on the eye is trained for an ever *more impersonal* appraisal of deeds, even the eye of the injured one himself.

(*GM* II. 11)

On the other hand, the vital contrast between Nietzsche's view and Rée's is that Nietzsche wants to explain the achievement of this impersonal justice in terms of the 'active and aggressive' imposition of power by a stronger party. This is indeed his account of state formation, which he vividly describes as the work of 'some pack of blond beasts of prey' laying its paws on a formless populace, or of 'violence-artists and organizers' hammering into it shape (*GM* II. 17–18). As Heraclitus might have said, the stability of a law-governed community is an equilibrium resulting entirely from warlike aggression.[39] For Rée, by contrast, the state that imposes punishments is something useful that comes about as a way of neutralizing harmful instincts and cooling activity down for the benefit of all. Once again Rée is at fault in Nietzsche's eyes for giving primacy to affective coolness, self-suppression, passivity, and peaceableness—at fault not just because activity, self-expression, and so on are more to Nietzsche's taste, but because Rée's account remains captive to the features that became valorized in Christian morality, and so mistakes the eventual local meaning of something for what explains its origin.

[39] 'You should know that war is comprehensive, that justice is strife, that all things come about in accordance with strife and with what must be' (Heraclitus, frag. B 80, in Barnes 2001: 71).

6

Good and Evil: Affect, Artistry, and Revaluation

1 Nietzsche as Artist and Psychologist

If one were setting out to pose fundamental evaluative questions about the system of moral attitudes prevalent in contemporary culture, would it help to adopt an artistic approach? Probably there could never be a general answer to this question, even if it were perfectly clear what is meant by 'artistic'. It would be a bold theorist who ventured that such a revaluative project, a project falling within ethics in the broadest sense, necessitated writing in the form of poem, drama, or opera, or at least borrowing elements of style or rhetoric from some such art. It would be almost as bold—though, one suspects, more common among philosophers—to hold that in such a critique of moral values any artistic endeavour must always be an inessential embellishment, an attractive but discardable clothing, a mere means of presentation for what could be stated without artistic devices. Must philosophy be such that fictional representation, dramatic dialogue, unexplicated metaphor, and sheer delight in wordplay are eliminable from it without loss of anything essential? Much of Plato's work would not stand this test. Yet his writing is paradigmatically philosophical and offers a critique of the values of many of his contemporaries.

Nietzsche's mature writings, and the *Genealogy* in particular, aim to release the reader from the 'illness' allegedly manifest in adhering to moral evaluations of a Christian or post-Christian nature. The first part of the therapeutic process is to diagnose the functions that such evaluations (concepts, beliefs, desires, emotional attachments, and aversions) fulfil for those who make them. In describing these functions Nietzsche typically uses the terminology of drives and affects whose activity is furthered by the adoption of evaluative attitudes. The second part of the therapeutic process is to overcome the need to hold the evaluative attitudes one has inherited, and to create new evaluations which are expressive of one's own strength, unity of character, or affirmation of life. I have argued that a consequence of some of Nietzsche's descriptive hypotheses—would-be truths—about the mind and the way our evaluations are formed is that an affective reorientation is required in order for his therapeutic, revaluative project to work; and that Nietzsche's way of writing is well directed to the task of such an affective reorientation. Here I shall use the specific example of the *Genealogy*'s First Treatise to explore this contention.

I shall not offer an argument that Nietzsche's mature prose works are art—though, for all I know, a good case could be made for saying just this—only that they are essentially artistic in some of their methods. A prima facie case for regarding Nietzsche's later writings as artistic is fairly easy to make in view of certain pervasive features which even the casual reader will identify: the wide range of grammatical devices he uses, including exclamation, incomplete sentences, and the insertion of direct speech to shift the centre of gravity away from the single authorial voice; the combination of meticulous care and playfulness in the use of language, that makes the linguistic texture of his writing call attention to itself as much as to its contents (we might say that Nietzsche thematizes his medium of representation). To this we may add the kind of irony that deliberately misleads the reader, and the use of a multiplicity of rhetorical devices for provoking the affects of the reader. It is the latter feature on which I shall concentrate most attention here. It is not far-fetched to say that Nietzsche sets out to embarrass, amuse, tempt, shame, and revolt the reader—to test our attractions and aversions. My claim is that provoking such responses is an integral part of Nietzsche's revaluative procedure. If his reader has arrived at and adheres to his or her values in the manner hypothesized by Nietzsche's moral psychology, then Nietzsche's chosen way of writing is well calculated to begin the process of detaching him or her from those values and enabling the revaluation he prefigures in the Preface to the *Genealogy*.

Recall Nietzsche's résumé of the *Genealogy* in *Ecce Homo*:

Regarding expression, intention, and the art of surprise, the three inquiries which constitute this *Genealogy* are perhaps uncannier than anything else written so far. [...] Every time a beginning that is *calculated* to mislead: cool, scientific, even ironic, deliberately foreground, deliberately holding off. Gradually more unrest; sporadic lightning; very disagreeable truths are heard grumbling in the distance—until eventually a *tempo feroce* is attained in which everything rushes ahead in a tremendous tension. In the end, in the midst of perfectly gruesome detonations, a *new* truth becomes visible every time among thick clouds.

(*EH*, 'On the Genealogy of Morals')

Three times here Nietzsche tells us that each treatise contains or reveals some truth. Other parts of the passage, especially 'three decisive preliminary studies for a psychologist', make it clear that psychological truth is at stake. About the First Treatise in particular Nietzsche says:

The truth of the *first* inquiry is the birth of Christianity: the birth of Christianity out of the spirit of *ressentiment*, not, as people may believe, out of the 'spirit'—a countermovement by its very nature, the great rebellion against the dominion of *noble* values.

What is now of interest is *how* this truth is to be revealed by the treatise. What is deliberately misleading about the beginning of the treatise? What is its uncanny surprise? Where is the unrest? What gruesome detonations occur? Why is the new truth among thick clouds?

I shall sketch my answer first, and attempt to support at least part of it in what follows. The misleading beginning is the discussion of philological and historical origins of words such as 'good'. This makes it appear that we are in a scientific, objective study of the past, a sort of history or anthropology, cool and *wissenschaftlich*, as Nietzsche says. But, as I shall argue, what will really be transacted is a calling into consciousness of the reader's affects. The thuggish behaviour of the nobles is portrayed in vocabulary calculated to make the modern, post-Christian reader wince with apprehension and bristle with indignation, at the same time, perhaps, as admiring the psychic health of the self-legislating aristocrat. The slaves are presented so as to arouse contempt, but also admiration for their ability to create new values. In the artistic culmination of the essay, the disgust that we feel for brutal discharge of power towards the weak is harnessed into a disgust at the ultimately similar discharge of power in which the creators of Christianity set out to subjugate their masters, an affective disgust dramatized through the 'Mr Rash and Curious' figure, the reader's representative who descends into the cavernous workshop where moral ideals are fabricated, and leaves because of the bad smell (*GM* I. 14). The uncanny surprise of the treatise is that what initially seem opposites—the noble mode of evaluation and the slavish morality of *ressentiment*—will provoke in the reader a similar mixture of disquiet and admiration. Hence the growing unrest. The reader will find his or her own attachment to Christian or post-Christian moral values hard to stomach. Gruesome detonations occur in that the reader can be expected to suffer under the violence of this reversal in his or her affects. The new truth is among thick clouds because these freshly aroused feelings are at first hard to integrate with the rest of the reader's attitudes.

In the passage from *Ecce Homo* Nietzsche mentions features of his writing that are self-consciously artistic: the use of irony and deliberate false scents for the reader, the careful concern with the expressive power and emotional effect of his narrative, and finally the claim to achieve an overall architecture that is conceived not, say, in terms of premises and conclusions, or evidence and explanation, or even narrative coherence, but in terms of mood and musical pace: a cool beginning gradually giving way to a hectic and ferocious tempo. But can Nietzsche's enterprise be essentially artistic if it is first and foremost concerned with the probing of human psychology and the revelation of truths? Someone might consider that these are not per se artistic aims. However, such an objector would most likely be operating with an unduly narrow concept of the artistic, perhaps in the grip of what Noël Carroll has recently diagnosed as the pervasive tendency in philosophical aesthetics to reduce art to beauty, or to the aesthetic, conceived in such a way that moral, political, and historical concerns, as well as audiences' emotional involvement and even authors' intentions, can come to seem extraneous to art.[1] But Nietzsche himself never belonged to that theoretical tradition, and never really conceives art in that way. He does not put forward a theory of aesthetic experience as such, and in the *Genealogy* criticizes both Kant and Schopenhauer for their reliance on the notions of passivity, disinterestedness, and impersonality in accounting for the aesthetic (*GM* III. 6, 12). In *Twilight of the Idols* he decries one influential conception of the autonomy of art:

When one has excluded from art the purpose of moral preaching and human improvement it by no means follows that art is completely purposeless, goalless, meaningless, in short *l'art pour l'art*—a snake biting its own tail [...] A psychologist

---

[1] See Carroll (2001, esp. 20–41, 215–35, 270–93).

asks on the other hand: what does all art do? does it not praise? does it not glorify? does it not select? does it not highlight? By doing all this it *strengthens* or *weakens* certain valuations [...] Art is the great stimulus to life: how could it be thought purposeless, aimless, *l'art pour l'art*? [...] art also brings to light much that is ugly, hard, questionable in life.

(TI, 'Expeditions of an Untimely Man', 24)

The last clause here must signify the revelation of truths through art. Yet, by contrast, other Nietzschean remarks can seem to point in an opposed direction. In the *Genealogy* Nietzsche portrays 'art, in which precisely the *lie* hallows itself, in which the *will to deception* has good conscience on its side' as the antithesis of the truth-obsessed 'ascetic ideal' (*GM* III. 25). How then could Nietzsche's own truth-directed investigations be properly artistic? A Dostoevsky or a Shakespeare might probe the human psyche and bring to light much that is hard or questionable in life; they might even be said to strengthen or weaken valuations. But, the objector might say, what makes these writers artists is their deliberate and central use of artifice or pretence, in that they produce fictions first and foremost—and Nietzsche differs crucially in that he does not normally produce fictions, except when writing about Zarathustra.

This raises a deep question about the interpretation of Nietzsche: accepting that his narratives (concerning slave morality in the *Genealogy*'s First Treatise, and the origins of guilt or bad conscience and the ascetic ideal in the Second and Third) are not, by his lights, straightforward fictions, where are we to locate them on the spectrum between sheer storytelling and literal presentation of truth? Supposing for now that we opted for the most extreme end of the spectrum in relation to the First Treatise, and decided that Nietzsche's account of the origins of morality in the *ressentiment* of those oppressed by an ebullient aristocratic culture was meant as a bald, literal truth-claim about the past: would this unlying, undeceiving aim militate against conceiving Nietzsche as artist-like in his method? Arguably not. When Nietzsche enlists art as the opponent of the ascetic ideal, it is because in art there is no unconditional faith in truth-telling as the single unquestionable and overarching value.[2] But we need not infer that in artistic endeavours there occurs an unconditional valuing of falsehood-telling. Art can reveal truths even if it also lies with

---

[2] For this characterization of the faith in truth as a form of the ascetic ideal, see *GM* III. 24.

a good conscience. So Nietzsche can proceed in a manner akin to that of an artist without losing his claim to put forward truths about the origins of our values.

2 Nietzsche's Choice of Style

There are passages in Nietzsche's mature works that are sometimes decried (more often ignored) as unnecessary rhetorical excesses. A prominent instance is this from the *Genealogy*'s First Treatise:

[the noble, the powerful] are not much better than uncaged beasts of prey toward the outside world [...] There they enjoy freedom from all social constraint [...] they step *back* into the innocence of the beast-of-prey conscience, as jubilant monsters, who perhaps walk away from a hideous succession of murder, arson, rape, torture with such high spirits and equanimity that it seems as if they have only played a student prank, convinced that for years to come the poets will again have something to sing and to praise. At the base of all these noble races one cannot fail to recognize the beast of prey, the splendid *blond beast* who roams about lusting after booty and victory; from time to time this hidden base needs to discharge itself, the animal must get out, must go back into the wilderness: Roman, Arab, Germanic, Japanese nobility, Homeric heroes, Scandinavian Vikings—in this need they are all alike.[3]

Thomas Mann found in this passage among others a 'clinical picture of infantile sadism' before which 'our souls writhe in embarrassment'.[4] Mann is too subtle a reader of Nietzsche to let it rest there: he later asserts that anyone who reads Nietzsche 'as he is' is lost, and that, in the light of Nietzsche's deeper concerns, 'the whole aesthetic phantasm of slavery, war, violence, glorious brutality whisks itself off to a realm of irresponsible play and scintillating irony'.[5] But still for Mann the violence in these texts

---

[3] *GM* I. 11. I shall not rehearse any of the debate about the infamous 'blond beast'. There is a firm consensus among recent commentators that Nietzsche despised both German nationalism and anti-Semitism (see Yovel 1994; Santaniello 1997: 23). *GM* III. 26 shows Nietzsche's contempt for the anti-Semites of his day. The extent to which Nietzsche's rhetoric itself is complicit in the development of National Socialism is another issue; Ken Gemes, for example, suggests, 'the real question of Nietzsche's culpability is best addressed in terms of his responsibility for fostering a set of metaphors, in particular, and most dangerously, the metaphor of degeneration' (Gemes 2001: 55 n. 14).

[4] Mann (1959: 165). *GM* II. 6–7 with its theme of 'without cruelty, no festival' provides a further example for Mann.   [5] Mann (1959: 174).

is something irresponsible and inessential, a superficial feature that a less enthusiastic genius might have curbed.

I have suggested a different approach. At least some of these uncomfortable passages are uncomfortable because the writing is openly concerned with probing *the affects of the reader*. To this end the literary violence is an effective means. Nietzsche's project of revaluing moral values contains as an essential part the uncovering of a multifarious affective life beneath our moral judgements. By provoking a range of affects in the reader, Nietzsche enables the reader to locate the target for revaluation, the 'morality' which comprises a complex of attitudes of his or her own, central to which are affective inclinations and aversions. If, as Nietzsche alleges, the prime material we have to work with in revaluing our moral evaluations is a wide range of affective attitudes whose existence in ourselves may be in some degree masked by the accretions of rationalizing interpretation, then discovering even *what our morality is* may have as a necessary condition our being prompted into a reflection upon the many and various affective attitudes in question. If we were to find that the only way to reflect on the relevant affects was by first feeling them, then Nietzsche's provocative rhetorical method could be seen not only as effective, but as essential to his task.

With some oversimplification, one might point to two basic versions of Nietzsche that have been on offer in recent commentaries. There has been the 'literary' or perhaps 'postmodern' Nietzsche whose prime concern is with style and rhetoric and with undermining the possibility of attaining truth or stable meaning. And there is the Nietzsche more congenial to analytical philosophers, who opposes transcendent metaphysics in a more or less neo-Kantian spirit, but is committed to there being empirical truths in the realms of the historical, cultural, and psychological, and who takes up coherent philosophical positions for which there are arguments (even if he does not always present them plainly as such). A problem confronting common 'postmodern' readings of Nietzsche is that they implicitly undermine his claimed 'revaluation of values'. This exercise has a diagnostic component, which consists in a description of the conscious and unconscious processes involved in the formation of those beliefs, desires, and other attitudes that combine to constitute moral evaluations. I argue that Nietzsche puts forward these descriptions as candidates for truth about the way human minds work. For, as he says quite bluntly, 'there are [...] truths' that are 'plain, harsh, ugly, unpleasant, unchristian, immoral' (*GM* I. 1). And indeed, unless Nietzsche can conceive of himself as uncovering truths, he cannot revalue the values of morality. If he is to carry out his diagnostic descriptions, then he must be 'allowed' to advance some truths (or hypotheses—a word he likes—i.e. candidates for truth). The 'postmodern' type of reading in which Nietzsche discards truth altogether will not allow us to make sense of his central project. On the other hand, a failing of those who allow truths to Nietzsche and concentrate on elucidating and finding arguments for his philosophical positions has tended to be their relative silence on questions concerning his literary methods. But it is essential to ask: Why does Nietzsche elect to write not in the form of philosophical or scholarly argumentation, but in his subtle, provocative, emotive manner? It would be an absurd mistake to think that Nietzsche was unable to write in the conventional form of connected arguments running from premiss to conclusion. It would be like treating Arnold Schoenberg as someone who never quite mastered major and minor scales, or de Chirico as someone who could not get the hang of conventional perspective drawing. (It would, in other words, be a kind of philistinism.)

In the firmament of the German academic world the young Nietzsche had been a star. He was a philologist who investigated the language, literature, and culture of the ancient world, studied with the strict systematician Ritschl,[6] and became a scholar so gifted that at the age of only 24 the academic establishment honoured him with a Chair at Basel. Nietzsche was an accomplished exponent of a *Wissenschaft*, a 'science' in a broad sense, or at any rate a *discipline*: a rigorous enterprise in which a body of knowledge was built up by argument from carefully sifted evidence, and findings presented for collective scrutiny. This philological discipline of nineteenth-century German academia became the foundation for much subsequent classical scholarship, including the study of the ancient philosophers. Perhaps it tends to be forgotten that for much of the twentieth century an education as a philosopher in the English-speaking world was likely also to be an education as a classicist. To that extent today's analytical philosophy owes some of its ingrained habits and assumptions to the very academic tradition in which Nietzsche was a prodigy—until he struck out in a new direction.

---

[6] 'Strict systematician' is the phrase used by Mann (1959: 143).

A new direction was evident in Nietzsche's first book, *The Birth of Tragedy*, which is arguably intended to be somewhat artistic in style and is preoccupied with art ancient and modern (and which was accordingly vilified by the academic establishment[7]). But it was through the sequence of works *Human, All Too Human, Daybreak,* and *The Gay Science* that Nietzsche developed his mature style. That he gave one of his works the title *Die fröhliche Wissenschaft*—the gay or joyful *Wissenschaft*—may be taken as emblematic of the new course Nietzsche hoped to follow.[8] We might also recall that in the middle of writing *The Gay Science* Nietzsche composed *Thus Spoke Zarathustra*, a book with evident artistic pretensions (even if many nowadays would place the emphasis on the second of these words[9]), and that *The Gay Science* itself begins and ends with poems, in the very last of which Nietzsche reflects on his methods thus:

> Let us dance in every manner,
> free—so shall be *our* art's banner,
> and *our* science—shall be gay!
>
> (*GS*, 'To the Mistral. A Dance Song')

A presupposition, then, for reading the mature Nietzsche of the 1880s is to recognize his shift in method away from analytical argument as a deliberate choice of style. But why, with what aims, did Nietzsche make this move? I believe that the appropriateness of Nietzsche's later style is more than just a matter of philosophizing in a new mood or 'conveying a certain spirit'.[10] Nietzsche moved deliberately towards a rhetoric of imaginative provocation of the affects, and certain aspects of this mode of writing flow naturally from his descriptive moral psychology.

---

[7] For a thorough discussion of this controversy, see Silk and Stern (1981: 90–131).

[8] Bernard Williams's elucidation of the title is helpful: 'It translates a phrase, "gai saber", or, as Nietzsche writes on his title page, "gaya scienza", which referred to the art of song cultivated by the medieval troubadours of Provence [...] just as the troubadours possessed not so much a body of information as an art, so Nietzsche's "gay science" does not in the first place consist of a doctrine, a theory or body of knowledge. While it involves and encourages hard and rigorous thought, and to this extent the standard implications of "Wissenschaft" are in place, it is meant to convey a certain spirit, one that in relation to understanding and criticism could defy the "spirit of gravity" as lightly as the troubadours, supposedly, celebrated their loves' (Williams 2001, pp. x–xi).

[9] See Tanner's assessment (1994: 46).   [10] Williams (2001, p. xi; quoted in n. 8 above).

3 Responding to the Slaves and Nobles

Earlier we saw that Nietzsche's end was to make us 'feel differently', changing or reversing our inclinations and aversions, losing our habitual or inherited attachment to the attitudes that comprise the morality of selflessness. How, then, would Nietzsche think that his envisaged end could be brought about, and how might his own writing contribute to that end? Here is a programme that would at least make sense: Detach people from their practice of making moral judgements, thereby enabling them to feel non-moral inclinations and aversions. How to detach people from making moral judgements? Show them the inherited affects of which these judgements are the *ex post facto* rationalizations. How to show people the affects they have inherited? Provoke affective responses in them, and invite them to reflect on the explanation for their having them.

How would this work if applied to the particular example of the First Treatise of the *Genealogy*? Nietzsche's target for revaluation here is the pair of concepts 'good' and 'evil', which are used in making moral judgements about persons, their actions, and other states (such as character traits and emotions). According to the narrative he gives, there was a time when there was no pair of concepts 'good' and 'evil', and morality as such did not exist. There were modes of evaluation, but they were not, strictly speaking, moral (despite his occasional use of the expression 'noble morality' for what precedes morality proper[11]). The pair of concepts 'good' and bad' originally existed, forming the basis of a noble or aristocratic form of evaluation: the good are those who are capable, strong, powerful, those to be admired for what they have and are; the bad are simply those who no one would have wanted to be if he or she had the power—the weak, the incapable, the subservient. In the story that Nietzsche tells morality was an invention in human history, and the driving force behind this invention was the class of people who were weak and marginal according to the aristocratic value system. Morality resulted from a Judaeo-Christian 'slave revolt' which creatively fashioned a new pair of values, and finally convinced even the powerful that to exercise their power over others weaker than themselves was 'evil', and that to be powerless—or not to exercise power—was 'good'.

---

[11] Cf. *GM* I. 10 and especially *BGE* 260. The line I am following is that of Clark (1994: 16–17).

At the earlier stage of the history we are asked to imagine here prominent affects are at work—hatred, thirst for revenge, and *ressentiment*: 'The slave revolt in morality begins when *ressentiment* itself becomes creative and gives birth to values: the *ressentiment* of beings denied the true reaction, that of the deed, who recover their losses only through an imaginary revenge' (*GM* I. 10). The morality of 'good' and 'evil' is a conceptual construction which meets the need for an affective release of hatred and revenge indirectly, not by attacking or defeating the hated object, but by redescribing it according to a new system of concepts.

The passage quoted above concerning 'uncaged beasts of prey' is part of Nietzsche's description of the 'nobles' in this narrative about the origins of 'good' and 'evil'. What sometimes goes unnoticed is the complexity of the affective response Nietzsche prompts to this description. The nobles, as he here describes them, are 'monsters', their behaviour is 'hideous', their lightheartedness 'appalling', their effect one of 'horror' (*GM* I. 11). Nietzsche also conspicuously uses words such as 'splendid'—but he knows that his reader will be horrified and appalled. Or indeed the reader's response may also be mixed. And this mixed response is, I think, what Nietzsche hopes to elicit—for soon he talks of 'the contradiction posed by the glorious but likewise so gruesome, so violent world of Homer' which the later poet Hesiod had to process into separate eras, the age of heroes and the age of bronze, in order to make a more comfortable historical narrative.[12] If it was already hard for Hesiod to integrate admiration and terror, it has surely become very difficult for the modern, post-Christian reader. But this combination of affects is what Nietzsche encourages in the same section, asking: 'who would not a hundred times sooner fear if he might at the same time admire, than *not* fear [...]?'

Readers will be indignant about the nobles as Nietzsche describes them. They will react with fear and disquiet, and moreover a disquiet that, on behalf of the imagined victims, gives rise to a desire to judge the nobles' behaviour wrong. Nietzsche must know this because he knows that the value system that originated with those who feared and recoiled from the nobles 'has been victorious' (*GM* I. 7). The reader's cultural inheritance includes this reactive value system, and so its characteristic aversions are

---

[12] *GM* I. 11. Note that Nietzsche transposes the order of Hesiod's age of bronze and age of heroes (see Hesiod, *Works and Days*, lines 134–65, in Caldwell 1987: 104–5).

likely to be salient in the reader's response. Thus Nietzsche prompts the reader to become conscious of himself or herself as an inheritor of affects whose origin is 'slavish'. But he does not leave matters there. In particular, note two further effects on the reader that he provides for in *GM* I: (1) The reader is given the opportunity to become conscious of himself or herself as the inheritor of some attitudes more in line with a noble mode of evaluation. (2) The reader is encouraged to question the polarized affective responses he or she has towards elements in the narrative: in particular, the reader is later encouraged to recognize that slave morality shares the same ultimate origin as the noble mode of evaluation, and to reorient his or her feelings accordingly.

On the first point compare *Beyond Good and Evil* 260:

in all higher and more mixed cultures, attempts to negotiate between these moralities also appear, although more frequently the two are confused and there are mutual
misunderstandings. In fact, you sometimes find them sharply juxtaposed—inside
the same person even, within a single soul.

So someone who winces at the description of the nobles in *GM* I might also be someone whose reaction is tinged with a kind of admiration or awe. Similarly, Nietzsche points up the complexity of our likely reaction to the 'slave revolt' against the nobles. If we feel contempt at the weakness and hypocrisy of the slaves as portrayed in the narrative, we may also admire them for the creative act which changes history, the 'truly *great* politics of revenge' (GM I. 10) which creates values, and makes mankind interesting.

The second point, about questioning the polarized nature of our responses, can best be elucidated by pointing to another passage in *Beyond Good and Evil*:

'How *could* anything originate out of its opposite?' [...] The fundamental belief of
metaphysicians is the *belief in oppositions of values* [...] [But] it could even be possible
that whatever gives value to those good and honorable things has an incriminating
link, bond, or tie to the very things that look like their evil opposites; perhaps they
are even essentially the same. Perhaps!

(BGE 2)

Nietzsche is only pretending to be tentative here, for the First Treatise provides a clear example of his last point. Morality is founded on a fundamental opposition between 'good' and 'evil', but the essay locates the origin of the 'good' in just the same kind of drive to dominate as is abhorred under the description 'evil'. The difference is that in the 'good' the drive to dominate is overlain with mendacity and ends up justifying itself with metaphysics. That is why, as I shall argue, in the rhetorical climax of the treatise in section 14, a glimpse into the way the ideal of the good is manufactured fills the reader (or the reader's representative, 'Mr Rash and Curious') with disgust. Barbaric domination over others makes us uneasy; a value system whose origin is in a drive to domination over others, but which pretends that its origin is in something 'higher', should trouble us as much, or more.

4 Nietzsche's Dialogue with 'Mr Rash and Curious'

Section 14 of the First Treatise is a good example of Nietzsche's use of artistic methods in pursuit of his diagnostic and therapeutic aims. He invents a character with whom the essay's narrative voice suddenly enters into comic dialogue. It is like calling for a volunteer from the audience: 'Would anyone like to go down and take a look into the secret of how they *fabricate ideals* on earth? Who has the courage to do so?' The supposed volunteer is addressed as mein Herr Vorwitz und Wagehals—rendered by translators variously as Mr Rash and Curious, Mr Nosy Daredevil, Mr Daredevil Curiosity, or Mr Wanton-Curiosity and Daredevil.[13] The narrator affects to send this member of the public down into a fetid, cavernous workshop, reminiscent of Wagner's Nibelheim, where morality is cobbled together by shadowy, stunted creatures brimming with *ressentiment*. The authorial voice receives reports from the front-line emissary as if from the safety of surface daylight, goading him on until what he witnesses becomes unbearable and he demands to be returned to the open air.

This is a striking, virtuosic piece of writing, but also perhaps a good example of the embarrassment commentators can feel through apparently having no purchase on why it might benefit Nietzsche to write in this way. I assume that virtually everyone who writes about Nietzsche, from undergraduates on, has read the passage. It has scathing humour, deadly

---

[13] See the translations respectively of Kaufmann and Hollingdale, Diethe, Smith, and Clark and Swensen.

similes, a novel dramatic structure, and great rhetorical power. So why are it and its role in the treatise as a whole not remarked upon more frequently? The very power of the imagery in the little drama may be inhibiting to interpreters. Aaron Ridley has called it 'one of Nietzsche's less attractive passages'.[14] Most commentators apparently say nothing. The simplest explanation, once again, is that people believe Nietzsche goes too far in this section and becomes unnecessarily unpleasant—so best not mention it. (Delving a little deeper, if we are right in finding here some echo of the sweatshops of the Nibelungs in *Das Rheingold*, familiar worries about the anti-Semitism of Wagner's symbolism may intrude, and threaten to render the least subtle of Nietzsche's similes in this section, where as narrator he speaks of 'these artists of black magic who produce white, milk, and innocence out of every black [...] cellar animals full of revenge and hate', unbearably nauseating, especially in view of later anti-Semitic propaganda. In fact, the target group for revulsion is quite clearly Christians, albeit as inheritors of the Jewish revolution in values.)

Whatever the reasons behind the comparative neglect of Herr Vorwitz und Wagehals, I would like now to examine the *Genealogy*'s First Treatise precisely from the perspective of the section in which he features. It could be regarded as the rhetorical climax of the whole treatise, firstly because, after only one more section (*GM* I. 15) that offers corroboration in Christian texts for what Mr Rash and Curious discovers, Nietzsche rounds off with 'Let us conclude' (*GM* I. 16)—and secondly because of its heightened tone and emotional urgency, which might support the contention that this above all is the passage of *tempo feroce* in which the gruesome detonations are to occur and the new truth become visible.

What does Nietzsche achieve in casting section 14 in this vivid, dramatic form? My answer, in outline, is twofold. I suggest (1) that Nietzsche here completes the transformation of his treatise from a past-directed enquiry into a critique whose focus is the here and now, the present attitudes of his reader; (2) that his emotive rhetoric aims at harnessing the reader's own disquiet over the untrammelled exercise of power by the overtly powerful—a disquiet he elicited and carefully nurtured earlier in the text—and converting it into a still greater disquiet over the covert desire to exercise power that drives Christianity and the post-Christian moral

---

[14] Ridley (1998: 25).

attitudes which are likely to persist in the reader. Nietzsche uses this dramatic characterization to enact disgust on the reader's behalf.

The fact of dramatization itself switches attention to a present shared by the author and his interlocutor. But there are other contributory features with a similar effect: the section talks very much of 'here' and 'now'—'now for the first time I hear', says Mr Rash and Curious at one point. There is an emphasis on what can be detected immediately by the senses: 'the view [...] is unobstructed here', 'I don't see anything, but I hear all the more', 'it stinks of sheer lies', 'I'll open my ears once again (oh! oh! oh! and *close* my nose)'. And since Mr Rash and Curious is explicitly 'anyone' who is brave enough to investigate the murkier parts of the psyche, he must be read as the representative of you and me, the present readers of Nietzsche's text.

Mr Rash and Curious perceives the affective states of the fabricators of the ideal of the good—their fear, hate, misery, revenge, hope, comfort—and his own affective reaction is shown through the sustained metaphor of smell, stink, 'Bad air!': he is disgusted. But what disgusts him most is the lies involved in fabricating the ideal of the good. The desires that are born out of the affective states of the oppressed are for revenge, justice, judgement, kingdom—in short, power over those that oppress them. Frustrated by lack of actual power, but still desiring it, the Christian fabricates two things: a redescription in which failure to exercise power in this world has positive value ('weakness is to be lied into a *merit* [...] fearful baseness into "humility"; subjection to those one hates into "obedience" ' and so on), and a fantasy revenge located in another world 'beyond' this one. So Mr Rash and Curious realizes (enacts for us the realization of) what Nietzsche has elsewhere said about opposites: that 'whatever gives value to those good and honorable things has an incriminating link, bond, or tie to the very things that look like their evil opposites; perhaps they are even essentially the same'—the basis for the Christian system of values is no different from that of the noble mode of evaluation: it resides in the tendency towards power.

5   Conclusion

Let us finally ask how the rhetoric of the First Treatise—according to our partial and schematic account of it—would engage with the reader's moral feelings and moral evaluations in the manner discussed above. While initially directed towards investigating past stages of history, the reader has been prompted to feel anxiety at the untrammelled exercise of power by the nobles, and to experience the urge to condemn this exercise of power as wrong. The reader receives an explanation of his or her aversion to the nobles: it exists because of the invention of a moral system of value concepts 'good' and 'evil' which the reader has inherited—but the explanatory basis of this system of concepts is once again affective, in that it arises out of the fear, hatred, *ressentiment*, and the power-drive of the oppressed. That is one part of the mechanism for detaching the reader from making moral judgements, preparing the way eventually for what Nietzsche called 'feeling differently' on the part of the reader. The second part of this mechanism of detachment is the attempt to elicit at the same time an affective inclination in favour of the nobles, to show that one has also inherited from earlier value systems an excitement and attraction for heroism, prowess, and the exercise of power with aristocratic disdain. (A moment's reflection on some elements of contemporary popular culture might suggest that this is indeed a long-lasting and stubborn inheritance.) So our inheritance is mixed: at the same time we fear and admire, condemn and wish to emulate. Nietzsche's reader might be pictured as reflecting as the treatise progresses: 'Suppose I adhere to the concepts "good" and "evil" because I have inherited certain inclinations and aversions from a prior stage of development in which forming the concepts "good" and "evil" answered the affective needs of *ressentiment*. Suppose that I also recognize in myself some inclination—mixed with aversion—towards the noble mode of being and valuing. Do I wish to continue adhering to the system of judging according to the concepts "good" and "evil"?'

Then the culmination of Nietzsche's rhetoric in section 14 functions to prompt in the reader a new and decisive affective reaction. Already averse to actions driven by the desire for power over others (because of his or her 'slavish' Christian inheritance), the reader is now led to understand how a desire for power also truly explains the invention of the categories 'good' and 'evil'. As I have said, Nietzsche enacts disgust on the reader's behalf, but it is a disgust with a specific and complex object: *that a system of values which exists to fulfil (in imagination) the drive towards power should falsely pass itself off as in opposition to the drive towards power.* At this point Mr Rash and Curious shouts 'Enough! Enough!' Nietzsche perhaps hoped that evoking this disgust might be enough to break the reader's allegiance to judging things good or evil, preparing the way one day for new combinations of affects for and against that he would regard as healthier.

7

Free Will, Autonomy, and the Sovereign Individual

Nietzsche talks of free will towards the end of the First Treatise of the *Genealogy* and towards the beginning of the Second, and may appear to contradict himself within the space of a few pages. He describes as nonsensical and false the belief in a 'neutral "subject" with free choice' standing behind an individual's actions (*GM* I. 13); yet he says there has existed or may exist a type of individual who 'has become free' and is a 'lord of the *free* will' (*GM* II. 2). Any reading of the *Genealogy* ought to address this apparent tension. Whatever else the mysterious 'sovereign individual' is, he is not supposed to be a nonsense or a falsehood. Nietzsche must regard the sovereign individual's achievement of freedom as something other than his becoming a neutral subject with free choice.[1] Here I want to address two chief topics. First, I document a change in Nietzsche's writing about free will between the earlier *Human, All Too Human* and the period of the *Genealogy* and *Beyond Good and Evil*, a change which I shall argue corresponds with the development of his genealogical method.[2] Secondly, I shall argue that Nietzsche should attribute a kind of autonomy to those of his readers whom he imagines being cured of their attachment to morality and creating their own values.

1 Acting Otherwise

Let us return once more to Schopenhauer and Rée. Both thinkers deny free will in a specific sense: they claim that for any particular action *A* of

---

[1] A distinction made by Ken Gemes between deserts' free will and agency free will is an appealing way of resolving the tension; see Gemes (2006*a*), to which this chapter was originally written as a companion piece.

[2] See Owen (2003) for an account of the development of the genealogical method.

any human individual, if the individual's character and all the circumstances in which he or she acts are assumed unchanged, then no action other than *A* is possible for that individual. No one could have done otherwise on some occasion than they in fact did on that occasion. For both, the notion of responsibility for human actions becomes unsustainable as a result. And yet the Nietzsche of the *Genealogy* reports himself as 'struggling almost solely with' Schopenhauer over the value of morality, and as 'saying no' to everything in Rée. If it were a high priority for him to argue that no one could have acted otherwise, might Nietzsche not have tempered the stark antithesis in which he sets himself to these two clearly determinist thinkers? Nietzsche's driving concern in the *Genealogy*, I have argued, is with analysing and questioning the morality of selflessness. Along the way he is critical of the radical metaphysical conception of free will as possessed by a 'neutral subject of free choice', but chiefly because he wishes to explain it as an invention of the slave morality that valorizes selflessness. The value of selflessness itself is the bigger issue, so that theorists who deny free will but continue to equate the good with the unegoistic, as Schopenhauer and Rée do in their different ways, are still fundamentally at odds with Nietzsche.

Schopenhauer's argument for determinism is clear and effective: a free will would be a will from which all necessity is absent, but nothing that occurs in the empirical world is without a cause that makes it necessary (one instance of the principle of sufficient reason). Human actions are events in the empirical world, and are caused by the interaction of the individual's character and the motives or mental representations that occur to him or her. So it is an error to think that 'contrary to all the laws of the pure understanding and of nature, the will determines itself without sufficient reasons, and that under given circumstances its decisions could turn out thus or even in the opposite way in the case of one and the same human being'.[3] Nowhere does anything determine itself, nor act without sufficient reason. We do not understand all the causal connections between our character and experiences and the actions that issue from them, because they are of greater complexity than other observable connections in nature, and because the effects can be remote and heterogeneous from their causes. We rightly believe in many instances that *if* we will to do *A*, we can do it.

---

[3] Schopenhauer (1999: 36).

But that does not make it true that we control whether it is *A* that we will rather than *B*.[4] Schopenhauer imagines a man deliberating:

'It is six o'clock; the day's work is over. I can now go for a walk, or go to the club; I can also climb the tower to see the sun set; I can also go to the theater; I can also visit this or that friend; in fact I can also run out by the city gate into the wide world and never come back. All that is entirely up to me; I have complete freedom; however, I do none of them, but just as voluntarily go home to my wife.' This is just as if water were to say: 'I can form high waves (as in a storm at sea); I can rush down a hill (as in the bed of a torrent); I can dash down foaming and splashing (as in the waterfall); I can rise freely as a jet into the air (as in a fountain); finally, I can even boil away and disappear (as at 212 degrees Fahrenheit); however, I do none of these things now, but voluntarily remain calm and clear in the mirroring pond.' Just as water can do all those things only when the determining causes enter for one or the other, so is the condition just the same for the man with respect to what he imagines he can do. Until the causes enter, it is impossible for him to do anything; but then he *must* do it, just as water must act as soon as it is placed in the respective circumstances.[5]

Nevertheless, Schopenhauer believes that there is moral responsibility. We feel guilt, and have an irremovable sense that 'we ourselves are *the doers of our deeds*'.[6] Schopenhauer argues that since we feel responsible, but cannot be genuinely responsible for our actions, we must be feeling a deeper responsibility for our very character, for what we are, our being (*esse*). A person realizes that the action that issued from him was not absolutely necessary; it was necessary relative to the circumstances and to his character, but it might not have occurred 'if only he had been another person'.[7] Schopenhauer's idea is that we truly feel guilty for being that out of which a harmful action emanates, despite the fact that we could not have acted otherwise. From this notion of responsibility for our being he argues, questionably, to the conclusion that there must be a kind of freedom residing in our character. Using the Kantian distinction between empirical and intelligible characters, the latter supposedly what I am in myself beyond the forms of space, time, and causality,[8] he suggests that my moral freedom is transcendental and lies in my non-empirical essence. The suggestion is hard to grasp. The intelligible character could be a locus of responsibility only if there is some sense in which it involves a free act, or a choice to have

---

[4] Ibid. 16–17.   [5] Ibid. 36–7.   [6] Ibid. 83.   [7] Ibid. 84.   [8] Ibid. 86.

such-and-such character (as Schopenhauer sometimes claims[9]). But how I could have chosen my own innate, unchanging, non-empirical character by some kind of act lying outside time is never explained.

Rée dismisses this notion of intelligible freedom: 'we have received our innate character not through any fault of our own; our remorse is not a feeling of regret over the fact that, by virtue of this intelligible freedom, we have chosen just this character and not some better one'.[10] With Schopenhauer's only refuge for responsibility and freedom thus blocked, Rée holds that we have neither, and the rest of his discussion of free will could be described as a thoroughly naturalized version of Schopenhauer's. 'I could have acted differently' is true only if it means 'The capacity for acting differently was also in my nature at that time, and my nature could have been swayed by it under other circumstances (that is, if a thought or a sensation had been different)'.[11] I could have acted differently only under different causal input, just like any animal. Responsibility falls immediately:

we hold others responsible for particular blameworthy actions they have committed, although they were able, as we suppose, to have acted differently.

Holding others responsible is thus based ... on the error of supposing that the human will is free.

In contrast, when we have understood that every person is born with certain characteristics, that circumstances act on these characteristics, and that certain thoughts and feelings necessarily emerge from the conjunction of these two factors, which in turn necessarily give rise to certain actions—when we have understood the necessity of all human actions, we will no longer hold anyone responsible.[12]

Responsibility is a plain illusion for Rée, though people do not often acknowledge it as such because they fear 'that those they have punished might say: Why are you punishing me? I had to act in that way', and 'are afraid of the conclusions of the mob: if everything is necessary, then, giving in to our instincts, we will steal, pillage, and murder'. This fear, which Rée says is 'often perhaps well-founded', leads philosophers to hide from the truth that there is no free will.[13]

---

[9] See ibid. 87: 'the whole being and essence ... of the human being himself ... must be conceived as his free act'; and Schopenhauer (1969: i. 289): 'the intelligible character of every man is to be regarded as an act of will outside time'.

[10] Rée (2003: 108).   [11] Ibid. 106.   [12] Ibid. 111.   [13] Ibid. 106–7.

Earlier in his career Nietzsche's thinking on free will was largely in step with Rée's and not especially original. In *Human, All Too Human* he consistently describes the belief in free will as an error and refers to the *unfreedom* of the will as 'total' and 'unconditional'.[14] Human beings are no more free than animals (*HA* I. 102), or indeed than a waterfall in which we may 'think we see [...] capriciousness and freedom of will' (*HA* I. 106). In a section entitled 'The Fable of Intelligible Freedom' (*HA* I. 39) he elegantly recaps the argument for determinism and Rée's rejection of Schopenhauer's attempt to save responsibility from it. The fable culminates in Schopenhauer's inference that because we feel guilt we must be responsible and must have freedom in some sense; but the inference is faulty, argues Nietzsche in clearly Rée-inspired mode:

it is because man *regards* himself as free, not because he is free, that he feels remorse and pangs of conscience.—This feeling is, moreover, something one can disaccustom oneself to [...] No one is accountable for his deeds, no one for his nature; to judge is the same thing as to be unjust. This also applies when the individual judges himself. The proposition is as clear as daylight, and yet here everyone prefers to retreat back into the shadows and untruth: from fear of the consequences.

However, I shall claim that a decade later in the *Genealogy* Nietzsche does not offer arguments against free will in the 'acting otherwise' sense, and that he attaches little thematic importance to the question whether there is free will in this sense.

2 The Doer and the Deed

In the opening of *GM* I. 13 Nietzsche's rhetoric, as often in the *Genealogy*, aims to tease out fundamental inclinations and aversions in the reader, probing those habitual affects which, for Nietzsche, are the bedrock of our attachment to the values of morality. Our instinctive reaction to the mini-parable in which lambs feel anger at birds of prey, but the birds of prey love lambs, may be to sympathize with both affective standpoints in quick succession, revealing how readily we understand the morality of *ressentiment*

---

[14] See *HA* I. 18, 39, 99, 102, 106; II/1. 33, 50; II/2. 12.

from within and how absurd we can also find it. Nietzsche goes on to spell
out the absurdity of the radical conception of freedom as unconstrained
by causal factors. He suggests that language may provide a kind of passive
platform for all sorts of reification, and hence for the construction of the
fiction that the agent, the 'doer', is some thing distinct from the sum total
of his or her actions or doings. But his explanation here includes a more
precisely motivated element, namely the will to power of the weak, whose
affects actively exploit the tendency to believe in metaphysical 'subjects' in
order to gain a kind of mastery over the naturally strong by persuading them
that to exercise their strength is evil, and to refrain from exercising it good:

> small wonder if the suppressed, hiddenly glowing affects of revenge and hate
> exploit this belief and basically even uphold no other belief more ardently than this
> one, that *the strong one is free* to be weak, and the bird of prey to be a lamb:—they
> thereby gain for themselves the right to hold the bird of prey *accountable* for being a
> bird of prey … When out of the vengeful cunning of powerlessness the oppressed,
> downtrodden, violated say to themselves: 'Let us be different from the evil ones,
> namely good! And good is what everyone is who does not do violence, who injures
> no one, who doesn't attack, who doesn't retaliate [...]' as if the very weakness of
> the weak [...] were a voluntary achievement, something willed, something chosen,
> a *deed*, a *merit*. This kind of human *needs* the belief in a neutral 'subject' with free
> choice, out of an instinct of self-preservation, self-affirmation, in which every lie
> tends to hallow itself.

> (*GM* I. 13)

Nietzsche's thought is that prior to the invention of the idea that we are
free to be other than we in fact are—that our essence resides elsewhere
than in the sum of our actual behaviour and underlying drives—we could
not have believed in accountability or blame in the manner required to
maintain the moral practice of judging actions good and evil. The notion of
a radically free subject of action is required in order to make human beings
controllable, answerable, equal, and in particular to redescribe inaction as a
virtue of which all are capable and dominant self-assertion as a wrong for
which all are culpable. Note the role of feelings in Nietzsche's explanation.
It is the reactive affects of the weak, described as 'hiddenly glowing',
that drive the need to assign blame and call to account. This accords
with the wider tendency of Nietzsche's genealogical explanations to trace
moral beliefs and conceptual distinctions back to more basic feelings.
Present-day adherents of morality have inherited affective habits because of

the prevalence of the system of evaluative concepts good, evil, blame, guilt, and so on, and that system of concepts came to exist because of *ressentiment*, hatred, revenge, fear, joy in inflicting cruelty, at earlier historical stages.

Bernard Williams provides a convincing discussion of Nietzsche's analysis of free will here. We have the metaphysical idea of the 'pure will', or of the wholly free or indifferent 'doer' that lies somewhere behind the deed, detached from all contingencies that could push it one way or the other, and Nietzsche's question is: What might have motivated this way of thinking about actions? His answer is (in Williams's phrase) that there needed to be a target for blame. Injured parties had (as I would suggest) a *felt need*, closely associated with the feeling of *ressentiment*, to locate an absolute responsibility in the other, who could then be conceived as having freedom to bring about a radically different course of events that resulted in no injury. Williams describes this as

a fantasy of inserting into the [other] agent an acknowledgement of me, to take the place of exactly the act that harmed me ... The idea has to be ... that I, now, might change the agent from one who did not acknowledge me to one who did. This fantasied, magical, change ... requires simply the idea of the agent at the moment of the action, of the action that harmed one, and the refusal of that action, all isolated from the network of circumstances in which his action was actually embedded.[15]

The salient point is that the redescription of the agent as existing in isolation from the pressures of nature, culture, and circumstance is *already a moralized description*, one you would make only if you already thought in terms of moral goodness and responsibility, and hence sought a target for blame. The human being naturalistically described, as the product of actual physical and cultural forces, does not provide a proper target for blame, so we have to resort to metaphysics. This reinforces Nietzsche's idea, expressed so clearly in section 6 of *Beyond Good and Evil*, that no metaphysics is morally neutral.

One difference between this treatment of free will and the earlier discussion influenced by Rée is that the conception of the radically free agent is assigned a genesis firmly within the slavish morality of the weak who are afflicted by *ressentiment*. The needs of a specific psychological type in a specific set of power-relations motivate the invention of the metaphysical concept of free agency. It is just '*this kind* of human' who

---

[15] Williams (1994: 245).

needs the belief in a neutral 'subject' with free choice—a more pointed explanation of its genesis than Rée's idea that humans think there is free will because of generalized habits of association and error. But note also a second difference. Nietzsche is now focusing on 'could have acted otherwise' in a different sense. What concerns him is whether the strong could have acted other than strongly, other than in their own character. The question is not whether a Homeric warrior could have done action *B* rather than action *A* in a particular circumstance—spared an enemy with aristocratic magnanimity, say, rather than killing him with aristocratic disdain or enslaving him with aristocratic contempt—but whether the hero was 'free' to run away whimpering like a weakling, to shrug off all concern for honour and victory, or otherwise act out of character. In order to blame the strong for failing to behave weakly, the weak need to believe in these latter possibilities, which Nietzsche claims are merely invented or fantasized. True, once you believe in the radical metaphysical conception of the free, neutral subject, you will become like Schopenhauer's man deliberating at six o'clock, and hold that an individual could indeed have done any possible *B* rather than their actual action *A*. But it would be a fallacy to infer from the falsity of the radical metaphysical conception to the falsity of 'I could have done otherwise'. Nietzsche's position in this passage needs to be read, therefore, as embodying only the claim that our repertoire as agents is circumscribed by our character, not the claim that particular actions are necessitated. The passage leaves it open that Achilles could have refrained, in character, from killing Hector.

Against this, however, it might be argued that there can be no free will at all unless there is a radically indifferent subject of the kind Nietzsche rejects. Schopenhauer takes this line, saying that unless we define free will as the classical *liberum arbitrium indifferentiae*, or free choice determined by nothing at all, we give up 'the only clearly determined, firm, and settled concept' of freedom of the will, and fall into 'vague and hazy explanations behind which lurks a hesitant insufficiency'.[16] If this is the only proper sense of free will, and if in this sense there is no free will, then there is no free will at all. Brian Leiter also subscribes to what is effectively this line,[17] and attributes it to Nietzsche: 'Nietzsche argues that an autonomous agent would have to be *causa sui* (i.e. self-caused, or the cause of itself); but since nothing can

---

[16] Schopenhauer (1999: 8).   [17] See Leiter (2002: 88, 90).

be *causa sui*, no one could be an autonomous agent.'[18] But does Nietzsche argue that there is no free will at all from the premisses that free will entails being *causa sui* and that being *causa sui* is a contradiction? In *Beyond Good and Evil* 21 he unequivocally states that the notion of being self-caused is a contradiction. However, that passage contains no premiss that resembles 'there can be free will only if there is a *causa sui*'. Here Nietzsche is not even pursuing the question whether there is or is not free will. Rather he is at his usual genealogical business: flushing out an underlying affective state—'*the longing for* "freedom of the will" in the superlative metaphysical sense'—and hypothesizing an explanation for its genesis and persistence. How do we come to have a thirst for this extremity of metaphysics, a self that makes itself out of nothing, and why is this extreme view lodged so firmly in the modern consciousness? Nietzsche's answer here is that we cannot stomach any sense that we are not *wholly* in control of ourselves. Nietzsche is not doing metaphysics, rather unearthing the valuations of ourselves that underlie our inclining to a certain metaphysical position.[19]

So far this is, admittedly, compatible with Nietzsche's rejecting free will altogether. However, the remainder of *Beyond Good and Evil* 21 signals a radical change from the *Human, All Too Human* passages discussed above. There Nietzsche harped on about the total unfreedom of the will and the illusoriness of responsibility; now he asks his reader 'to rid his mind of the reversal of this misconceived concept of "free will": I mean the "un-free will" [...] The "un-free will" is mythology'. There is reason to believe, Nietzsche now argues, that in nature itself there is no 'causal association', 'necessity', or 'psychological un-freedom'; we merely project such notions onto reality. When he asks why we make this projection, he is again seeking psychological explanations for some feelings that lie beneath our thoughts:

It is almost always a symptom of what is lacking in a thinker when he senses some compulsion, need, having-to-follow, pressure, un-freedom in every 'causal connection' and 'psychological necessity'. It is very telling to feel this way—the person tells on himself. And in general, if I have observed correctly, 'un-freedom of the will' is regarded as a problem by two completely opposed parties, but always in a profoundly *personal* manner. The one party would never dream of relinquishing

---

[18] Ibid. 87. The ensuing discussion of Leiter and *BGE* 21 is indebted to Owen and Ridley (2003).

[19] Other metaphysical beliefs receive analogous treatment by Nietzsche. For instance, we do not find him arguing against the existence of God; instead he asks what affective states explain our attachment to belief in God.

their 'responsibility', a belief in *themselves*, a personal right to *their own* merit (the vain races belong to this group—). Those in the other party, on the contrary, do not want to be responsible for anything or to be guilty of anything; driven by an inner self-contempt, they long to be able to *shift the blame* for themselves to something else.

(*BGE* 21)

Nietzsche does not direct these diagnostic (and condemnatory) words towards the total theoretical rejection of responsibility perpetrated by Rée and his former self; but he could well ask himself what affects that episode in his career had been symptomatic of, or what had been lacking in himself. The Nietzsche of *Human, All Too Human* asserted the total unfreedom of the will and the illusoriness of responsibility. But the Nietzsche of this text, Nietzsche the genealogist, asks instead what affective psychological states explain the origination of these extreme metaphysical pictures of ourselves. Similarly, in *Genealogy* I. 13 he asks for the psychological origins of belief in the indifferent subject unconstrained by nature and circumstances, and finds the answer in *ressentiment* and its outgrowth, the felt need for a target for blame.

3 The Free Will of the Sovereign Individual

Sections 2–3 of the Second Treatise introduce the 'sovereign individual', but the text leaves us uncertain about who this individual is, was, or might be. He or she is described as an end-product of the conformist 'morality of custom', a mode of evaluation prior to the Christian morality Nietzsche is out to re-evaluate in the *Genealogy*.[20] But are 'sovereign individuals' supposed to have existed after the age of the morality of custom was over or during its later stages? And are they supposed to have existed once and then faded away into history, or are there sovereign individuals around today? Or have they never existed? The tone suggests that Nietzsche may be describing an ideal type, giving us what Aaron Ridley has called 'a sort of foretaste of the (enlightened) conscience of the future'.[21] But many such questions are left open.

[20] Nietzsche introduces the 'morality of custom' (*Sittlichkeit der Sitte*) in D 9.
[21] Ridley (1998: 18).

It has been claimed that being a sovereign individual is for Nietzsche constitutive of being truly human.[22] But this is difficult to support. For although Nietzsche attributes to the sovereign individual a 'feeling of the completion of man himself' (*GM* II. 2), he emphasizes the distinction and superiority of the sovereign individual over other types of human individuals who lack power, pride, and autonomy.[23] In the sense of free will at issue here not every human being will have free will, or at least not to the same degree.[24] Nietzsche again ignores the global, metaphysical question whether absence of necessity is possible in human agency, and poses a cultural and psychological question about qualities and conditions that mark out certain human beings as peculiarly admirable or valuable. Free will in this sense is a variably realizable condition, not a universal one. It is an achievement, or a blessing, of the few, and can occur only in some cultural circumstances with people of certain character-types.

A further pointer in this direction appears right at the end of the Second Treatise, where Nietzsche envisages a different creative kind of spirit, a rare and exceptionally strong 'human of the future', a 'bell-stroke of noon and of the great decision, that makes the will free again, that gives back to the earth its goal and to man his hope; this anti-Christ and anti-nihilist; this conqueror of God and of nothingness' (*GM* II. 24). Such talk of making the will free *again* suggests a fall and redemption pattern: at some time in the past, as a product of the harshly repressive 'morality of custom', there became possible sovereign individuals with the characteristic quality of having a free will. Since that time the post-Christian morality of selflessness has been victorious, positing the desirability of guilt and self-suppression and the conception of the non-self-suppressing individual as blameworthy for not making the supposedly available choice to be harmless. In some future we might cast off this conception of morality, and the will could be free again.

The individual with free will contrasts starkly with the morality of custom (*die Sittlichkeit der Sitte*) because, as Nietzsche provocatively puts it, ' "autonomous" and "moral" are mutually exclusive' (*GM* II. 2). For there to be values at all, Nietzsche suggests, there had to be a long prehistory in which simple conformity to tradition determined what was good, departure

---

[22] See Havas (2000: 94–5).

[23] The point is made in reply to Havas by Ridley (2000: 106–7).

[24] This is a central point in Gemes (2006*a*).

from tradition what was bad and fit to be curbed. Civilization begins with the proposition 'any custom is better than no custom', and tradition is a 'higher authority that one obeys [...] because it *commands*' (D 16, 9). Yet the end-product or 'fruit' of this whole constraining process is an individual 'resembling only himself', having the capacity to be 'free again from the morality of custom', to have an 'independent [...] will' and be 'autonomous'. Nietzsche says much in a short space here, perhaps grasping for a vocabulary that will capture his insights. The sovereign individual's will is 'free', 'his own', 'independent', 'long', and 'unbreakable'; and in virtue of this will the sovereign individual is permitted to promise, has 'mastery over himself', has his own standard of value, is permitted to say yes to himself,[25] and has a consciousness of his 'superiority' and 'completion'. To be *permitted* to make promises, one must not only be minimally capable of promising but have the power to fulfil one's promises and the integrity to promise only what one genuinely has the will to do. This suggests a kind of self-knowledge in which one is properly conscious of what it is that one wills, and confident of the consistency with which one's will is going to maintain itself intact until the moment at which it can be delivered upon. The sovereign individual can count upon himself to act consistently, to be the same in the future when the time comes to produce what he promised in the past. Understanding oneself in this way, one will presumably attain a justified sense of satisfaction in one's power and integrity, and value others, not according to their conformity to some general practice imposed from without, but according to their manifestation of the kind of power and integrity one recognizes in oneself.

This positive conception of free will, then, involves acting fully within one's character, knowing its limits and capabilities, and valuing oneself for what one is rather than for one's conformity to an external standard or to what one ought to be. In the later *Twilight of the Idols* Nietzsche eulogizes Goethe as 'a spirit *become free (freigewordner)*', who 'dares to allow himself the whole compass and wealth of naturalness, who is strong enough for this freedom' and 'stands in the midst of the universe with a joyful and trusting fatalism'.[26] One becomes free in accepting and affirming oneself as

---

[25] GM II. 3. All immediately surrounding quotations and paraphrases are from GM II. 2.

[26] TI, 'Expeditions of an Untimely Man', 49; my trans. of *freigewordne*, in preference to Hollingdale's 'emancipated'.

a whole, and rather than seeing the necessity or fatedness of one's character as an inhibition or obstacle to action, one sees it as the condition of and opportunity for true self-expression. In another passage about artistic creativity Nietzsche emphasizes how much the right kind of freedom stems from acknowledging and submitting to constraints:

everything there is, or was, of freedom, subtlety, boldness, dance, or masterly assurance on earth [...] has only developed by virtue of the 'tyranny of such arbitrary laws.' And, in all seriousness, it is not at all improbable that *this* is what is 'nature' and 'natural'—and *not* that *laisser-aller*! Every artist knows how far removed this feeling of letting go is from his 'most natural' state, the free ordering, placing, disposing and shaping in the moment of 'inspiration'—he knows how strictly and subtly he obeys thousands of laws at this very moment.

(BGE 188)

These are among the harder parts of Nietzsche's philosophy to feel one has understood or re-expressed faithfully. There is a vagueness in Nietzsche's evocations of what future values and future individuals will be once they have liberated themselves from moral self-descriptions. We may excuse the vagueness to some extent: Nietzsche is writing of a mere aspiration that he thinks has rarely, if ever, been realized, he is writing in the midst of a moralized vocabulary that by his own lights is all-pervasive, and *ex hypothesi* he cannot give a general or formulaic account of the values of his future individuals because of their very individuality, their intensely personal, self-legislating nature that must resist universalization. But we might be able to conceive of something like the following as an approximation to Nietzsche's sovereign individual: someone who is conscious of the strength and consistency of his or her own character over time; who creatively affirms and embraces him- or herself as valuable, and who values his or her actions because of the degree to which they are in character; who welcomes the limitation and discipline of internal and external nature as the true conditions of action and creation, but whose evaluations arise from a sense of who he or she is, rather than from conformity to some external or generic code of values. This is a glimpse of the sense in which free will might be attained, or regained for Nietzsche. But to gain even this glimpse we must step outside our learned moralistic preoccupation with blame and with the neutralizing of character differences in explaining action, and look beyond the dichotomy between the notion of *causa sui* or radical independence from nature and the 'total unfreedom' of Rée's naturalism: a dichotomy between two myths, as Nietzsche has warned us, myths that prevail because they are driven by differing affective impulses within us.

4 Autonomy and the Achievement of New Values

Nietzsche is hoping for a revaluation of values: he wants some of us at least to change our allegiance away from the values of selflessness as he has diagnosed them, and to regard them as symptoms of sickness and decline which we will do our best to distance ourselves from in future. But what is this change in allegiance, and how might it occur?

An important aspect to revaluation is the claiming of values as one's own. Rather than adhering to values which are received, traditional, generic, universal, one is to discover one's own personal values. For example, Nietzsche says:

Let us [...] *limit* ourselves to the purification of our opinions and value judgements and to the *creation of tables of what is good that are new and all our own*: let us stop brooding over the 'moral value of our actions'! Yes, my friends, it is time to feel nauseous about some people's moral chatter about others. Sitting in moral judgement should offend our taste.

(GS 335)

Discovering truths about the psychological origins of our evaluations does not as such revalue them, but, as Nietzsche says in a notebook entry,[27] 'for our feelings [...] [it] reduces the value of the thing which originated that way, and prepares a critical mood and attitude towards it'. He also puts this by saying, 'Your insight into *how such things as moral judgements could ever have come into existence* would spoil these emotional words [such as "duty" and "conscience"] for you' (GS 335). The effect, I take it, could also be described as a loss of one's more or less automatic emotional alignment with received values, a suspension of the single-dimensional 'pro and contra' inherited from the Christian culture of Nietzsche's most typical readers. This suspension allows a space for a new evaluation and a shift or reversal in

---

[27] *WLN* 95 (n. 2 [189] (1885–6), previously pub. as *WP* 254).

values, which Nietzsche often describes in ways which seem to presuppose agency, judgement, and choice.

A relevant example comes at the end of the *Genealogy*'s Second Treatise. Here Nietzsche takes himself to have shown that guilt came to be regarded as a good in the Christian world-view because the conception of our natural instinctual selves as an ultimate transgression against God allowed us the most powerful guarantee of being able to vent our inbuilt drive towards cruelty upon ourselves. Nietzsche evaluates this state of self-torture as 'the most terrible sickness that has thus far raged in man' (*GM* II. 22). But then he offers us the healthy alternative, 'a reverse attempt [...] namely to wed to bad conscience the *unnatural* inclinations, all those aspirations to the beyond, to that which is contrary to the senses, contrary to the instincts, contrary to nature' (*GM* II. 24)—though he doubts that any but that most exceptional human being of the future, the redeeming, creative spirit of *great health*, will be able to accomplish this.

How to characterize the change of allegiance in values that Nietzsche here imagines someone undergoing? We start with the observation that people feel guilt and regard life lived with an enduring guilty conscience as having positive value. We offer to explain these phenomena in terms of historical psychological states: in brief, an instinctual drive to inflict cruelty, internalization of the instincts, and rationalization of self-cruelty by the invention of a theistic metaphysics. We judge this psychological complex a sickness, allowing ourselves, as Nietzsche says, to feel horrified and unnerved by the sadness of it (*GM* II. 22). Although we are the inheritors of Christian attitudes of disapproval to what is labelled egoistic, we can take a step back from our accustomed valuations, and then—if strong enough—try to bring ourselves to feel negatively towards ourselves if we experience any continuing temptation to despise our natural instincts and inclinations, or to hope for a higher, otherworldly order of values. So the process of reversal Nietzsche envisages is cognitive at many stages. One *comes to believe* a certain explanation as true, one *judges* a set of psychological states as unhealthy, one *tries* to feel a new set of affects, and *identifies oneself with* specific critical second-order attitudes regarding certain of one's feelings.

In *Daybreak* Nietzsche describes the change in valuation he seeks with the phrase 'we have to *learn to think differently*'—i.e. outside the moral evaluative oppositions of good and evil, egoistic and selfless—'in order at last, perhaps very late on, to attain even more: *to feel differently*' (*D* 103). Also in *Daybreak* Nietzsche adumbrates a kind of liberation of the individual's thinking, not from feelings per se, which for him would be impossible and undesirable,[28] but from feelings which are not original or appropriate to the individual. Instead of carrying around 'valuations of things that originate in the passions and loves of former centuries' (*GS* 57) and giving 'obedience to one's grandfather and grandmother and their grandparents', one is to honour what he strikingly calls 'the gods which are in *us*: our reason and our experience' (*D* 35). Other passages suggest that a revaluation of values will be an act of placing trust in values that are authentically one's own, an autonomous decision taken in the light of self-understanding.

> It is selfish to consider one's own judgement a universal law, and this selfishness is blind, petty, and simple because it shows that *you haven't yet discovered yourself or created for yourself an ideal of your very own* [my emphasis] [...] No one who judges, 'in this case everyone would have to act like this' has yet taken five steps towards self-knowledge. [...] We, however, want to *become who we are*—human beings who are new, unique, incomparable, who give themselves laws, who create themselves! To that end we must become the best students and discoverers of everything lawful and necessary in the world.
>
> (*GS* 335)

Nietzsche here predicates both self-knowledge and autonomy of those who would successfully follow him. Against this one may range many passages in which Nietzsche asserts that self and will are illusions, that there is no internal 'helmsman' controlling one's actions, no unitary subject of thought or action known to oneself by privileged access, only a subterranean multiplicity of competing or hierarchically organized drives, of which one's knowledge will always be incomplete.[29] However, the fact that self-knowledge (likewise selfhood as such, as Gemes shows[30]) is hard, that most have very little of it, and even that no one ever attains it completely—none of this shows that self-knowledge is impossible: only that it is rare among

---

[28] As witness the famous passage in *GM* III. 12, where Nietzsche urges that 'there is [...] *only* a perspectival "knowing"; and *the more* affects we allow to speak about a matter [...] that much more complete will our "concept" of this matter, our "objectivity" be. But to eliminate the will altogether, to disconnect the affects one and all, supposing that we were capable of this: what? would that not be to *castrate* the intellect?'

[29] See *D* 109, 116, 119, 129; *GS* 335, 360; *BGE* 16, 17, 19, 34, 54; *TI*, 'Reason in Philosophy', 5; 'The Four Great Errors', 3.   [30] Gemes (2006a).

human beings, that it is a task set for a few of us rather than a given, and that its achievement is a matter of degree.

Nietzsche imagines that by examining our own deep-seated attitudes of inclination and aversion, by accepting hypotheses about their origin in past psychological configurations such as those of the ancient masters and slaves, by reflecting on which values we feel as most congenial to our characters, we may attach ourselves to a new set of values. The latter step of becoming free from the inherited values of morality requires, I argue, the conception of oneself as deciding, choosing, and trying as a genuine agent. Such genuine agency does not require that one be a neutral subject of free will that has unlimited possibility of action unconstrained by character and the causal order. In that sense there is no free will. But it does require, as Nietzsche says, that we rid ourselves of the other myth, that of the total unfreedom of the will. To those who incline to think that Nietzsche's denial of radical *causa sui* free will leaves him no room for such autonomous, transformative choice of values,[31] his own words may perhaps be addressed:

In human beings, *creature* and *creator* are combined: in humans there is material, fragments, abundance, clay, dirt, nonsense, chaos; but in humans there is also creator, maker, hammer-hardness, spectator-divinity and seventh day:—do you understand this contrast?

(*BGE* 225)

The extent to which Nietzsche succeeds in combining a naturalistic account of the human 'material' with an account of creative agency may be a subject for debate. But it is wrong to think that he wishes to exclude creative agency from his picture of humanity, because without it his proposed critique of moral values and his project of learning to think and feel in healthier ways would make little sense.

---

[31] As argued especially by Leiter (1998; 2002: 81–101).

8

Guilt, Bad Conscience, and Self-Punishment

1 Cruelty that Turns Back

The Second Treatise of the *Genealogy*, entitled '"Guilt", "Bad Conscience", and Related Matters', has been comparatively poorly served by extended commentary.[1] The treatise admittedly follows a winding path even by Nietzsche's standards, but I hope to reveal a central train of thought from which its many byways branch off. The central train of thought is that having a bad conscience or feeling guilty is a way in which we satisfy a fundamental need to inflict *cruelty*. This is achieved by turning the exercise of cruelty *inwards*, upon the self rather than others, and by interpreting such cruelty as a legitimate form of *punishment* of oneself.

In *Ecce Homo* Nietzsche sums up the Second Treatise as follows:

The *second* inquiry offers the psychology of the *conscience*—which is *not*, as people may believe, 'the voice of God in man': it is the instinct of cruelty that turns back after it can no longer discharge itself externally. Cruelty is here exposed for the first time as one of the most ancient and basic substrata of culture that simply cannot be imagined away.[2]

Not the voice of God, but a human instinct. Each of the *Genealogy*'s three treatises, I would argue, illustrates a point that Nietzsche makes towards the beginning of *Beyond Good and Evil*: 'The fundamental belief

---

[1] It is perhaps symptomatic of the slight attention *GM* II has generally received that the introduction of the excellent edition by Clark and Swensen (1998) includes only a single paragraph of commentary on the essay, contrasted with a whole section devoted to each of *GM* I and *GM* III. Some recent exceptions to the general neglect are: Ridley (1998, chs. 1–2; 2005*b*); Risse (2001, 2005); May (1999, ch. 4); Leiter (2002, ch. 7); Soll (1994); Havas (1995, ch. 5).

[2] *EH*, 'Genealogy of Morals'. My emphasis on the word *not* is introduced to reflect the emphasis present in the German text.

of metaphysicians is the *belief in oppositions of values*.' Metaphysicians ask: 'How *could* anything originate out of its opposite?' But, Nietzsche counters, 'It could even be possible that whatever gives value to those good and honorable things has an incriminating link, bond, or tie to the very things that look like their evil opposites; perhaps they are even essentially the same' (*BGE* 2). The First Treatise provides a good example of this: morality is founded on a fundamental opposition between 'good' and 'evil', but that essay locates the origin of the moral description 'good' in just the same kind of drive to dominate as is abhorred under the description 'evil'. In the Second Treatise likewise we start with morality's tacit assumption that cruelty is an evil thing, whereas feeling guilty and having a bad conscience about one's actions, especially those that spring from natural instincts, is something good: the opposite of cruelty, and therefore (by a metaphysician's false inference) something with a different or higher origin. The essay tells us that feeling guilty or having a bad conscience is a more perverse and disguised way *of inflicting cruelty*. Feeling guilty is insidiously, incriminatingly, related to cruelty, and is even the same as it is in essence.

The Second Treatise is structured around two central thoughts concerning cruelty and its 'turning back' against the self. The first, which Nietzsche calls 'an old powerful human-all-too-human proposition' (*GM* II. 6) might be put as follows:

(A) Because of an instinctive drive, human beings tend to gain pleasure from inflicting suffering.

We might call this the 'pleasure-in-cruelty' thesis. The second thought, which I shall state also in my own formulation, posits a psychological process which Nietzsche calls *Verinnerlichung* or internalization (see *GM* II. 16):

(B) When the instinctive drives of a socialized human individual are prevented from discharging themselves outwardly, they discharge themselves *inwardly, on the individual him- or herself.*

Nietzsche's 'own hypothesis' concerning the origin of 'bad conscience', a pivotal hypothesis of the whole essay, makes use of both these thoughts and might be expressed thus:

(C) Because human beings have an instinctive drive that leads them to gain pleasure from inflicting suffering, human beings subjected to the restrictions of civilized society, and so constrained to internalize their instincts, satisfy their instinctive drive *by inflicting suffering on themselves.*

In Nietzsche's own words: 'Hostility, cruelty, pleasure in persecution, in assault, in change, in destruction—all of that turning itself against the possessors of such instincts: *that* is the origin of "bad conscience" ' (*GM* II. 16). We might pause to consider the idea of experiencing pleasure in making oneself suffer. Nietzsche does not need to claim that human beings feel pleasure in *undergoing* suffering. That might also be true sometimes, but, if it is, Nietzsche does not use it here. He relies on the proposition that human beings find pleasure in *inflicting* suffering on themselves. We are gratified as instigators, agents, of suffering in his account, not as its recipients. The relevant proposition thus has the same interesting form as one of Nietzsche's pithier epigrams in *Beyond Good and Evil*: 'Anyone who despises himself will still respect himself as a despiser' (*BGE* 78). Being despised is unpleasant and distressing, and being despised by oneself instead of another presumably does not alter that fact; but in so far as one identifies with the subject of the despising relation, to some extent split off from oneself as its object, one can stand in a positive affective attitude to oneself, that of respecting. Compare the thought in *GM* II. Self-inflicted suffering is, like any suffering, a painful and negative experience. But a pleasure or gratification is possible for one who identifies with the inflicter of suffering, to some extent split off from him- or herself as the suffering object.

A pre-echo of this position is found in *Daybreak* 113:

the *ascetic* and martyr [...] feels the highest enjoyment by himself enduring [...] precisely that which [...] his counterpart the *barbarian* imposes on others on whom and before whom he wants to distinguish himself. The triumph of the ascetic over himself, his glance turned inwards which beholds man *split asunder into a sufferer and a spectator* [my emphasis] [...] this is a worthy conclusion and one appropriate to the commencement: in both cases an unspeakable happiness at the *sight of torment!*

Here the ascetic enjoys as spectator 'precisely that which' the barbarian enjoys inflicting on others: the two are the opposite ends of a single continuum or 'ladder'. The barbarian enjoys seeing another suffer, the ascetic enjoys seeing a sufferer suffer, but the sufferer is himself. Asceticism is a more sophisticated form of enjoying-seeing-suffering, and to sustain it one must be 'split asunder', identifying with the spectator of suffering rather than merely with the sufferer. That this passage talks of spectating suffering rather than inflicting it, as I have done so far, does not affect the essential point. Both the pleased spectator and the pleased inflicter are cruel. And in the *Genealogy*'s Second Treatise, Nietzsche often treats them in one breath. His original statement of the point I expressed as (A) is 'Seeing-suffer feels good, making-suffer even more so' (*GM* II. 6), and he further plays up the role of spectatorship by dwelling on cruelty 'as festival' and on the public enactment of punishments. I shall retain the formulation given in (A) because, as I shall argue, in the inward turn from ordinary cruelty to bad conscience around which the whole of the Second Treatise coheres, it is pleasure in *inflicting* suffering on oneself that must be present.

Finally, is it plausible that Nietzsche would hold that the drives of human beings are so constituted that there is such a pervasive tendency towards pleasure in being cruel? He elsewhere makes clear his view that human beings do not have a basic drive towards pleasure as such—compare the unpublished note in which he says, 'What man wants, what every smallest part of a living organism wants, is an increment of power. Striving for this gives rise to both pleasure and unpleasure.'[3] The constancy of the need to inflict cruelty therefore has a deeper explanation in the supposed truth that 'above all, a living thing wants to *discharge* its strength—life itself is will to power'.[4] And in the Second Treatise, Nietzsche confirms that the force that leads to acts of dominance and state-building 'is basically the same force that here—inwardly [...] creates for itself the bad conscience [...] namely that *instinct for freedom* (speaking in my language: the will to power)' (*GM* II. 18). So simply as living creatures we seek to discharge our strength, and when the opportunity to discharge it outwardly is denied, we discharge it inwardly. Our earlier (A) and (C) should therefore be replaced by

(A′) Because of the instinctive drive of all living things to express power, human beings tend to gain pleasure from inflicting suffering.

(C′) Because human beings have the instinctive drive of all living things to express power, which leads them to gain pleasure from inflicting suffering, human beings subjected to the restrictions of civilized society, and so constrained to internalize their instincts, satisfy their instinctive drive *by inflicting suffering on themselves.*

---

[3] *WLN* 264 (n. 14 [174] (1888), previously pub. as *WP* 702).
[4] *BGE* 13 (see also 23, 259).

As Ivan Soll has argued, psychological hedonism, 'the theory that the deepest motive of all human behavior is the attainment of pleasure and the avoidance of pain',[5] is false for Nietzsche, and to be replaced by the doctrine of will to power. Pleasure is merely a by-product, the subjective result of the natural discharge of power. This, however, does not prevent Nietzsche from emphasizing the pleasure involved in inflicting suffering and the transference of this pleasure to the case of self-inflicted suffering. The vocabulary of pleasure, joy, satisfaction, or feeling good in relation to cruelty is prevalent throughout the essay.[6]

2 Some Questions of Interpretation

The Second Treatise raises numerous large-scale issues of interpretation which make it difficult to go into detail beyond the level of the 'mission-statement'. Such issues should not be multiplied beyond necessity, so I shall mention just the following: (1) Is 'bad conscience' a form of the 'conscience' that Nietzsche attributes to the 'sovereign individual' in the essay's opening sections? (2) Are 'consciousness of guilt' and 'bad conscience' two separate phenomena, or one and the same? (3) Is the process of internalization of the instincts which Nietzsche describes as the 'origin of bad conscience' already an instance of 'bad conscience' or merely a precondition for it? (4) What is the process of 'moralization' which results in a particularly Christian form of bad conscience towards the end of the essay?

---

[5] Soll (1994: 169).

[6] See section 5: 'the creditor is granted a certain *feeling of satisfaction* as repayment and compensation,—the feeling of satisfaction that comes from being permitted to vent his power without a second thought on one who is powerless, the carnal delight "*de faire le mal pour le plaisir de le faire*," the enjoyment of doing violence'; section 6: '*cruelty* constitutes the great festival joy of earlier humanity [...] Seeing-suffer feels good, making-suffer even more so—that is a hard proposition, but a central one, an old powerful human-all-too-human proposition'; section 7: 'this pleasure in cruelty needn't actually have died out: but [...] it would need a certain sublimation and subtilization'; section 16: 'Hostility, cruelty, pleasure in persecution, in assault, in change, in destruction—all of this turning itself against the possessors of such instincts: *that* is the origin of "bad conscience"'; section 18: 'this uncanny and horrifying—pleasurable work of a soul compliant—conflicted with itself, that makes itself suffer out of pleasure in making-suffer [...] and we know [...] what kind of *pleasure* it is that the selfless, the self-denying, the self-sacrificing feel from the very start: this pleasure belongs to cruelty'; section 22: 'a kind of madness of the will in psychic cruelty that has absolutely no equal: the *will* of man to find himself guilty and reprehensible to the point that it cannot be atoned for'.

Recall that in sections 1–3 the 'sovereign individual' is 'the human being who *is permitted to promise*', in virtue of the memory developed by a prior history of pain-infliction, but also in virtue of the exceptional aristocratic strength to maintain a single will unchanged over time and to 'uphold it even against accidents, even "against fate"'. The 'consciousness of this rare freedom, this power over oneself and fate' Nietzsche calls the sovereign individual's *conscience*. However, section 4 begins with a question that introduces, seemingly for the first time, the topics contained in the essay's title: 'But how then did that other "gloomy thing," the consciousness of guilt, the entire "bad conscience" come into the world?' Taken simply on its own, this sentence suggests clear answers to two of our questions of interpretation, namely (1) Is 'bad conscience' a form of the 'conscience' that Nietzsche attributes to the 'sovereign individual' in the opening sections? Answer: No, it is an 'other' thing. And (2) Are 'consciousness of guilt' and 'bad conscience' two separate phenomena, or one and the same? Answer: They are the same, announced here as a single topic for investigation. Nothing Nietzsche says about the sovereign individual in sections 1–3 implies that he or she must feel guilty or suffer from a bad conscience. And nothing from section 4 onwards (the sovereign individual not as such being mentioned again) implies that those who suffer from bad conscience are sovereign individuals.[7] Guilt, or bad conscience, is a condition in which we fall well short of any ideal Nietzsche entertains. I suggest that we can grasp the central train of thought of the treatise from section 4 onwards without trespassing further into an elucidation of the sovereign individual.

But are 'consciousness of guilt' and 'bad conscience' the same thing for Nietzsche? A contemporary reader of Nietzsche might well have expected the terms to be more or less synonymous. For example, in his book on the origin of conscience published two years earlier, Rée had written that the knowledge or consciousness which blames us for our own wrongdoing is called 'punishing conscience, also pang of conscience, or guilt-consciousness', adding that 'if one nevertheless wanted to make a difference between pangs of conscience and guilt-consciousness, it can only

---

[7] Risse gives an account of the development of guilt and bad conscience in *GM* II, stating (2001: 56) that he does not deal with sections 1–3. This is an appropriate division to make, in my view.

reside in duration. Guilt-consciousness is a longer pang of conscience.'[8] Later in the Second Treatise, Nietzsche also sometimes appears to treat the two as equivalent:

Punishment is supposed to have the value of awakening in the guilty one the *feeling of guilt*; one seeks in it the true *instrumentum* of that reaction of the soul called "bad conscience," "pang of conscience." [...] Precisely among criminals and prisoners the genuine pang of conscience is something extremely rare. [...] But if we think, say, of those millennia *before* the history of man, then one may unhesitatingly judge that it is precisely through punishment that the development of the feeling of guilt has been most forcefully *held back*.

(*GM* II. 14)

It is hard to follow this passage except on the assumption that 'feeling of guilt', 'bad conscience', and 'pang of conscience' are being equated. Then, when using the conception of internalization to give his 'own hypothesis on the origin of the "bad conscience"', Nietzsche appears content to switch to talk of 'this whole development of guilt-consciousness' (*GM* II. 19). Finally, the 'man of bad conscience' who achieves the maximum of internalization of cruelty tortures himself with the painful feeling of 'guilt before God' (*GM* II. 22).

Recent writers have stated that there is an important Nietzschean conceptual distinction between bad conscience and guilt-consciousness, though there appears no clear consensus across the accounts as to the nature of the distinction.[9] At least two commentators, Risse and May, agree that the true target of Nietzsche's critique is bad conscience in its moralized and Christianized form, which is indeed *a pervasive feeling of guilt*: one feels a mental pain because one represents oneself as perpetually failing to fulfil an obligation or state of indebtedness which one conceives oneself to stand in towards the all-powerful God (an anguished state presented with inimitable eloquence in *GM* II. 22).

On Risse's account the distinction between bad conscience and the feeling of guilt is as follows. After centuries of Christianity, we now have 'bad conscience *as a feeling of guilt*', which is the notion Nietzsche wishes to uncover in the essay as a whole, 'but in section 17, Nietzsche talks about an *older form* of the bad conscience that *precedes* Christianity and is not

---

[8] Rée (1885: 212).   [9] See May (1999); Risse (2001); Leiter (2002).

connected to guilt at all. This older form arises through the internalization of instincts and is a remote ancestor of the bad conscience as a feeling of guilt.'[10] In sum, for Risse, 'late' bad conscience—Nietzsche's true target for criticism—is identical to the feeling of guilt, while 'early' bad conscience is not yet guilt, but is simply the internalization of cruelty. One might point out, on the other hand, that Nietzsche frequently talks of internalization in various qualified ways as 'the *origin* of bad conscience' or 'bad conscience *in its beginnings*', or '*animal's* "bad conscience" ',[11] all of which are compatible with internalization's being simply a preliminary and necessary component of bad conscience, not bad conscience as such.[12]

So it is hard to assert either that Nietzsche consistently distinguishes bad conscience from the feeling of (or consciousness of) guilt, or that he sees bad conscience as consisting *simply* in internalization of instincts, lacking a further component present in guilt. But rather than pursuing these issues, I shall proceed under the following assumptions: (1) internalization of the drive to express power and hence to inflict cruelty is one crucial component in the genesis of guilt-consciousness; (2) such internalization is not identical to guilt-consciousness proper; (3) guilt-consciousness proper is the most fully developed form of bad conscience and the true target of Nietzsche's critique.

3 What Explains Guilt-Consciousness?

In the discussion above we reached the idea that, because of a standing human tendency to gain pleasure from inflicting suffering and an enforced incapacity to inflict it outwardly, human beings who are subjected to the conditions of a settled society gain pleasure from inflicting suffering on themselves. Internalization of cruelty means that we must discharge power somehow by inflicting suffering upon ourselves in a manner that produces gratification. But there are plenty of imaginable ways in which such a

---

[10] Risse (2001: 58).   [11] *GM* II. 16, 17; III. 20; my emphases.

[12] Nietzsche sometimes discusses guilt in a similar way. In *GM* III. 20 he refers back to the discussion of the 'animal psychology' of internalization and glosses it with 'there the feeling of guilt first confronted us in its raw state as it were'. Priests exploit this already existing kind of guilt feeling by reinterpreting it as 'sin', he says, 'for thus reads the priestly re-interpretation of the animal's "bad conscience" (cruelty turned backwards)'. Here Nietzsche describes the state of internalization of the instincts indifferently as 'bad conscience' and as 'guilt'.

mechanism could work without the suffering's being the specific one of feeling *guilty*. Human beings, when faced with society's confines, could have aggressed against themselves by inflicting the pain of *fear* on themselves, becoming afraid of one another or of the untamed natural environment or of some imagined predatory beings. Or they might have made themselves suffer from painful *jealousy* of other beings whose instincts did not need to be curbed. Or they might have suffered from crippling *shame* or been *angry* at their own impotence. These would all have been ways (compatible with our propositions (A′), (B), and (C′)) in which to 'torture' or 'persecute' themselves. So even if we accept that internalization of hostile instincts dictates that socialized human beings must gratify themselves through self-inflicted suffering, we still do not have to accept that such human beings must feel guilt, have guilt-consciousness, or indeed that they must suffer the pangs of bad conscience in any usual sense. And that creates a gap for Nietzsche to bridge. If the internalization of cruelty is not yet the feeling of guilt, then how do we reach there from here?

A potentially even more serious problem for the overall train of thought in the treatise is that Nietzsche gives what looks like a quite different explanation of the origin of the feeling of guilt: 'The feeling of guilt [...] had its origin [...] in the oldest and most primitive relationship among persons there is, in the relationship between buyer and seller, creditor and debtor' (*GM* II. 8). One of the main sources of explanatory energy for the whole essay is the repeated play on *Schuld, Schulden, Schuldner* (guilt, debt, debtor), at its most salient in Nietzsche's thought that 'that central moral concept "guilt" had its origins in the very material concept "debt"' (*GM* II. 4). One is a debtor when one is under an obligation, such that something is rightly claimed by someone as a conventional equivalence for a detriment one has caused them. But if *this* is the origin of the consciousness of guilt, why give us also the apparently quite separate hypothesis that consciousness of guilt originates in internalization of the instincts of hostility? The two explanations are not only distinct but of different kinds, the one invoking a psychological process supposed to occur in each individual as a consequence of the adaptation of the instinctual nature of humans to a socialized environment, the other a cultural regularization of exchange between individuals.

And finally there is a further difficulty. The debtor–creditor relationship operates independently of any *feeling* of guilt by those party to it—as

Nietzsche points out with great clarity. If one is punished as a debtor, it is essential that one suffers a pain which is, according to some institutional rule, equivalent to the harm inflicted on one's creditor. But throughout the majority of human history—Nietzsche makes clear—arousing the *feeling* of guilt has been neither the purpose nor the characteristic effect of punishment. My standing in what we can call 'objective guilt',[13] my *being* guilty, in the sense of someone's having the right to pay back some punishment to me, is emphatically independent of my having any *feeling* or *consciousness* of guilt: 'no other "inner pain"' need be felt than sorrow and fear over one's impending ruin. That one suffers at the hands of one's creditor may present itself to one only as a matter of grave misfortune, little different from facing 'a plummeting, crushing boulder against which one can no longer fight' (*GM* II. 14).

So our difficulties have been compounded. Nietzsche appears to give two independent explanations for the origin of guilt-consciousness. And of the would-be explanations—internalization of instincts and the debtor–creditor relationship—neither on its own takes us near to the explanandum.

4 Self-Punishment

If we are to regain coherence for the central train of thought in the Second Treatise, the 'two explanations' of the origin of guilt-consciousness must be parts of a single more subtle story. This can be the case, I suggest, if at some stage the cruelty that is internalized takes the form of a putative redress for transgression or payment of what is owed—if, in other words, we fulfil our alleged instinctive need to inflict suffering by conceiving the pain inflicted on ourselves as legitimate, because rightfully inflicted as a *punishment*. A further advantage of this reading, I maintain, is that the notion of *inflicting suffering on oneself because one conceives it as legitimate that one suffer* goes some way towards a believable characterization of the feeling of guilt.

We must, incidentally, say something about the role of punishment in the Second Treatise. One of the most substantial and convincing aspects

---

[13] A succinct statement by Card (1998: 139) is helpful here: ' "Guilt" is ambiguous between emotional self-punishment for having wronged others (internal guilt; guilt feelings) and the fact or finding of a transgression (objective guilt; a verdict).'

of the essay is Nietzsche's reconstruction of the birth of punishment as a legitimization of cruelty by the introduction of equivalences between harms incurred and degrees of suffering owed to the perpetrators of harm (sections 4–15). Nietzsche leads us down something of a blind alley, since in sections 14 and 15 we discover that punishment was neither the direct origin of, nor a deliberate instrument towards, making people feel guilty. But, given the richness and prominence of the material on punishment, the essay achieves more cohesion if punishment plays a role, albeit relatively indirectly, in the development of guilt-consciousness.[14]

The reading I wish to defend is, schematically, as follows: the consciousness of guilt is a means of punishing oneself, and punishment originates in the debtor–creditor relationship; hence it makes sense for Nietzsche to say that consciousness of guilt originates in the debtor–creditor relationship. But self-punishment is also a form of self-cruelty or self-persecution, an outlet (or inlet) for the instinctive drive of living beings to dominate over something. Hence, if consciousness of guilt is a form of *self-punishment*, then Nietzsche can intelligibly claim both that it originates in internalization of the instincts and that it originates in the debtor–creditor relationship.

It may help to put the same point in another way. Nietzsche talks of internalizing cruelty, or reversing its direction: the self replaces others as the object on which suffering is inflicted. But in the passages on punishment he talks also of the legitimization of cruelty:

Through his 'punishment' of the debtor the creditor participates in a *right of lords*: finally, he, too, for once attains the elevating feeling of being permitted to hold a being in contempt and maltreat it as something 'beneath himself' [...] The compensation thus consists in a directive and right to cruelty.

(*GM* II. 5)

So internalization and legitimization are two processes by which the expression of cruelty may be modified. If we think of them as two dimensions of transformation we arrive at the schema shown in Figure 1. There is a standing need to express power and hence to inflict cruelty, which adapts to socialization by inflicting the suffering on the self. Then there is the debtor–creditor relationship, which interprets the infliction

---

[14] Leiter (2002: 225–6) calls the material on punishment 'somewhat tangential' to *GM* II's argument. Risse (2001: 57–8) points out that punishment already plays another role, in that it coerces the populace's internalization of their instincts in *GM* II. 16.

	non-legitimized →	legitimized
non-internalized	(a) simple cruelty to others	(c) punishment of others (conceived as rightful recipients of suffering)
↓ internalized	(b) simple cruelty to self	(d) punishment of self (conceived as rightful recipient of suffering)

Figure 1. Internalization and legitimization of cruelty.

of suffering as rightful or permitted. In the transformation from (a) to (c) the primitive standing need to inflict cruelty co-opts the institutional debtor–creditor relationship so as to legitimize cruelty towards others, giving permission to despise and maltreat them. My suggestion is that in the transformation (b) to (d) the same primitive standing need to inflict cruelty co-opts the debtor–creditor relationship so as to legitimize the internalized version of itself. We are being cruel to ourselves because, given our instincts as living beings, we are driven to be cruel to something, but we interpret the self-cruelty as deserved and rightful, as punishment of ourselves by ourselves. We give ourselves permission to despise and maltreat ourselves.

Why should we do this? Because of a further need thematized in the *Genealogy* as a whole, the need to give meaning to suffering. Nietzsche observes that 'what actually arouses indignation against suffering is not suffering in itself, but rather the senselessness of suffering'.[15] The relation between a primitively existing suffering and an interpretation imposed upon it appears in Nietzsche's substantive discussion of punishment as a series of reinterpretations of, or givings of meanings to, the relatively permanent 'drama' of inflicting a measured amount of cruelty (*GM* II. 12–13). See also the discussion in the Third Treatise, where the priest imposes upon the basic suffering that arises from 'animal psychology' a 'reinterpretation [...] into feelings of guilt, fear, and punishment' so that the self-torturing human

---

[15] *GM* II. 7; see also III. 28.

is to seek 'the "cause" of his suffering [...] in *himself*, in a *guilt* [...] he is to understand his suffering itself as a *state of punishment*' (*GM* III. 20). As a way of giving meaning to a self-inflicted suffering that has to occur when our nature as living beings is subjected to socialization, we interpret that suffering as deservedly inflicted upon ourselves—an interpretation which, as we shall see, motivates the subsequent invention of reasons to regard ourselves as deserving to suffer.

I have argued so far that (*b*) and (*c*) in our schema are insufficient for the feeling or consciousness of guilt. In (*d*) we have in play both the adaptive mechanism of internalization and an interpretation which applies to self-cruelty the conception of punishment. I now want to suggest that (*d*) is at least a plausible candidate as an analysis of the feeling or consciousness of guilt.

What differentiates the feeling of guilt from other kinds of psychological pain? It must be the way the subject represents herself: she must at least take herself to have done harm, to have transgressed, usually against some other agent, in such a way as to violate an obligation she accepts herself to be under. To feel guilty requires an inner suffering that one represents as undergone because one has departed from what one believes one ought to do, in a way that is likely to cause anger or resentment from others,[16] and would permit them to despise or maltreat one. Something Nietzsche does not explicitly provide for in his analysis—but which must be there nevertheless for guilt to occur—is the conception of oneself as a transgressor in one's own eyes. I cannot feel guilty unless I believe that there is something I have done which I truly ought not to have done, that I have violated an obligation that I conceive myself genuinely and rightly to be under. It is plausible that the feeling of guilt is a process whereby some putatively permitted or rightful punishment is exacted internally by means of a partial identification with those whom one conceives as angered by one's transgression. As Bernard Williams has put it, feeling guilty involves the internalization of a figure who is an ideal 'victim' or 'enforcer' (in contrast to shame, which internalizes the figure of the watcher or witness).[17] One allows oneself to be punished *by oneself* on behalf of those one pictures either as harmed or as charged with punishing the

---

[16] See Williams (1993: 89–90); Gibbard (1990: 126–40); Rawls (1971: 445, 484).
[17] Williams (1993: 219).

transgressive harm. Assuming for now that this is somewhere near correct, then if Nietzsche puts forward self-punishment as a characterization of the feeling of guilt, he makes, if not a full analysis of the phenomenon, at least a claim about it with some plausibility.

A noteworthy feature of Nietzsche's account is that the need to inflict cruelty on oneself comes first, the incentive to conceive oneself as a legitimate recipient of cruelty comes second as a way of giving meaning to self-cruelty, and the invention of reasons why one deserves cruelty comes last in the story. We interpret ourselves as 'transgressors' or 'sinners' in order to make our suffering meaningful in that we can conceive it as rightful or permitted. We make suffering thus meaningful in order to perpetuate our primitive cruelty to ourselves, in order to satisfy our even more primitive need to inflict suffering, in order to continue to satisfy our natures by discharging power.

5 Christian Bad Conscience

By the time Nietzsche reaches the end of his narrative and his true analysandum—the moralized Christian form of bad conscience which is a pervasive guilt-consciousness—it is clear that the subject of this state is indeed a self-punisher. The Christian has a concept of God as judge and executioner, which fulfils 'the *will* of man to find himself guilty and reprehensible to the point that it cannot be atoned for; his *will* to imagine himself punished without the possibility of the punishment ever becoming equivalent to the guilt' (*GM* II. 22). This God is part of a very ambitious interpretation of suffering: one punishes oneself because one interprets one's self-cruelty as a punishment that one deserves for being inherently unworthy in the sight of an absolute being. On this theistic interpretation there exists a world-order containing a divine or absolute being of whom we are not worthy, and before whom we are wrongdoers; so we will always do wrong, so we will always feel guilty. Nietzsche reverses the direction of explanation: we need to be cruel to ourselves, so we invent the notion of ourselves as wrongdoers in order to legitimize the self-cruelty; then in order to sustain the notion of ourselves as wrongdoers we resort to a metaphysical picture in which we are bound to transgress against something absolute that is placed there for that very purpose. Cruelty is the base: the rest is interpretation in the service of giving meaning to the suffering we cannot help giving ourselves once society boxes us in.

Section 19 of the Second Treatise begins a final assault on the development of the 'sickness' of bad conscience, promising to explain how it reached its 'most terrible and most sublime pinnacle'. Nietzsche takes up the debtor–creditor relation again, and tells how in earlier times human communities interpreted themselves as indebted to figures in their distant past, the ancestors who founded their clan. Over time these ancestors are conceived as ever more powerful and the clan's indebtedness to them as greater and harder to pay off. The ancestor eventually becomes transfigured into a god. Nietzsche then presents the Christian god as the end-point of this process: 'The rise of the Christian god as the maximum god that has been attained thus far [...] also brought a maximum of *Schuldgefühl* into appearance on earth.'[18]

Even now Nietzsche alerts us that we do not yet have an account of the 'moralization' of 'the concepts "*Schuld*" and "duty"'.[19] Nietzsche's glosses on 'moralization' are brief and confusing, so that it is much easier to describe the end-result of this process than the process itself. He does appear, however, to make the maximal Christian God a presupposition of the process.[20] I have already referred to section 22's devastating description of Christian self-torment. The end-result of moralization is that God is conceived as an absolute and all-powerful being to whom one is indebted for everything, but to whom it is impossible to discharge one's obligations or make adequate reparation. In Christianity man 'erect[s] an ideal—that of the "holy God"—in order, in the face of the same, to be tangibly certain of his absolute unworthiness'. In particular, man's 'actual and inescapable animal instincts' are the antithesis of the perfect God. As Risse puts it, 'man's nature is full of dispositions to violate the divine order'.[21] In this

---

[18] *GM* II. 20. *Schuldgefühl* is most naturally translated as 'feelings of guilt', as by Clark and Swensen. Risse (2001: 61–2) urges the translation 'feelings of indebtedness', because of his view that feelings of guilt do not pre-date the Christian God for Nietzsche—but see the discussion below.

[19] *GM* II. 21. Clark and Swensen have 'guilt' for *Schuld* here. Risse argues for 'debt' as the right translation—again, see below.

[20] See *GM* II. 21: moralization of the concepts *Schuld* and *Pflicht* is 'their being pushed back into conscience, more precisely the entanglement of *bad* conscience with the concept of god'; and 'faith in our "creditor," in God' is a 'presupposition' of the moralized concepts. On 'moralization' and the elusive notion of 'pushing back', see Risse (2001: 63 ff.) and May (1999: 70 ff.).

[21] Risse (2001: 65).

conception it belongs to the human essence to be transgressive against absolute values, and so the consciousness of guilt is inbuilt, perpetual, and profound.[22]

Section 22 marks a magnificent rhetorical climax to the essay (presumably this is what Nietzsche later meant in *Ecce Homo* by the *tempo feroce* of this treatise, 'in which everything rushes ahead in a tremendous tension'); but notice too how carefully Nietzsche recapitulates the earlier features of his psychological narrative and incorporates them in the picture of the Christian self-torturer:

> that will to self-torment, that suppressed cruelty of the animal-human who had been made inward, scared back into himself [...] who invented the bad conscience in order to cause himself pain after the *more natural* outlet for this *desire to cause pain* was blocked,—this man of bad conscience has taken over the religious presupposition in order to drive his self-torture to its most gruesome severity and sharpness. Guilt before *God*: this thought becomes an instrument of torture for him.
>
> (*GM* II. 22)

There is still the standing tendency towards pleasure-in-cruelty. But we must inflict suffering on ourselves, because our drive to cruelty has undergone internalization. But in order to continue inflicting suffering on ourselves meaningfully, we must interpret ourselves as transgressors in a debtor–creditor relationship who are granted the permission rightfully to despise and maltreat ourselves, to inflict self-punishment. And in order thus to interpret ourselves we must fabricate a creditor residing in another realm of values which absolutely guarantees that we continue to deserve punishment. In short, we use the invention of God as an elaborate and disguised way of being intensely cruel in perpetuity.

6 Guilt without God?

So how, for Nietzsche, does the feeling of guilt relate to belief in a single all-powerful God? Mathias Risse puts forward the following analysis of the development of bad conscience in the Second Treatise:

---

[22] In May's formulation: 'moralization is defined ... by the idea that one's human nature is essentially and undischargeably guilty and *hence defective*' (1999: 70–1).

We have followed Nietzsche through his discussion of the two elements from which the current meaning of bad conscience descends, the bad conscience as the result of the internalization of instincts and the indebtedness to the gods.... [The] third element is *Christianity*, and it is through the interaction of Christianity with the early form of the bad conscience [i.e. internalization] and the indebtedness that the bad conscience as a feeling of guilt arises.[23]

This would give Nietzsche quite an extreme position: no one has feelings of guilt until the advent of Christianity. And it is a surprising position, given our analysis so far. If feeling guilty is self-punishment, one might expect it to be possible for someone who (*a*) conceives himself to have obligations of some kind, (*b*) conceives himself to be legitimately punished for transgressing his obligations, and (*c*) has undergone internalization of the hostile instincts, planting the punishing agency within. Hence the conditions for guilt-consciousness or guilty bad conscience are present before the Christian world-picture arrives, indeed before any concept of a god.

Certainly Nietzsche believes that bad conscience persists once the conception of the maximum god perishes (*GM* II. 21), and explicitly urges the reader to try feeling bad conscience towards his or her yearnings to side with the transcendent against the natural human inclinations.[24] This, however, is not inconsistent with the idea that human beings had the general capacity to feel guilt only once they became believers in some monotheistic religion. But does Nietzsche really hold that? First, as we have said, it seems an implausible position, but secondly, as Aaron Ridley has pointed out,[25] we can construct a much more plausible Nietzschean narrative in which an already existing propensity to feel guilt—whose psychological and institutional origins we have seen traced in the internalization of instinctual drives and the debtor–creditor relationship—is subsequently exploited to particular ends by Christianity. When in section 22 our belief in God functions to push our 'self-torture to its most gruesome severity', what is being intensified is most naturally taken to be the general propensity to feel guilty. This fits with Nietzsche's view that man here fulfils a pervasive 'will to find himself guilty and reprehensible'. And the emphasis in 'Guilt before

[23] Risse (2001: 63).
[24] *GM* II. 24. This point is urged against Risse's reading by Ridley (2005*b*: 38).
[25] Ridley (2005*b*: 40).

God: this thought becomes an instrument of torture for him' similarly indicates the use of the idea of God to tighten the screws on an already present feeling of guilt.[26] Therefore, the presence of guilt feelings prior to the belief in the Christian God is not only possible in Nietzsche's account, but needed to make sense of it.[27]

7 The Goodness of Guilt

What then of 'moralization'? A simple but unremarked characteristic of 'moralizing' a concept is making it fit to take its place in an overall conception of the morally good. This suggests that in the final step of Nietzsche's narrative 'feeling guilty' and 'having a bad conscience' become part of what the morally good person does or is. Earlier in the narrative human beings cannot be said to have regarded the self-cruelty and self-punishment into which they fell as anything particularly good per se. Suffering in this way began as an enforced psychological adaptation, then became a kind of burden or sickness. There were good, even spectacularly good, consequences of internalization: Nietzsche mentions the development of the inner mental life, creativity, beauty, and the promise of self-overcoming (*GM* II. 16, 18). But implicit in his account is that no one prior to Christianity conceived self-cruelty or self-punishment as a good per se.

It is, I suggest, the supposed *goodness* of feeling guilty that Nietzsche thinks requires metaphysical underpinning. This provides a clearer sense in which moralization of guilt presupposes an 'entanglement with the concept of god', as Nietzsche says in section 21.[28] It is a good thing to punish myself

---

[26] Note that Nietzsche writes 'Schuld gegen *Gott*': guilt against or in the face of God. So the 'before' in the English translation 'guilt before *God*' does not in itself connote any temporal priority of guilt.

[27] Risse (2005: 46–7) has countered criticisms by saying that the guilt-consciousness that arises solely with the belief in the Christian God is 'existential guilt', as opposed to the more ordinary responsive attitude which he calls 'locally-reactive guilt', guilt felt concerning some particular act of putative transgression by the agent. In these terms, however, Nietzsche's account is best read as explaining the origins of locally reactive guilt in internalization and the debtor–creditor relation, and the subsequent intensification of locally reactive guilt into existential guilt by means of the Christian metaphysical picture.

[28] Ridley (2005*b*) and Risse (2005) disagree as to whether 'moralization' of the concept *Schuld* presupposes belief in the Christian God; yet both take the moralization in question to be the transformation of indebtedness into guilt feeling. I have followed Ridley in arguing that that transformation does not require belief in God. But I take moralization to be something that happens to guilt feelings further down the track, and to be a process in which the concept of God is indeed implicated.

if I deserve punishment in principle and essentially. And the Christian conception of the self and its place in the world—the infinite all-valuable divine order and the pernicious animal self in perpetual transgression against it—provides the guarantee of punishment's being wholly deserved. Moralization is the elevation of feeling guilty into a virtue, its incorporation into what the morally good individual is or does, into a conception of the kind of person one should want to be, by means of the rationalizing metaphysical picture in which the individual's essential instinctual nature *deserves* maltreatment, because it stands in antithesis to an infinite creditor.

Why is the self-punishment of feeling guilty construed as a good? Because our natures are conceived as evil. Why are our natures conceived as evil? Because of their animal drives towards aggression and cruelty. But what is feeling guilty? An outlet—or again an inlet—for these same drives. If we find the story credible, we may incline towards a wry smile at the expense of the inflated Christian conception of the good. And if, as Nietzsche says in *Ecce Homo*, a new truth becomes visible in his essay, it must be a version of his 'opposites' point from *Beyond Good and Evil*: 'what gives value to that good and honorable thing, bad conscience, has an incriminating link to what looks like its evil opposite, the drive towards inflicting cruelty; perhaps they are even essentially the same'.

9

Will to Power in the *Genealogy*

1 Will to Power as Psychological Explanation of Moral Phenomena

In Nietzsche's writings, and even more in other people's interpretations of them, the will to power presents itself in various guises: it appears sometimes to offer a global metaphysics, sometimes to be an explanatory term specific to Nietzsche's psychology of drives, and at other times to give a criterion for his own evaluations—the latter most blatantly in the late passage 'What is good?—All that heightens the feeling of power, the will to power, power itself in man' (*A* 2). I want to start by showing how the concept of will to power unifies the psychological explanations we have seen Nietzsche offer in the first two treatises of the *Genealogy* concerning the origins of our concepts 'good' and 'evil' and the genesis and moralization of guilt and bad conscience.

It is in the Third Treatise that Nietzsche makes the generalization that 'every animal [...] instinctively strives for an optimum of favorable conditions under which it can vent its power (*Kraft*) completely and attain its maximum feeling of power (*Machtgefühl*)' (*GM* III. 7). In the Third Treatise will to power emerges as the 'strongest, most life-affirming drive', and acquires a variety of further explicit roles, appearing as the paradoxical self-overcoming and self-domination of the ascetic, as the tyranny of the sick over the healthy, as the self-preserving drive that leads the weak to form communities in which to shelter, and as the explanation of the happiness in feeling superior that arises from doing good to others.[1] But it would be wrong to think that will to power is invoked in an explanatory role only

---

[1] See *GM* III. 11, 14, 15, 18. The ascetic ideal is the priest's 'tool of power' in III. 1; and 'feeling of power' and 'consciousness of power' (*Machtgefühl*, *Machtbewusstsein*) feature in III. 7, 9, 10, 14, 19.

in the Third Treatise.[2] 'Will to power' does not occur by name in the First Treatise, and makes appearances only in three sections of the Second (three times as *Wille zur Macht*, once as 'power-will' (*Macht-Wille*), and once as the 'will of life which is out after power' (*Lebenswille, die auf Macht aus ist*); GM II. 11, 12, 18)—though in one of these sections it receives prominence among the most thorough methodological reflections in the whole book (of which more below). Nevertheless, it is quite easy to show how the explanations given in the first two treatises count as instances of explanation through will to power.[3]

The first and second treatises, as I have argued, instantiate a point made about opposites in *Beyond Good and Evil* 2. In both treatises, Nietzsche reveals that 'good and honorable' things have an incriminating link to 'the very things that look like their evil opposites', and that they are one with them in essence. As part of the project of 'translating man back into nature', Nietzsche criticizes the metaphysicians' prejudice that the good must have a separate ('higher') origin from what we suppose is its opposite, but the point is not solely that the good has a natural rather than supernatural explanation—it is that the very same human drives may explain superficially opposite evaluations. Without doubt Nietzsche presents the nobles in the First Treatise as human animals instinctively striving for conditions in which to express their strength and gain a maximum feeling of power, and therefore as manifesting will to power. And similarly in the Second Treatise cruelty represents a basic human tendency to release one's power to the detriment of another and temporarily at least 'become master' over them. But there is a shock in each essay: the slaves' invention of the good–evil opposition and labelling of themselves as good is driven by the need to overpower the powerful in a more subtle and underhand way, and the imposition of guilty bad conscience on ourselves is an inward deflection of cruelty, the instinct to release power at the expense of something else. The interiority, complexity, conceptual sophistication, and subsequent rationalization of these moral phenomena disguises the sameness

---

[2] As in Leiter's statement (2002: 173): 'It is, in short, naturally occurring psychological mechanisms—*ressentiment* (GM I), internalized cruelty (GM II), the will to power (GM III), that suffice to explain morality's origin in Nietzsche's view.' It is more accurate to say that throughout the three treatises morality is explained by psychological mechanisms which are *diverse manifestations of will to power*: *ressentiment*, internalized cruelty, and the conscious adoption of self-denial as an ideal.

[3] The same point is made by Reginster (2006: 139).

of their origins with brutality and cruelty, and Nietzsche's unmasking of these disguises is a project that unifies the *Genealogy*. In the Third Treatise, Nietzsche describes asceticism as

a self-contradiction: here a *ressentiment* without equal rules, that of an unsatiated instinct and power-will that would like to become lord not over something living but rather over life itself [...] an attempt is made here to use energy to stop up the source of energy.

(*GM* III. 11)

He thereby completes a single arc of explanation that began on the battlefields and hunting grounds of the early simple-minded 'nobles'. Morality's various phenomena are explained as ways in which human beings, like all animals, strive to discharge their power and maximize their feelings of power under the exigencies of their own characters and externally imposed constraints.

There are a number of dimensions of variation in the way will to power operates in Nietzsche's psychological explanations. First, will to power may be *outward-directed* or *inward-directed*, showing up on the one hand as the more obvious interpersonal domination, competition, or superiority, on the other hand as a state in which one sub-personal part or drive dominates, harnesses, or lives at the expense of another. Making oneself suffer feelings of guilt is one example of the latter; having a policy of despising and suppressing one's natural instincts is another. Outward-directed will to power may be either *active* or *reactive*, as witness the obvious central contrast between the spontaneous, self-defining behaviour and values of the noble mode of evaluation and the invention of the good–evil morality out of a need to redefine and blame one's masters.

Another variation is that will to power may result in the achievement of actual *power*, or only in the gratifying *feeling* of power.[4] Thus, Christians who envisage the humiliation of the strong in the afterlife (and whose emotional investment in this 'overpowering' attitude is so graphically invoked in *GM* I. 14 and 15) attain a feeling of power with respect to others, but without necessarily altering the real power-relations that obtain between themselves and those others. Again (as in *GM* I. 13), by forming the belief that a transgressor acts out of a neutral, characterless freedom, the victim

---

[4] I am helped here by Owen (2003: 257–8).

can portray the other as choosing to inflict harm with full responsibility, and thereby feel the superiority of blaming the other as 'evil'. Although no actual power is so far gained over the other, because one has simply painted a false picture of him, the *feeling* of power is strong enough to provide compensation for the inability to retaliate. In due course, however, this mode of evaluation genuinely becomes victorious. The weak, through the reinterpretations offered by the ascetic priest, whose overcoming of his natural self is a genuine exercise of inward-directed power, in fact become masters over the strong by teaching them to be restrained by guilt and to think of their natural ability to be strong as blameworthy and wrong.

Will to power may manifest itself in healthy or unhealthy ways, creating either *unity* or *conflict* in the psyche. The ascetic is sick, because he is split against himself by his need to locate ultimate value in despising and denying himself. Opposed to this are those 'rare cases of powerfulness in soul and body, the *strokes of luck* among humans' (*GM* III. 14), whom Nietzsche portrays as well-formed and healthy expressions of will to power. Yet Nietzsche's thought tracks the intricacies of psychology with a subtlety that strains the boundaries of such classifications. Of the ascetic he says, for instance:

we stand here before a conflict that *wants* itself to be conflicted, that *enjoys* itself in this suffering and even becomes more self-assured and triumphant to the extent that its own presupposition, physiological viability, *decreases*.

(*GM* III. 11)

Nietzsche calls the ascetic a paradox and a self-contradiction, meaning not that the ascetic is an impossibility, but that he genuinely grows in power (over himself) as he dissociates from and destroys his natural strength. The ascetic ideal gives its proponent a unity of purpose and strength of will, so that there is a real 'triumph' and 'victory', not a mere illusion of one. Yet this is a personality type—to which most of us belong in the modern world, according to Nietzsche—whose strength and unity consist in self-opposition and denial of one's own most natural functions. The complexity of the phenomena here is mirrored in Nietzsche's attitudes too: he admires the magnitude of the ascetic's achievement while lamenting its unhealthy devaluing of the natural self.

Such ambivalence characterizes also his attitude to the slave revolt in morality and the internalization of instincts. The slave revolt, though it demeaned the simple, healthy, outward-directed expression of power, was itself a *successful* exercise of will to power, daring, fear-inspiring, ideal-creating, value-reshaping, and victorious over other forces that, left to themselves, would have rendered human history 'too stupid'.[5] A similar ambivalence permeates the description of the will to power that is at work in the internalization of the instincts that leads to bad conscience:

> this artists' cruelty, this pleasure in giving oneself—as heavy resisting suffering matter—a form, in burning into oneself a will, a critique, a contradiction, a contempt, a 'no'; this uncanny and horrifying–pleasurable work of a soul compliant–conflicted with itself [...] this entire *active* 'bad conscience', as the true womb of ideal and imaginative events, finally brought to light [...] a wealth of new disconcerting beauty and affirmation and perhaps for the first time beauty *itself* ...
>
> (*GM* II. 19)

The will to power, directed inward, violently reorganizes the self, giving it positive form and purpose that was lacking before, but again at the expense of losing for ever a more primitive unity and health.[6]

2 Will to Power and Interpretation

In addition to using the notion of will to power in these many forms of psychological explanation, Nietzsche sometimes seeks to embed human psychology within a broader picture of organic nature as will to power. The most theoretical discussion of will to power in the *Genealogy* occurs at the centre of the book's central essay, in sections 12 and 13, where Nietzsche uses the case of punishment to show why his genealogical method is needed, in the light of the way phenomena in human culture are subjected to endless reinterpretation. Nietzsche points out the error of confusing the function or use of a thing at some point in its history with the cause of its coming into existence. In punishment there is something fixed, a practice, act, drama, or procedure—that is, the regularized infliction of suffering in connection with some harm perpetrated—and something fluid, the various 'meanings' or 'purposes' or 'uses' or 'utilities' this procedure acquires when harnessed by different cultural practices. Thus the point of punishment is

---

[5] See *GM* I. 7 and 8 for all these descriptions.   [6] See also *BGE* 188.

successively to impose justice, to deter, to isolate and defuse a harmful influence, to attain retribution, and so on. Working backwards in the text, we find in section 12 Nietzsche's more general description of the process of change by which such a fluid plurality of meanings and purposes is generated:

For history of every kind there is no more important proposition than [...] that the cause of the genesis of a thing and its final usefulness, its actual employment and integration into a system of purposes lie *toto caelo* apart; that something extant, something that has somehow or other come into being, is again and again interpreted according to new views, monopolized in a new way, transformed and rearranged for a new use by a power superior to it; that all happening in the organic world is an *overpowering*, *a becoming-lord-over*; and that, in turn, all overpowering and becoming-lord-over is a new interpreting, an arranging by means of which the previous 'meaning' and 'purpose' must of necessity become obscured or entirely extinguished. [...] all purposes, all utilities, are only *signs* that a will to power has become lord over something less powerful and has stamped its own functional meaning onto it.

What, then, is Nietzsche's most important proposition for history? The well-taken point about the difference between genesis and use slides (without even a sentence-break) into a general theory of will to power, which, as we read through the whole of section 12, is accorded the following prominent characteristics: it consists in something's 'becoming lord over' something else, it involves something's giving 'meaning' or 'purpose' to an extant thing, and it is 'the essence of life' that 'plays itself out in all happening'.

There appears to be a dual use of the concept of will to power in this account. First, will to power belongs to the nature of human beings; it belongs to them qua members of the 'organic world'. It is in our nature that we tend to act, think, and feel in ways which enhance mastery over something. But secondly, our nature is continually reinterpreted by culture. Cultural institutions of punishment, for example, are set up to fulfil diverse surface objectives, but can be explained more fundamentally by their function of providing opportunities to take pleasure in being master over someone on whom one can legitimately inflict suffering. Cultural interpretation (as will to power) appropriates and assigns successive meanings to the act of punishing, and thereby enables our nature (as will to power) to go on expressing itself. Yet even to separate will to power into a cultural and a natural aspect is not quite in tune with Nietzsche's thinking here. For him the natural and cultural realms seem to interpenetrate. Biological forms of description reach up into the cultural sphere, and conversely in nature itself organisms and their drives are already interacting in such a way as to impose form and meaning upon one another. Nietzsche mingles 'power' vocabulary and 'meaning' vocabulary indiscriminately, saying that, in not recognizing will to power as the essence of life, one misses 'the spontaneous, attacking, infringing, reinterpreting, reordering, and formative forces'. His terms stretch in a continuum from the 'attacking' and 'infringing' which connote a release of power or activity that might apply uncontentiously to all living things, to the 'reinterpreting' which we must think of as primarily an intentional, culturally embodied relation. The concepts of 'ordering' and 'forming' mediate between the two extremes, because they can apply both to the generation of meaning and to the forceful impingement of one part of nature upon another.

Nietzsche collapses the natural and the intentional into one another when he claims that all happening in the organic world is a form of interpretation of one thing by another (this by straight inference from 'all happening in the organic world is an over-powering' and 'all over-powering is a new interpreting'). Then later he shifts again without comment from 'all happening in the organic world' to 'all happening'. As we remarked above, this whole passage puts in some doubt the claim that Nietzsche is a naturalist in the specific sense that he seeks continuity of results with the empirical sciences.[7] For his preferred view would seem essentially to import the notions of overpowering and interpretation into the biological realm and perhaps even into nature at any level of description. It is from this position that he attacks science for its 'democratic idiosyncrasy against everything that rules and desires to rule', and for excluding all active appropriation from its picture of nature. To describe the mechanistic ideology he opposes as having 'become lord over the whole of physiology and the doctrine of life' is a typically clever reflexive move: the mechanistic ideology has appropriated the various phenomena of living beings and pressed them into the service of something more powerful, thus exemplifying the very process it refuses to find in nature as a whole. Nor is this an isolated passage. In *Beyond Good and Evil* too Nietzsche offers will to power in opposition

---

[7] See Leiter (2002: 7–8) and the discussion in Ch. 3 above.

to science's 'plebeian antagonism against all privilege and autocracy' (*BGE* 22). When in that work he recommends translating the human being back into nature, he is, as numerous passages testify, conceiving nature as will to power.[8] It is by understanding that we are like the rest of organic nature in manifesting will to power in a bewildering variety of guises that we may truly penetrate beneath the misleading scrawlings that distance us from the truth about ourselves.

3 The World as Will to Power?

It is a matter of some contention how straightforwardly we should take Nietzsche's talk of the world or nature as will to power. In the context of the *Genealogy* he is overwhelmingly concerned with psychological explanation of the origins of moral attitudes, and to this concern the global theory that every happening is the playing out of a power-will is not directly relevant. The counter-theory Nietzsche cites—that all happening is mechanistic, passive, and non-hierarchical—is indeed a global one. An appropriate strategy for Nietzsche would be to point out that, under pressure of this orthodoxy, one may falsify the description of what matters to him, namely the explanations of human psychological attitudes in terms of will to power. But then we are left wondering: If Nietzsche has no need of a power-theory of the whole world, why does he talk about it at all?

   In works slightly earlier than the *Genealogy* Nietzsche has a tendency to make pointed juxtapositions between 'will to power' and Schopenhauer's central notion 'will to life', and arguably the whole set of 'will to ...' locutions so favoured by Nietzsche has its origins in a critical appropriation at least of Schopenhauer's terminology.[9] Schopenhauer thinks that the metaphysical core of human beings, what they are in themselves, is will. We discover in the immediate certainty of inner experience that we are subjects of willing, and this provides, he argues, the key to discovering our essence (*Wesen*). This essence is to strive, desire, pursue ends, be aggressive, and flee from harm. But conscious willing is only the tip of the iceberg

---

[8] See *BGE* 13, 22, 23, 36, 186, 259.

[9] Nietzsche uses such expressions plentifully and somewhat playfully: e.g. will to truth (*BGE* 1), will to deception (*BGE* 2), will to negate (or deny) life (*BGE* 259), will to contradiction and anti-nature (*GM* III. 12).

in Schopenhauer's conception of humanity. Our very bodies are the will made manifest: heart, limbs, genitalia, brain, and so on are expressions of our organic directedness towards *life*, which we instinctively seek both to preserve in the individual and to reproduce in further individuals. Schopenhauer's way of putting this is to say that each human being manifests will to life (*Wille zum Leben*).

Will to life gives us continuity with beings in the rest of the organic world. In the rest of nature, and even in the majority of its expressions in human beings, will to life is what Schopenhauer calls a 'blind striving', a process akin to end-seeking, but unconscious and without a proper subject. Even my intellect and rational capacity are brain functions, and hence explicable through the will to life manifesting itself in my organism. To reflect this, my ordinary perceptions and calculations are shot through with the ends of the will that ultimately explains their existence. Schopenhauer likes to think that, working outwards from human phenomena of willing, we can embrace *all* phenomena in the same account, so that everything in the world is ultimately will. And he means this in a metaphysical sense: the will must be seen as the thing in itself that is distinct from any empirical phenomena, and is an undivided, non-spatial, non-temporal, non-causal essence to the world.[10] He thinks that scientific explanations of phenomena must eventually run out and require grounding in this unified trans-empirical account of reality in itself.

In Nietzsche's *Thus Spoke Zarathustra*, life speaks to Zarathustra at one point, referring in veiled fashion to Schopenhauer's doctrine:

'He who shot the doctrine of "will to existence" at truth certainly did not hit the truth: this will—does not exist! [...]

'Only where life is, there is also will: not will to life, but—so I teach you—will to power!

'The living creature values many things higher than life itself; yet out of this evaluation itself speaks—the will to power!'

Thus life once taught me: and with this teaching do I solve the riddle (*Räthsel*) of your hearts, you wisest men.

(*Z* II. 12, 'Of Self-Overcoming')

---

[10] Though see Schopenhauer (1969: ii. 196–8), where Schopenhauer insists that the thing in itself is absolutely unknowable and that will is its most general manifestation in appearance. For discussion, see Young (1987: 29–32); Atwell (1995: 126–7). See also Janaway (1999: 158–65).

Schopenhauer, with his ambition to be the 'unriddler of the world' (*GS* 99), thought he had found the answer by saying that each living thing was in essence will to life, being a manifestation of the will that was the thing in itself underlying all phenomena. We could perhaps be tempted for a moment to think that for Nietzsche 'will to power' is meant to solve a similar puzzle—although care is required here.

In *Beyond Good and Evil* too Nietzsche contrasts will to power with will to life:

> Physiologists should think twice before positioning the drive for self-preservation as the cardinal drive of an organic being. Above all, a living thing wants to *discharge* its strength—life itself is will to power—: self-preservation is only one of the indirect and most frequent *consequences* of this.
>
> (*BGE* 13)

And in the same vein we find more juxtapositions of 'life' and 'power': 'Life *is* precisely will to power [...] "exploitation" [...] belongs to the essence (*Wesen*) of being alive as a fundamental organic function; it is a result of genuine will to power, which is just the will of life.'[11] Will to power appears to be in some sense a competitor to Schopenhauer's metaphysics of the will,[12] but what features, if any, do the rival doctrines share, and how does Nietzsche's doctrine supplant that of his predecessor?

We may distinguish three large-scale interpretative questions about the doctrine of will to power:

1. What type of doctrine is it? Is it designed, for example, to be an empirical generalization about a range of phenomena, or to give a metaphysical theory of the nature of things in themselves underlying phenomena?

2. What is the doctrine's scope? Supposing that the doctrine says that every phenomenon of kind K is an instance of will to power, how wide a swathe of phenomena are to be gathered within K?

3. What is its content? In saying of any phenomenon that it is an expression of will to power, what are we really predicating of that phenomenon?

---

[11] *BGE* 259. Also, upon dismissing Schopenhauer's attempt to found ethics on the principle 'injure no one, but rather help all those you can', Nietzsche comments 'how inanely false and sentimental this claim is in a world whose essence is will to power' (*BGE* 186)—not only inserting the reference to will to power into a discussion of Schopenhauer, but pointedly calling it the world's essence (here *Essenz*).

[12] See also Reginster (2006: 11, 105, 124).

On the basis of passages in Nietzsche one might argue for various permutations of answers to these questions. One permutation yields a theory that most contemporary readers of Nietzsche would regard as an appalling embarrassment, namely a global metaphysical volitionalism, according to which the essence of the world *in itself* is will to power, and *every* phenomenon is a species of *wanting* or *desiring* power. Recent commentators have tried to stave off this embarrassment in a number of ways.

The most readily available distancing move consists in denying that Nietzsche intends a metaphysical theory applying to things in themselves. Although Nietzsche sometimes speaks of will to power as the essence of the world (*BGE* 186) and says that the world 'seen from inside [...] determined and described with respect to its "intelligible character" [...] would be just this "will to power" and nothing else' (*BGE* 36), the rhetorical juxtaposition of these passages with Schopenhauer's overtly metaphysical doctrine of will as thing in itself makes them likely to be parodic rather than straightforward assertions of doctrine. The overwhelming evidence is that in his mature writings Nietzsche's aim is to undermine the enterprise of transcendent metaphysics, conceived as knowledge of a real, enduring essence of the world that lies beyond its representation in experience. Nietzsche's stance towards metaphysics is so forcibly presented in texts such as 'On the Prejudices of the Philosophers' (Part One of *Beyond Good and Evil*) and the section of *Twilight of the Idols* entitled 'How the Real World Finally Became a Fable' that anyone championing a literally meant Nietzschean metaphysics of the in-itself around the time of the *Genealogy* has a virtually impossible task. We may proceed, then, on the assumption that will to power is meant at most to be something empirical, something inhabiting 'this' (the observable, scientifically tractable) world, and playing some kind of explanatory role within it.

Maudemarie Clark has labelled as the 'cosmological' doctrine of will to power the view that 'the world, or at least the organic world, is will to power'.[13] Clark claims that Nietzsche espouses no such cosmological

<hr />

[13] Clark (1990: 205). Clark's bracketing together of the propositions 'The world is will to power' and 'The organic world is will to power' reflects an apparent willingness on Nietzsche's part to keep simultaneously in play the thoughts 'Life is will to power' and 'The world is will to power', which mimics Schopenhauer's habit of flitting back and forth between saying that my inner nature is will to life (an essence shared with the organic world) and that it is simply will (an essence shared with everything).

view. For her 'the world is will to power' and even 'the organic world is will to power' are claims too wide in scope to be genuinely Nietzsche's. However, we need to probe this denial a little, addressing to it all three interpretative questions posed above. For instance, agreeing that Nietzsche does not espouse a metaphysics of the world in itself does not settle the issue concerning the *scope* of the will to power doctrine. It could be cosmological while strictly phenomenal—global in scope, including all empirical events in its purview, but intended to be founded on empirical evidence and leaving no room at all for talk of things in themselves. The 'power-will playing itself out in all happening' might well be something of that sort.

Clark places considerable weight on *Beyond Good and Evil* section 36, which she describes as 'the only passage in all of Nietzsche's published writings' to present 'a detailed argument for the cosmological doctrine of will to power'.[14] Here, with some omissions, is that section:

Assuming that our world of desires and passions is the only thing 'given' as real, that we cannot get down or up to any other 'reality' except the reality of our drives [...] aren't we allowed to make the attempt and pose the question as to whether something like this 'given' isn't *enough* to render the so-called mechanistic (and thus material) world comprehensible as well? [...] as a primitive form of the world of affect, where everything is contained in a powerful unity before branching off and organizing itself in the organic process [...] we must venture the hypothesis that everywhere 'effects' are recognized, will is effecting will—and that every mechanistic event in which a force is active is really a force and effect of the will.—Assuming, finally, that we succeeded in explaining our entire life of drives as the organization and outgrowth of one basic form of will (namely, of the will to power, which is *my* claim); assuming we could trace all organic functions back to this will to power and find that it even solved the problem of procreation and nutrition (which is a single problem); then we would[15] have earned the right to clearly designate *all* efficacious force as: *will to power*. The world seen from inside, the world determined and described with respect to its 'intelligible character'—would be just this 'will to power' and nothing else.—

Note the many Schopenhauerianisms: (1) the thought that what is 'given' in our self-consciousness might be the starting point for understanding material reality as a form of will; (2) the notion of a unitary 'will' expressing

---

[14] Clark (1990: 212).

[15] I substitute 'would' for Norman's 'will' as a translation of the subjunctive *hätte*. The modality is important for the construal (below) of this passage as not seriously asserting its conclusion.

itself in all organic functions; (3) the slide from 'all organic functions' to 'the world'; and (4) the whole world 'seen from inside' so as to discern its 'intelligible character'.

But while on the surface of it there is an argument here that parallels Schopenhauer's move from the premiss that we have immediate certainty of (and only of) our own willing to the conclusion that the whole world is in itself will, Clark argues persuasively that section 36 does not implicate Nietzsche in any assertion that the world as it is in itself (or the world's inner nature, or the intelligible character of the world) is will to power,[16] nor in any acceptance of the premises which appear to lead to that conclusion. In this section there is really no argument of Nietzsche's at all. There is ironic distancing in his use of 'assuming...we could'—signalling that he accepts none of the premises thus introduced; in his use of quotation marks around 'intelligible character' in the putative conclusion; and in the modal 'would have earned the right' that attaches to it.

Nietzsche rejects not only the metaphysical destination of Schopenhauer's philosophical enterprise, but also his would-be initial datum of 'willing' from self-consciousness. In general for Nietzsche subjective consciousness has no primacy in the discovery of the natural, even within ourselves, and indeed it often has to be ignored as erroneous.[17] So we cannot 'understand nature from ourselves' in the way Schopenhauer hoped we could.[18] Nietzsche says, 'Assuming that our world of desires and passions is the only thing "given" as real', but if this means a Schopenhauerian 'given immediately in self-consciousness', then, for Nietzsche, it is simply not true that nothing else is 'given as real'. In an earlier section he opposes 'harmless self-observers' who still 'believe in the existence of "immediate certainties", such as "I think", or the "I will" that was Schopenhauer's superstition' (BGE 16), and again he objects to 'philosophers [who] are accustomed to speak of the will as if it were the best-known thing in the world', adding that 'Schopenhauer has given us to understand that the will alone is really known to us, absolutely and completely known.'[19] These self-observers and accustomed philosophers are wrong, according to Nietzsche. Why? Because in Nietzsche's lengthy description of what

[16] See Clark (1990: 212–18).   [17] See GM II. 16; GS 354; D 119.
[18] See Schopenhauer (1998: i. 466); Janaway (1999).
[19] BGE 19. I use Kaufmann's translation here in preference to that of Norman, who chooses 'familiar' to translate bekannt.

happens during what we call 'willing', there occur thinking, a host of different feelings, and in particular a feeling of being in command over something (also within ourselves) that has to obey, but no act of willing as such. Nietzsche's preferred description of such an episode is that various of the drives that constitute the human being have won out temporarily over others, while what constructs itself in consciousness is a picture that allows the 'I' to identify itself with the victorious forces in the sub-personal struggle. Schopenhauer attempted to take as foundational the will known immediately in the consciousness of the acting subject. But Nietzsche cannot do so: what is 'given' in our self-consciousness as agents is no privileged guide even to our nature, let alone to that of the world as a whole.

So we may agree with Clark that Nietzsche's apparent published argument for the cosmological doctrine of will to power in *Beyond Good and Evil* 36 does not genuinely parallel Schopenhauer's argument for the metaphysical will, and is not really a literally meant argument at all. Yet Nietzsche still uses that section to float an idea which is emphatically his own—*his* claim of will to power—and to entertain a hypothesis that all mechanical events are will operating on will. This is in tune with the numerous other passages where he just asserts (with no obvious undermining rhetorical pointers) that will to power has global scope. We may have removed an apparent argument for will to power as a generalization about all organic happenings, perhaps even all empirical happenings, but we have not shown that this is not Nietzsche's view. Against an interpretation of this kind put forward by Walter Kaufmann (that for Nietzsche will to power might be 'the one and only interpretation of human behavior [and reality in general] of which we are capable when we consider the evidence and think about it as clearly as we can'[20]), Clark argues that Nietzsche could not plausibly see everything even in human behaviour as explained by a *desire* for power, since to do so would be an empty claim: unless power were contrasted with some other possible motives, it would be uninformative to claim that all behaviour had power as its motivation.

However, at this point the delayed and vexed question of the content of the theory of will to power must come to the fore. In her argument against Kaufmann, Clark assumes that in psychological contexts 'will

---

[20] Clark (1990: 209), quoting Kaufmann (1974: 206).

to ... ' is equivalent to 'desire for ... '.[21] But I object that we should not make that assumption. To the extent that Nietzsche is adopting a post-Schopenhauerian terminology, even if parodically, we can take a lead from Schopenhauer here. In Schopenhauer's doctrine of will to life 'will' is not a psychological term, and is certainly not equivalent to 'desire'; it denotes a tendency to end-directed behaviour throughout nature, only one of whose manifestations—albeit the most familiar to us because of its occurrence in self-consciousness—is the psychological phenomenon of desire. Schopenhauer would say that desires are but one specialized instance of the will in nature, and indeed he remarks as misguided the attempt to see every kind of will throughout nature as a kind of desiring.[22] Even in the human case, the will to life does not manifest itself primarily as a desire for life. We do desire life, both instinctively and rationally, but in Schopenhauer's scheme will to life is an organizing principle that is explanatorily more basic than any desire—the principle that organizes the human organism so as to fit it for survival and reproduction. So when Nietzsche asks us to replace 'will to life' with 'will to power', he may count on our complicity with the notion that some natural tendency more primitive, less psychological than desiring is meant. In that case, desires may manifest will to power, but not all human phenomena that manifest will to power are desires or result from desires. Thus when Nietzsche gives psychological explanations of human behaviours and valuations in terms of will to power, he need not be explaining them in terms of a *desire* for power.

A related point is that the bearers (or perhaps units[23])of will to power are not exclusively or primarily individual agents or human beings, but rather sub-personal elements which Nietzsche calls drives (*Triebe*). Drives 'constitute the being (*Wesen*)' of someone.[24] For example, in the philosopher 'his morality bears decided and decisive witness to *who he is*—which means, in what order of rank the innermost drives of his nature stand with respect to each other'.[25] The person is a synthesis of drives, or is composed

---

[21] See Clark (1990: 208, 210).   [22] Schopenhauer (1969: i. 111).
[23] See Richardson (1996: 21).
[24] D 119: 'However far someone may drive his self-knowledge, nothing can be more incomplete than the picture of the collective *drives* that constitute his being (*Wesen*)' (my trans.). *Daybreak* Book 2 contains many sections relevant to the present discussion—see esp. sections 109, 115, 129—though Nietzsche has not yet reached his formulation 'will to power'.
[25] *BGE* 6. I substitute 'morality' here for Norman's translation 'morals'.

of drives in the way a political unit such as a state is composed of human individuals.[26] Nietzsche also refers to the body as a social structure of 'under-wills' or 'under-souls' (*BGE* 19). The drives are frequently anthropomorphized:

Anyone who looks at people's basic drives (*Grundtriebe*) [...] will find that they all practiced philosophy (*Philosophie getrieben*[27])at some point—and that every single one of them would be only too pleased to present *itself* as the ultimate purpose of existence and as rightful *master* of all the other drives. Because every drive craves mastery, and *this* leads it to try philosophizing.

(*BGE* 6)

But it would be sensible to think that the drives themselves do not literally 'seek', or 'crave', or 'try' this or that in the way agents do; rather, desires, tryings, actions, occur in the person because of the way the multiple, and changing, drives of his or her nature are disposed.

We might think that to say a drive exhibits will to power means that power is the end that a drive serves. But this would make a nonsense of the idea that 'every drive craves mastery'. For we have to consider what distinguishes one drive from another. If every drive simply *consisted in* 'wanting to be master', none of them would truly be a drive distinct from the others. The most plausible way with this passage is (applying a proposal of John Richardson's[28])to construe it as saying: the drive towards *X*, the drive towards *Y*, and the drive towards *Z* are disposed to dominate over one another. What distinguishes the drives is what they are the drive for (we might for the purposes of the schema imagine such things as a sex drive, a survival drive, a pleasure drive, or whatever, though Nietzsche does not commit himself as to what the 'basic drives' are). What unites them is their mode of behaviour: each 'wants'—though not literally—to dominate over other drives within the same organism. And it is this latter 'wanting' that Nietzsche means when he attributes will to power to every drive. As Richardson puts it: 'Nietzschean power... is (roughly) improvement in whatever a drive's activity already is .... these drives "will power" inasmuch as they will the "full achievement" of their internal ends,

---

[26] See the accounts by Richardson (1996: 44–7) and Thiele (1990: 51–65).

[27] It is hard to bring out this pun. All of the drives have 'driven philosophy'—though *Philosophie treiben* is also the ordinary phrase for 'doing philosophy', or 'practising philosophy'.

[28] See Richardson (1996: 21–8).

at the expense, if need be, of all competing drives' efforts.'[29] So Nietzsche's empirical generalization about will to power would at least say that all human behaviour is explained by the competitive activity of drives that compose the individual, each of which functions so as to preserve and intensify its own activity against other drives; and that the individual as such tends towards different forms of increase or mastery in accordance with the antagonistic disposition of his or her drives.

But then it seems less strange that Nietzsche should think of human behaviour as like 'all happening' in organic nature. Scientific works of the day would readily have encouraged such a thought. For, in the words of Gregory Moore, 'while contemporary sociologists likened society to an organism, biologists compared the organism itself to a community'.[30] Moore's thorough study of the scientific background to Nietzsche's conception of will to power draws on Nietzsche's notes and information about the books he was reading, and shows how many components of the will to power notion were lying in wait in the literature. For instance, the embryologist Wilhelm Roux proposed that the whole organism be viewed as resulting from the internal struggle between its parts—organs, tissues, cells, and molecules—their temporary equilibrium resulting in the sound functioning of the overall organism, which in order to survive must dominate its parts through a capacity for self-regulation.[31] The physiologist Michael Foster proposed that volition was present at low levels of biological organization, 'the will of the individual being the co-ordinated wills of the component cells'.[32] The zoologist William Rolph argued, like Nietzsche, that there is no primary drive to self-preservation because living beings strive above all to expand themselves, appropriating in the right conditions far more than they would need simply to survive.[33] Nietzsche read many such theories and made extensive notes on them. He came to the idea of an inner, active tendency towards increase and competition between parts of an organism, which had to be viewed as will-*like* or soul-*like* in the sense that they are in some sense striving in competition with one another.

---

[29] Ibid. 23–4. Cf. Schacht (1983: 242): ' "will to power" is not a teleological principle, identifying some state of affairs describable in terms of "power" as a goal to which all forms of behavior of living creatures are instrumentally related'. [30] Moore (2002: 36).

[31] See ibid. 37–8, 43. Nietzsche drew heavily on Roux's book *Der Kampf der Theile im Organismus* (1881).

[32] See Moore (2002: 39). Nietzsche's source here was Foster's 1877 *A Text Book of Physiology*.

[33] See Moore (2002: 47–53). Nietzsche owned and used Rolph's *Biologische Probleme* (1884).

His model for the way the organism's parts interacted was hierarchical: the parts are centres of power that command and obey one another, and the higher functions of the organism rule over the lower as if they were social subordinates. Whatever degree of unity, strength, or health was achieved in the organism as a whole would depend on the extent to which it could harness, govern, or give new purpose to the warring 'under-wills' of which it was composed.

It is difficult to say just how Nietzsche regarded his vocabulary of 'under-wills' 'seeking' this or that, 'interpreting' and 'becoming lord over' one another: are these pure metaphors when applied to organic nature, Nietzsche hoping that some totally non-mentalistic literal account could be given of the processes he thus describes? Or are they metaphors that are for some reason ineliminable? Even granted that the mentalistic 'wanting', 'trying', and so on, are just metaphors, they have a point only if the literal truth is something like the social interrelation of competing wills.[34] And in practice Nietzsche repeatedly resorts to descriptions which apply intentionalistic, anthropomorphic language to sub-personal and organic processes, and seems unable to do without them. This is a feature he shares not only with the contemporary sources I have mentioned, but more broadly with Schopenhauer's notion of the will in nature and (as Moore suggests[35])with the *Bildungstrieb* of the earlier Romantic *Naturphilosophie*. In this context it is hard not to see the will to power in nature as a piece of serious theorizing which, while not seeking to attribute mindedness as such to nature, points to an analogy or continuum between mind and organic nature, positing relations that can only be described as dominance, submission, competition, and interpretation.

Richardson has more recently offered a reading of will to power that would save it (or rather us) from all embarrassment, a 'non-psychic, non-vitalist will to power' that would 'play the role of an internal amendment to Darwinism'.[36] He proposes that we can read will to power *not* as a primitive explanatory concept for Nietzsche, i.e. not as something 'uncaused and unexplainable', nor as a 'universal force more basic than Darwinian selection';[37] rather, he proposes reading will to power as a product of natural selection. In a detailed discussion to which I cannot do justice here,

---

[34] Cf. Poellner (1995: 220).　　[35] Moore (2002: 8, 55).　　[36] Richardson (2002: 546–7).
[37] Richardson (2004: 12).

Richardson argues that we can construe a Nietzschean drive in Darwinian fashion as 'a disposition that was selected for a certain result; this result is its individuating goal, which explains its presence and its character'.[38] However, for all the ingenuity of this account, the most Richardson can urge is that this is a 'recessive' view, 'sometimes' taken by Nietzsche, while the majority of Nietzsche's references to will to power better fit the 'dominant' view of will to power as an explanatory principle in nature that is fundamental and not itself explicable through selection.[39] For Richardson the dominant view 'leaves Nietzsche with no alternative to a mental vitalism, reading mind into all things'.[40] Though we may not need to see Nietzsche as literally doing that, I have suggested that, at the very least, Nietzsche finds something mindlike in natural processes, some kind of interpretation and dominance that it makes sense to treat as analogous to genuine striving.

Clark, however, has another argument which challenges this reading head-on. She suggests that Nietzsche sometimes offers descriptions of the world that are not meant as literal truth-claims, but are purely metaphorical and 'inspired ... by a will to construct the world in the image of his own values'.[41] Just as all previous philosophies have been expressions of prejudices and valuations masquerading as value-neutral knowledge-claims about reality,[42] so Nietzsche wants to show us his own value-preferences by producing a kind of mock cosmology which he does not put forward as true. The best passage in support of this reading is *Beyond Good and Evil* 22, briefly mentioned above, where Nietzsche contrasts the 'plebeian antagonism against all privilege and autocracy' that reigns in scientific enquiry with a different interpretation of the natural world:

somebody with an opposite intention and mode of interpretation could come along and be able to read from the same nature, and with reference to the same set of appearances, a tyrannically ruthless and pitiless execution of power claims. This sort of interpreter would show the unequivocal and unconditional nature of all 'will to power' so vividly and graphically that almost every word, and even the word 'tyranny', would ultimately seem useless [...] Granted, this is only an interpretation too—and you will be eager enough to make this objection?—well then, so much the better.

---

[38] Ibid. 39.   [39] Ibid. 46–65.   [40] Ibid. 64.   [41] Clark (1990: 221).
[42] See esp. *BGE* 5, 6.

According to Clark, Nietzsche's closing words here are 'an admission that his doctrine of the will to power does read his values into nature, that he therefore does not regard it as any truer than the idea that nature conforms to law, but that this is fine with him'[43]—fine because all philosophical theories of the essence of nature falsify reality out of some value-prejudice. Again, she claims, 'He pictures life as will to power because he values the will to power, not because he has reason to believe that life is will to power...his doctrine of the will to power is a construction of the world from the viewpoint of his moral values.'[44]

We can challenge this suggestion by asking in what sense Nietzsche 'values the will to power' in practice. His obvious and memorable slogan 'What is good?—All that heightens the feeling of power, the will to power' (*A* 2) fails to do justice to the ambivalences that permeate the psychological narratives of the *Genealogy*, where the range of human phenomena that Nietzsche attempts to explain through will to power is large, and includes, as I argued above, the contradictory sickness of the ascetic, the mechanism that internalizes the instincts and produces bad conscience, and the psychological process that leads from *ressentiment* to the invention of morality and the overpowering of the strong by stealthy means. The Jews and Christians in his story undoubtedly heightened their feeling of power by inventing the 'evil', accountable free-willed agent: was that good? Nietzsche is predominantly disparaging or critical of all these manifestations of will to power, or at least of their unhealthy and life-denying effects. At best, as I argued above, he displays ambivalence: we might concede that he is capable of admiring even deplorable and debilitating disasters inasmuch as they manifest an exercise of will to power on a sufficiently grand and triumphant scale, reinterpreting, reordering, or mastering the resources of a whole culture. Whether this mixed attitude of admiration and lament provides sufficient motivation for a rhetorical projection of the metaphor 'will to power' onto life and nature as a whole is less clear. But in general it is too simple to say that something's being an instance of will to power is sufficient for Nietzsche to be enamoured of it.

A further worry concerning Clark's suggestion is: where do we stop regarding Nietzsche as merely displaying his value-prejudices rather than making would-be explanatory truth-claims? For example, Nietzsche

---

[43] Clark (1990: 223).   [44] Ibid. 227.

appears to assert that a will to dominate over the naturally strong gave rise to Christian beliefs—but why do we not set this down as Nietzsche merely filtering the history of morality through his own value-prejudices, his inclination towards active nobility and aversion to reactivity and equality? Why, in other words, find any genuine truth-claim here, rather than simply a way of constructing history in accordance with Nietzsche's own values? Why not construe similarly the idea that Clark herself relies on as a truth for Nietzsche, that a spiritual will to power drives and explains the thinking of philosophers? There have been many interpreters who have wished to see Nietzsche as eschewing any notion of truth or literalness, so that none of his utterances can safely be read as an ordinary assertion. Clark resists this trend vehemently, and wishes to preserve a *psychology* of will to power which makes claims to genuine knowledge—quite rightly, since if Nietzsche makes no truth-claims at this level, then he can gain no knowledge of the conditions and circumstances out of which moral values have grown, and the project of the *Genealogy* is impossible (or at least has to be construed very differently from the way we have understood it). Clark wishes to sever the psychology of will to power sharply from what she calls 'metaphysics or cosmology'. Her criterion for discriminating Nietzsche's genuine theorizing from his 'reading his values into nature' is whether or not he offers a unitary description of nature as a whole: when he does that, he is in mock-assertion mode, but when he gives particular explanations of psychological phenomena in terms of will to power, he is making proper truth-claims.

If, however, as I suggested above, Nietzsche thought of his will to power theory along the lines of the contemporary theorizing of Roux, Rolph, and the like, he would not have seen a sharp line of severance between a psychology of will to power and an empirical theory that power-relations do explanatory work at all levels of organic reality. He would be inclined to think that human behaviour that showed up as motivated by power-seeking desires and psychological drives resulted from more basic natural units capable of analogous relations such as dominance and submission, and the imposition of meaning or purpose. When Clark urges that Nietzsche sticks at a will to power psychology, and all his utterances concerning the organic world as a whole are no longer attempts at explanation, but self-conscious exercises in value projection, the methodological cut-off point she alleges seems abrupt and arbitrary. An alternative view is that Nietzsche thought his psychological explanations would have more plausibility if they were embedded in an account of the whole organic world—perhaps even of all happenings—that used the same principles of explanation. I suggest that this alternative view is the more likely.[45] It is true that *we* do not find this wider conception of the world as will to power congenial, and true that Nietzsche's psychological explanations of morality can stand, if they stand, without need of its help. But neither of those facts allows us to conclude that Nietzsche did not genuinely assert, quite often, that all of empirical nature manifests will to power, and that the last line of explanation lies in the quasi-social interrelations of will-like, soul-like units whose activity is something analogous to interpreting and overpowering one another.

[45] For further criticism of Clark's view, see Owen (2003: 267–8 n. 56).

10

Nietzsche's Illustration of the Art of Exegesis

There is often a certain resistance to news that things are less extreme than people have thought. So there may be resistance to the main hypothesis of this chapter, which reduces the apparent outlandishness of one particular facet of Nietzsche's writings, namely the example he provides in the *Genealogy* of how to read or interpret an aphorism. I argue that Nietzsche's lesson for the reader is far more straightforward than has sometimes been supposed. At the end of the chapter I revisit the issue of possible resistance to my conclusion, and ask to what extent such resistance may be justified.

1 The Ascetic Ideal

The Third Treatise of the *Genealogy*, entitled 'What Do Ascetic Ideals Mean?', is Nietzsche's most densely organized and protracted diagnosis of the malaise of modern European culture. The intricate, evolving structure of this piece makes it impossible to summarize effectively. But let me offer the following as an initial interpretative sketch.

An ideal is some state conceived by its adherents to have the highest value for human beings, a state which can be erected as the single, ultimate goal of life, or the unique source of significance for life. Nietzsche alleges that everything that has seemed to be a goal for humanity and seemed to bestow significance on our existence has been an open or disguised form of one and the same ideal, which he calls the ascetic ideal. The ascetic ideal requires the positing of objects whose value transcends that of one's own ordinary existence or of human existence in general. It involves a kind of self-denial or self-belittlement, in which one considers oneself of low worth by comparison with the external entity whose value is supposedly absolute and unconditioned. But it also contains an aspiration to rise above oneself: provided that one operates a severe self-suppression, killing off many instincts and drives, one can improve upon the meagre value of one's existence and be brought closer to the thing that has transcendental value.

Many apparently diverse cultural manifestations have, according to Nietzsche, been driven by a need thus to devalue ourselves by comparison with some 'higher' realm. Nietzsche claims that the ascetic ideal has throughout enabled our sufferings to be meaningful. The real affront to humanity is not suffering itself, rather the prospect that suffering is meaningless (*GM* III. 28). The ascetic ideal, in all its manifestations, enables us to feel that our suffering is redeemed in the light of something higher than ourselves. Human beings, Nietzsche says, 'would much rather will *nothingness* than *not* will' (*GM* III. 28, 1)—where 'not willing' means, I take it, ceasing to strive towards any object of 'higher' value, the possibility of such value having evaporated; and 'willing nothingness' means giving oneself a meaning or direction through the extreme of nihilistic self-denial and self-suppression to which, in Nietzsche's eyes, post-Christian culture is tending, expressed most blatantly in Schopenhauer's philosophy.[1]

The Third Treatise is unusually long, and unusually slippery even by Nietzsche's standards. Lured prematurely into an 'oppositional' mode of thinking, the reader is liable to make such judgements as: 'Nietzsche is against the belief in God because it expresses the ascetic ideal, so he must be for scientific atheism' or 'Nietzsche lambastes philosophers who manifest the same ascetic drive as priests, so he must think his own position is already beyond the ascetic ideal'. But nothing is so simple here. Nietzsche wants to show firstly that the ascetic ideal has potentially an unlimited set of 'meanings': with careful enough analysis variations on the same ascetic structure may be discerned in very many cultural phenomena. He also wants to show how there is no simple division between progress and decline: both can coexist in the same phenomenon (I think of Rilke's line 'Blühn und verdorren ist uns zugleich bewußt'[2]). The spearhead of the ascetic ideal, as we learn in the final breathtaking phase of the essay, is 'will to truth'. It is by cleaving to the unconditional value of truth (as a

---

[1] On which, see esp. *GM*, Preface, 5.
[2] Flowering and withering is known to us at once: *Fourth Duino Elegy*.

kind of God-substitute) that we have been able to overcome the ascetic metaphysics of Christianity. Faith in the value of truth is carrying us yet further, allowing us to undermine the notions of Christian morality. But it is finally time to ask whether we can discard this last absolute, and 'experimentally call into question' the value of truth itself. Thus in the end we are to see the ascetic ideal, pared to its purest form in 'will to truth', as moving towards its own self-abolition, much in the manner (incidentally) of Schopenhauer's 'will to life'.

Some similar ideas occur in Nietzsche's other late works, but nowhere does he present a passage with quite the same degree of slow-moving, self-undermining intricacy. That, I suggest, is because this essay has the explicit didactic aim of providing a sample of 'reading' or 'exegesis'. And it is this use of the Third Treatise that I now wish to explore.

2 A Test for Readers

In the Preface of the *Genealogy* Nietzsche says that the Third Treatise gives an instructive example (*Muster*) of how to perform the 'art of interpretation' that is needed for a proper understanding of aphoristic writing. He has, he says, given us an 'aphorism' and a 'commentary' on it in which this art of interpretation or exegesis is carried out as he would like his readers to carry it out (*GM*, Preface, 8). The Third Essay itself is the commentary on the aphorism prefixed to it.

It has been commonly assumed[3] (wrongly, I shall argue) that the aphorism in question is the epigraph or motto which precedes the treatise, namely this sentence excerpted from *Thus Spoke Zarathustra*:

Unbekümmert, spöttisch, gewaltthätig—so will *uns* die Weisheit: sie ist ein Weib, sie liebt immer nur einen Kriegsmann.

(Carefree, mocking, violent—thus wisdom wants *us*: she is a woman, she always loves only a warrior.)

Now it is notoriously hard to see how the whole treatise on ascetic ideals is a commentary on this one brief metaphorical sentence, or

---

[3] Assumed by (for example) Nehamas (1985: 114); White (1990: 49); Magnus *et al.* (1994: 404); Danto (1988: 13); Scheier (1994: 451); Oliver (1993: 13; 1994: 66 n. 3; 1995: 17, 36)

how pairing this sentence with the treatise could demonstrate the art of exegesis. Yet commentators sometimes give this idea—which I shall call the 'standard view'[4]—a remarkably deadpan reception. Claus-Artur Scheier, for instance, thinks Nietzsche is offering a 'rather perplexing' hint, but then goes on to say that, notwithstanding,

> there might seem to be nothing special in this to worry about. The part of the *Genealogy* in question deals with the meaning of ascetic ideals, with their presence in modern science, with scientific truth as a means of degeneracy, with decadence as the way to final peace of mind, and with the hidden essence of the ascetic ideal or with the will to nothingness. (So much for wisdom, woman, war.)[5]

Is this parenthetical aside meant as a joke? So it sounds to my ear. But if not, the commentator achieves nothing but a restatement of the original enigma. How do the words inside the parentheses find their interpretation in the words outside? We are left with the same thing 'to worry about' as we had before.

The initial approach taken by Alexander Nehamas is more candid and more helpful, spelling out the disquiet that any reader is likely to feel:

> in what way is this essay an interpretation of the aphorism? It does not mention it again. It does not offer to explicate it. It does not even *concern* itself with it at all. In fact the essay almost seems designed to make its readers forget that it is intended as an interpretation of the sentence that stands at its head.[6]

This is an uncomfortable position. How does the little aphorism furnish material that finds its appropriate exegesis in the thought that Wagner intended *Parsifal* ironically, the thought that Plato versus Homer epitomizes the opposition between art and truth-seeking, the thought that Christianity as a dogma was destroyed by its own morality—and so on and so on, through seventy-odd pages of the most complex thought-constructions Nietzsche ever achieves? It is a mighty small hat for so many hundreds of lively rabbits. Maudemarie Clark observes that 'Nietzsche seems to have constructed this essay as a test for readers.'[7] But the situation seems to

---

[4] When I published the first version of this chapter in 1997, the view under discussion could rightly be called standard. The reading I support may now have sufficient currency that the 'standard view' is no longer so commonly held—but it still has its proponents, e.g. Marsden (2006).

[5] Scheier (1994: 451).   [6] Nehamas (1985: 114).   [7] Clark (1990: 168).

demand a feat so magical as to tax the reader's ingenuity not only to the limit, but well beyond.

3 Which Aphorism?

There is an alternative, however, and the alternative constitutes my hypothesis:[8] that the treatise is *not* intended as an illustrative commentary on the *Zarathustra* epigraph that stands at its head—that it is rather intended as an illustrative commentary on what is called section 1 of the treatise itself.

As a first step let us see how, in a straightforward way, the remainder of the treatise on ascetic ideals (sections 2–28) functions as a commentary on the succinct remark towards the end of section 1: '*That* the ascetic ideal has meant so much to man [...] is an expression of the basic fact of the human will, its *horror vacui*: *it needs a goal,*—and it would rather will *nothingness* than *not* will,' and as a commentary on the whole of section 1 leading up to that remark:

What do ascetic ideals mean?—Among artists nothing or too many different things; among philosophers and scholars something like a nose and instinct for the most favorable preconditions of higher spirituality; among women, at best, one *more* charming trait of seduction, a little *morbidezza* on beautiful flesh, the angelicalness of a pretty, fat animal; among the physiologically failed and out of sorts (among the *majority* of mortals) an attempt to appear to oneself to be 'too good' for this world, a holy form of excess, their principal instrument in the battle with slow pain and with boredom; among priests the true priests' faith, their best tool of power, also the 'most high' permission to power; among saints, finally, a pretext for hibernation, their *novissima gloriae cupido*, their rest in nothingness ('God'), their form of madness.

Not only does section 1 summarize a great deal of what comes in sections 2–28, but section 2 opens with the same sentence, 'What do ascetic ideals mean?', and section 28 closes with 'And to say again at the end what I said at the beginning: man would much rather will *nothingness* than *not* will.' With the same top and tail as the remainder of the treatise,

---

[8] Also the hypothesis of other scholars who have arrived at it independently on both internal and documentary grounds. See Clark (1997); Wilcox (1997, 1999). The original version of the present chapter was published independently of these studies, as Janaway (1997*a*). See also Clark and Swensen (1998: 148).

section 1 reads as a drastically compressed version of it. Further, Nietzsche lets it be seen that his initial presentation defies comprehension, and that the relationship of the remainder to section 1 consists in rendering more intelligible what is at first so condensed. He brings alive this relationship by means of the dialogue with an imagined reader which ends section 1: 'Am I understood? Have I been understood?... *"Absolutely not! dear Sir!"*—Then let us start at the beginning.' It is plain that the body of the treatise in sections 2–28 is a luxuriant elucidation of what is packed into section 1, and packed even more tightly into the single aphoristic pronouncement 'it [the human will] would rather will *nothingness* than *not* will'. Merely reading these words is not sufficient; they need deciphering, and we must start again from the beginning, following all the twists and turns of the treatise which eventually lead us back to the very same saying.

Obviously 'The human will would rather will *nothingness* than *not* will' is an aphorism. But section 1 itself is also an aphorism[9] on the familiar model of most of Nietzsche's publications since *Human, All Too Human* which commentators habitually classify as aphoristic. Now faced with the question 'Which aphorism does the essay explicate?' and asked to choose on internal evidence between the brief *Zarathustra* epigraph on 'wisdom as woman' and the section labelled '1' (minus the 'Am I understood?' dialogue), the choice of the latter could scarcely be better motivated. To put it at its bluntest, sections 2–28 are transparently about what is in the aphoristic section 1, and in no easily discernible manner about what is in the aphoristic 'wisdom as woman' epigraph.

4   Exegesis, Reading, and Cows

So let us look more closely at what Nietzsche says about the Third Treatise in his Preface to the *Genealogy*:

the aphoristic form creates a difficulty—it lies in the fact that we don't attach *enough weight* to this form today. An aphorism honestly coined and cast has not

---

[9] A slight variation on my hypothesis would make it quite indifferent as to whether the aphorism in question is the whole of section 1 (minus the closing link of 'Am I understood?' etc.) or any sub-part which includes the statement that the human will would rather will nothingness than not will.

been 'deciphered' simply because it has been read through; rather, its interpretation (*Auslegung*) must now begin, and for this an art of interpretation is needed. In the third treatise of this book I have offered a sample of what I call 'interpretation' in such a case:—an aphorism is placed before this treatise (*vorangestellt*), the treatise itself is a commentary on it.

(*GM*, Preface, 8)

Part of this goes extremely well for my hypothesis. The treatise is obviously (whatever else it is) an *Auslegung*—a laying out, unfolding, explication—of the statement that the human will would rather will nothingness than not will, and of various 'meanings' of the ascetic ideal taken from section 1's list. But the problem is surely that Nietzsche says an aphorism is *vorangestellt*—placed before or in front of the treatise. How can this refer to the first section of the treatise itself? Must it not refer to the epigraph from *Zarathustra*? Not necessarily, as a fleeting look at the history of Nietzsche's manuscript will show. In the original manuscript presented to the publisher the Third Treatise began with what is now section 2. This snippet of information can be found by consulting the editorial commentary in Colli and Montinari's *Kritische Studienausgabe* of Nietzsche's works.[10] That suggests that just before the book went into print it would have been natural for Nietzsche to regard the original piece comprising sections 2–28 as the treatise, and the fresh addition, section 1, as the aphorism that was *vorangestellt* in order to demonstrate the art of exegesis. One could argue exactly to the contrary that this reported absence of section 1 from the printer's manuscript indicates that section 1 could not have been the aphorism that was put in place to illustrate the art of exegesis—if it was not there when Nietzsche wrote section 8 of the Preface.[11] However, Clark provides what she rightly calls, 'overwhelming evidence'[12] against this argument from first-hand examination of the manuscripts and other documents relating to the publishing of the *Genealogy*. First, Nietzsche *had* indeed added the new section 1 and renumbered all subsequent sections before writing sections 24–8 of the treatise. So there was an unfinished Third Treatise

---

[10] Of section 1 they report: 'dieser Abschnitt wurde später hinzugefügt, §2 war in Dm [Druck-manuskript] der Anfang der dritten Abhandlung' (*KSA* xiv. 380). By 'Druckmanuskript' is meant 'die handschriftliche Vorlage zum Erstdruck' (ibid. 39).

[11] This line of argument is considered and carefully refuted by Clark (1997). Marsden (2006: 37 n. 5) repeats the line of argument, but does not mention Clark's evidence and is thus led to perpetuate the now discredited reading.   [12] Clark (1997: 614).

without section 1, but not a finished one. Secondly, the Preface originally ended with section 7, and section 8 is of a piece with the last-written final sections of the treatise. There never was any reference to 'an aphorism placed in front' until after the treatise had had its new section 1 put in place.

Our hypothesis therefore has the great advantage of bringing together a view Nietzsche would naturally have held about what he had added to his manuscript, and a reorientation which reveals 'the treatise' (sections 2–28) as a superb and truly exemplary *Auslegung* of 'the aphorism' (section 1) that stands at its head. We now achieve a sound grasp on what Nietzsche aims, by example, to cultivate in the reader: he is encouraging us to approach any Nietzschean aphorism as a distillation of protracted and diverse thought processes which themselves do not necessarily reach the page, but which must be reconstructed, or constructed *de novo*, or at least paralleled by protracted and patient thought processes in the reader. Reading as an art, he says, requires that one 'almost be a cow', and practise the process of rumination or repeated chewing (*das Wiederkäuen*) which 'modern man' has unlearned (*GM*, Preface, 8). On my view the treatise demonstrates the reader's interpretative task by leading her through a sample enactment of it. The test is: can you chew over my words long and hard enough (and I suppose—to use frequent Nietzschean figures—swallow and digest them efficiently enough) to be informed or nourished by an aphorism? (Note in addition that the recommendation of slow, circumspect reading is by no means out of character for Nietzsche. He comments elsewhere on the extremely slow 'tempo' demanded of reading ('or philology') as an art—'a goldsmith's art and connoisseurship of the *word*' which 'has nothing but delicate, cautious work to do and achieves nothing if it does not achieve it *lento*'.[13])

This view of the 'art of reading' up for illustration by the *Genealogy*'s Third Treatise can be confirmed in a little more detail. Section 1 of the treatise lists artists, philosophers, scholars, women, the physiologically failed and out of sorts, priests, and saints, and suggests that the 'ascetic ideal' has its specific meaning or meanings in each case. These several instances are taken up by the remainder of the essay as it progresses, though they are increasingly less easy to disentangle from one another.[14] In section 1 we

---

[13] *D*, Preface, 5. On tempo, see also *BGE* 28, 246.

[14] White (1990: 50) says: 'Of these six types of ascetic, *The Genealogy*'s Third Essay treats only three: i.e., artists, philosopher–scholars, and priests.' I disagree on two counts: *all* of them appear in the main body of the essay, and there are *seven* types. White counts 'philosopher–scholar' as one type.

are given the words 'among artists [ascetic ideals mean] nothing or too many different things', but as we cannot decipher that straight off, sections 2–4, using Wagner as an example of the artist, give us a direction, or a number of directions, in which our exegesis might proceed. Later sections offer expansions on other thoughts baldly stated in section 1: section 5 makes the transition, via the Wagner–Schopenhauer relationship, to the philosopher as exponent of the ascetic ideal. From section 10 onwards the figure of the ascetic priest emerges, often entwined with that of the philosopher. Section 1's 'physiologically failed and out of sorts' (the majority of mortals) are picked up in section 13 with the discussion of the 'sickliness of the type man' (a condition which produces the need for the ascetic priest), while in section 14 the 'sick woman' is placed at the furthest extremity of the 'will to power of the weakest', who instinctively seek to tyrannize the healthy.[15] In section 17 the notion of a self-denying 'sanctification' and union with God (or nothingness) expands on section 1's remarks about 'saints'; and the idea of scholars as manifesting the ascetic ideal comes to the fore in section 23.

In the treatise as a whole, then, Nietzsche sets us an example on which to model our own reading of any aphorism: it should proceed with the complexity, the ruminative pace, and the discerning eye for particular cases displayed in this rich, divergent, labyrinthine piece of writing. And he is demonstrating too how such ruminations are potentially endless: the treatise circles back repeatedly to its initial question, 'What do ascetic ideals mean?',[16] and in section 23 openly states, 'I will restrain myself from saying *what* all (when would I come to an end!).'

5 Difficulties with the 'Standard View'

Some commentators who have adhered to the 'standard view' have discerned certain kinds of linguistic self-reflexiveness in the relationship

---

But Schopenhauer is emphatically 'a *genuine* philosopher' in section 5, as he always is for Nietzsche. Schopenhauer is not classed as a scholar or a philosopher–scholar. These figures are distinct and come later in the essay.

[15] Cf. Plotnitsky (1994: 238).

[16] After sections 1 and 2, see sections 5 (beginning), 6 (end), 7 (end), 11 (beginning), 23 (beginning), 27 (beginning).

between the 'wisdom as woman' epigraph and the Third Treatise—but they have not, I argue, managed to explain satisfactorily how the latter relates to the former as its *commentary*. Arthur Danto thinks, 'This aphorism [i.e. the epigraph] has a complex pragmatics, since it is at once used *and* used to demonstrate what it means to use language in this way … The aphorism is a special use of the language it is also *about*.'[17] For Danto the aphorism is (at least partially) about the technique of using aphorisms, in preference to the ineffectual, clumsy[18] writing of the archetypal philosopher: 'if one's writings are to be mocking and violent, hence meant to *hurt*, the aphorism is a natural, obvious form to use; for, piercing like a dart the defenses of reason, it lodges inextricably in the mind's flesh, where it sticks as a perpetual invasion: like a barbed arrow, it cannot be extricated without tearing its host'.[19]

Let me raise a couple of worries about Danto's account. First, does it offer anything to clarify the alleged interpretative *relation* between epigraph and treatise? We are told that the 'wisdom as woman' epigraph is a special use of the language it is about: it is an aphorism, then, about the barbed, warlike nature of aphoristic writing. But how does the epigraph's having this property help to explain what it means for the treatise to be a commentary on it? That the epigraph–aphorism demonstrates the nature of aphoristic writing would make it interesting in its own right, perhaps. But presumably Danto ought to be saying either that *the treatise* demonstrates the use of language which *the aphorism* is about, or that *the aphorism* demonstrates the way language is used in *the treatise*. Otherwise he is saying nothing about the interpretative relation of one to the other, which, according to the 'standard view', is the point of Nietzsche's juxtaposing them.

Secondly, if the 'wisdom as woman' epigraph refers aphoristically to the aphoristic style itself, we might wonder how appropriate that would be as a reference to the style of the Third Treatise. Section 1 of the treatise is, as I have said, clearly aphoristic. But sections 2–28 are surely among the *least* aphoristic of all Nietzsche's writings. He uses the word *Abhandlung* (essay or

---

[17] Danto (1988: 14–15).

[18] Danto refers us here to the well-known passage in Nietzsche's Preface to *BGE*: 'Suppose that truth is a woman—and why not? Aren't there reasons for suspecting that all philosophers […] have not really understood women? That the grotesque seriousness of their approach to the truth and the clumsy advances they have made are unsuitable ways of pressing their suit with a woman?'

[19] Danto (1988: 14).

treatise) to denote this, the least compact, least pointed, most sustained and continuous piece of writing he has published for over ten years, since his *Untimely Meditations* (1873–6). The character of the treatise sits better with my earlier claim that sections 2–28 are offered not so much as themselves aphoristic in character, but rather as an expansive illustration of the complex of thoughts that may lie behind, or encoded in, an aphorism.

To this point, however, Danto has a reply. He says that 'the manner of the essayist is a marvelous camouflage for the sort of moral terrorist Nietzsche really was, as the essay itself is a kind of literary camouflage for the sharpened stakes of aphorism he has concealed for the unwary, making this in a deep sense the most treacherous book he ever compiled'.[20] I grant that this description has plausibility. So suppose we accept that the treatise is a crypto-aphoristic pseudo-essay, and combine that with the thought that the aphoristic epigraph is 'a special use of the language it is also about'. Then for Danto the *epigraph* will also be a use of, and be about, the style of language used in the *treatise*. That at least secures a stylistic link between the two. However, is it not still obscure how this explains the treatise's being *a commentary on* the epigraph? That should mean that, in some fashion, the treatise is 'about', or assists in the deciphering of, the epigraph. But it rather looks the other way round in Danto's account: if anything, he implies that the aphorism gives the stylistic clue to unlocking the treatise.

Alexander Nehamas's account improves a little on Danto's, I think, by making the relation between epigraph and treatise more explicit:

The third essay of this work is … primarily a self-reflexive application of the aphorism that precedes it, and it is by applying it that it interprets—that is extends, draws out, and complicates—it. The essay also in a way masters, or appropriates, the aphorism in that it gives this general and vague sentence a very specific sense and direction … The application is self-reflexive because Nietzsche interprets the aphorism by applying it within a text that is itself an interpretation of something else. The object of this interpretation is the ascetic ideal, against which this essay is explicitly a declaration of war.[21]

It is quite intelligible that the epigraph's warrior figure should illuminate the polemical method of writing that the treatise practises. But Nehamas specifies the interpretative relationship between treatise and epigraph more

[20] Ibid. 18.   [21] Nehamas (1985: 115).

precisely, saying that the treatise 'applies' the epigraph. This I take to mean that the treatise puts into operation, or complies with, an injunction issued by the epigraph, an injunction something like: 'Be unconcerned, mocking, and violent when you write, and write for robust and energetic readers, or you will fail to attain wisdom.' For Nehamas the treatise puts such an injunction into effect, while its internal train of thought makes war on the ascetic ideal. What rings false, though, is the outright equivalence this reading asserts between *interpreting* the epigraph and *complying with the injunction made by* the epigraph—that is, writing in the manner it enjoins. Nehamas expressly equates the two, saying, 'it is by applying it that [the essay] interprets' the aphorism, and 'Nietzsche interprets the aphorism by applying it' in the text. This is supposed to explain how, contrary to our initial bafflement, the treatise is after all 'an interpretation of' the 'wisdom as woman' aphorism.

My objection is that Nehamas plays on an ambiguity in the term 'interpretation', and essentially relies on the wrong sense of that term. What Nietzsche claims to give is a *Commentar* on an aphorism, which demonstrates how the process or activity of *Auslegung* should take place: this suggests an expansion or discursive elaboration of an aphorism. It suggests much less readily, if at all, the variety of 'interpretation' which consists in performing an activity that puts into operation the injunction an aphorism makes. That Nehamas fully realizes the potential of this distinction is shown by his claim that 'Nietzsche [...] does not consider interpretation to be only commentary, elucidation, or, as he once put it, "conceptual translation".'[22] This is meant to allow the species of 'interpretation' illustrated by the essay to be the applying of a method, or the compliance with a methodological or stylistic injunction. But the difficulty with this argument is that Nietzsche never claims the treatise is an 'interpretation' of an aphorism *except* in the sentence

Ich habe [...] ein Muster von dem dargeboten, was ich in einem solchen Falle 'Auslegung' nenne:—dieser Abhandlung ist ein Aphorismus vorangestellt, sie selbst ist dessen Commentar.

(I have offered a sample of what I call 'interpretation' in such a case:—an aphorism is placed before this treatise, the treatise itself is a commentary on it.)

(*GM*, Preface, 8)

22 Nehamas 114–15.

Nietzsche only ever claims to offer a paired aphorism and commentary, and to illustrate therewith a mode of exegetical activity—he therefore claims to be teaching the reader about 'interpretation' only in the very sense Nehamas licenses himself to discard. So I submit that Nehamas has not explained how the treatise can be what Nietzsche says it is, namely an illustration of the art of exegesis, by means of a commentary on an aphorism.[23]

By contrast, to recap, our hypothesis that section 1 is the aphorism on which sections 2–28 are a commentary yields a brilliant model of Nietzsche's preferred ruminative act, or art, of exegetical reading.

6 Wisdom as Woman: Free Associations

So what becomes of the *Zarathustra* extract at the head of the treatise's opening page?[24] I suggest that its lot is improved by my hypothesis. Liberated from the absurdly overtaxing double role of having some seventy pages of deliberation on a topic it does not even mention spun out of its meagre frame *and* thereby providing the hint from which a conception of textual *Auslegung* is to be learned, it can revert to its more plausible function as a pure epigraph or motto, of the kind sometimes used by Nietzsche elsewhere, and not, of course, by him alone. The first book of Schopenhauer's *The World as Will and Representation* is prefixed by a motto from Rousseau, 'Sors de l'enfance, ami, réveille toi!'—and we are not obliged to regard the ensuing defence of idealism and theory of knowledge as an exegesis of those few words. Nietzsche's *The Gay Science* of 1882 is not an exegesis of the quotation from Emerson on its title page, nor is its 1887 edition an exegesis of the different motto in verse that Nietzsche substitutes for it. It is conventional for such epigraphs to be pregnant and oracular,

[23] Another strategy from here would be to construe the talk of 'commentary' as merely a playful façade for some less straightforward relationship. This seems to be the line taken by Scheier (1994: 454–5). Scheier imagines Nietzsche 'looking for some lines he could *pretend* to have interpreted' in the Third Essay (my emphasis), and speaks of his 'calculated "rationalization" of the intense relation between the verse ... and the third part of the *Genealogy* as the ingenuous interpretation of an "aphorism"'. We know that Nietzsche loves masks, but he does not have to be behind one all the time, and this reading strikes me as rather desperate.

[24] Note, however, that, as Clark reports (1997: 613), the epigraph was originally on a separate title page.

putting the reader temporarily off balance, gesturing away from the work
they preface, creating a tension with it, or providing an indefinitely large
space for associations.

One easily accepted significance of the 'wisdom is woman' motto is
that it points to something outside the Third Treatise, but called for by
it, namely an antagonist for the ascetic ideal. When late in the treatise
Nietzsche asks, '*where* is the opposing will in which an *opposing ideal*
expresses itself?' (*GM* III. 23), the 'warrior', who does not appear in the
essay itself, stands ready as the opponent—carefree, mocking, violent—to
the ascetic, priestly men of learning, who are seen in contrast as meek,
non-impulsive, and self-renouncing, burdened by their solemn pursuit of
knowledge, and reverential towards truth. As Kelly Oliver puts it: 'The
ascetic ideal is not the mocking warrior loved by wisdom. The ascetic ideal
is impotent. It is not manly. It is not hard enough to love a woman.'[25]

Elsewhere Nietzsche uses different terms to pose a similar contrast. For
example, in *The Gay Science* he had recently written the passage we earlier
associated with the critique of Rée:

? weakened, thin, extinguished personality, one that denies itself and its own
existence, is no longer good for anything good—least of all for philosophy.
'Selflessness' has no value in heaven or on earth; all great problems demand *great
love*, and only strong, round, secure minds who have a firm grip on themselves
are capable of that. [...] even if great problems should let themselves be *grasped* by
them, they would not allow frogs and weaklings to *hold on* to them; such has been
their taste from time immemorial—a taste, incidentally, that they share with all
doughty females.

(*GS* 345)

A kinship between this passage and the 'wisdom as woman' sentence is
perhaps suggested in the German by the opening words here: the selfless
personality is *eine geschwächte, dünne, ausgelöschte*—a phrase whose musicality
seems to mirror the *unbekümmert, spöttisch, gewaltthätig* of the *Zarathustra*
epigraph. In terms of style and import this *Gay Science* extract might have
served roughly as well as the motto for the *Genealogy*'s Third Treatise,
at least if made a bit shorter and snappier. Let me propose the following
edited version:

[25] Oliver (1994: 66–7 n. 13).

Weakened, thin, extinguished—such men are not to philosophy's taste. Its problems demand *great love*, and of that only a strong, round spirit is capable; they do not permit frogs and weaklings to hold on to them—a taste they share with doughty females.

This motto, in inviting comparison with the gaining of a woman's love, could perhaps have been used, like the 'wisdom is woman' excerpt, to deny success in intellectual endeavour to the selfless and disinterested and vouchsafe it to the robust and self-assured, hinting at a counter-ideal we must begin to build for ourselves.

However, Nietzsche chose the 'wisdom is woman' epigraph—and I am happy to acknowledge its potential to deliver a set of resonances that are uniquely its own. For one thing, it reinforces the link between the *Genealogy* and *Thus Spoke Zarathustra* which Nietzsche is keen to promote in a number of ways. In the Preface to the *Genealogy* (section 8), expressing the assumption that the reader 'has first read my earlier writings', Nietzsche singles out *Zarathustra* as the work with which the reader should enjoy an extreme intimacy. The epigraph reminds us to look back again to *Zarathustra*, if we need reminding. Also in its new context the extract lies adjacent to the ending of the Second Treatise, which yearns for the coming of the 'human of the future who will redeem us [...] from the previous ideal', the younger, stronger figure who is none other than 'Zarathustra the godless' (*GM* II. 24–5). Zarathustra personifies a future ideal of which the *Genealogy* offers only slender clues, though we are liable to think first of the two great ideas in *Zarathustra*, the *Übermensch* and the eternal return.[26]

We can seek further insights by turning to the place in *Zarathustra* from whose midst the 'wisdom as woman' passage is taken, the section entitled 'Of Reading and Writing', which has been proclaimed nothing less than 'the literary program of the philosopher Nietzsche'.[27] There Nietzsche has Zarathustra say, 'I love only that which is written with blood' and 'Aphorisms (*Sprüche*) should be peaks, and those to whom they are spoken should be big and tall of stature' (*Z* I. 7). These peaks provide an exalted station, a distance from which one can laugh mockingly at what others take seriously, as does the 'warrior'.[28] So Nietzsche's chosen epigraph transports us into a context which again evokes allegiance to warlike writing and calls

---

[26] On this, see Loeb (2005).   [27] Scheier (1994: 454).
[28] This aspect is brought out by Oliver (1993: 17).

for a powerfully robust reader. And of course Nietzsche himself is openly writing a polemic (*eine Streitschrift*, the subtitle of the whole *Genealogy*), and in that sense adopts a warlike pose. He is making war on the ascetic ideal, and correspondingly a 'warrior' style of writing is the antithesis of the method of the ascetic scholar. These connections allow the epigraph to throw light on the manner of Nietzsche's writing and the manner of reading it calls for, but without forcing the treatise into the uncomfortable mould of 'commentary' upon it.

We need demand no single, settled significance for such an epigraph, and there is no lack of further angles we might superimpose upon one another. For instance, Oliver suggests it is the reader who must 'make war' on the Third Treatise: 'Nietzsche allows his reader to … take up the place of the warrior and do violence to the text.'[29] She also reflects that the aphorism assigns an active role to the 'woman' that is wisdom—it is wisdom that *wants* the male 'warrior', who despite his 'violence' is assigned a comparatively passive role vis-à-vis wisdom—and so disagrees with Nehamas's idea that 'the conception of the writer as warrior, and not the identification of wisdom with woman, is the crucial feature of this aphorism'.[30] As one becomes alert to other passages in Nietzsche's works where 'woman' is a metaphor, not only for wisdom, but for life, and for truth,[31] many fascinating connections suggest themselves. Metaphors are rarely superficial or gratuitous for Nietzsche, and anyone who seeks to appraise Nietzsche's far from one-dimensional views on women and his relevance for the feminism of his day and ours will probably wish to consider this aphorism in both its contexts.

7 Consequences of my Hypothesis

My view that the main body of the Third Treatise is an exegetical commentary on its own section 1 leaves intact whatever figurative connections radiate out from the 'wisdom is woman' image. And as far as the question of 'Nietzsche and woman' is concerned, my interpretation contradicts neither

---

[29] Oliver (1993: 13; 1995: 17).   [30] Nehamas (1985: 114)—see Oliver (1993: 21–2; 1995: 22).
[31] For some examples, see *BGE*, Preface (quoted above, n. 18); *GS*, Preface, 4; *TI*, 'How the "Real World" at Last Became a Myth'; *Z* II, 'The Dance Song'. See Staten (1990: 173–7) for probing analysis of the last-mentioned passage.

Walter Kaufmann's once fashionable statement that Nietzsche's judgements concerning women are 'philosophically irrelevant',[32] nor Peter Burgard's more recently fashionable verdict that 'He includes woman, accords the feminine a central role, in the articulation of his philosophy, even as his extreme sexism excludes woman.'[33] But just as nothing I have said could stem the metaphorical and intertextual energies emanating from the 'wisdom as woman' epigraph, so the existence of these metaphorical pathways through Nietzsche's œuvre does not constrain us to accept the 'standard view' of the epigraph–treatise relationship.

Acceptance of my hypothesis would, however, block some claims made within the tradition that was inaugurated some years ago when Jacques Derrida executed his famous acrobatic *saltus*: 'The title of this lecture was to have been *the question of style*. However—it is woman who will be my subject.'[34] This tradition, into which Nietzsche's writings were instantly co-opted, formed around the assumption of a close bond between a radical feminism and a radical, supposedly anti-authoritarian conception of language and meaning. This generated a readiness to maximize the theoretical import of any of Nietzsche's mentions of 'woman' or of 'style', 'reading', or 'interpretation'. So it is easy to understand how Nietzsche's claim to illustrate the art of exegesis and his 'wisdom as woman' epigraph (unaccountably absent from Derrida's essay) could come under strong pressure to coalesce in conformity with the expectations of this tradition.

Among the tradition's recent descendants—though by no means wholly uncritical of it—are writings by Kelly Oliver which focus explicitly on the 'wisdom as woman' epigraph. Oliver's account, which also assumes the 'standard view' of the essay–epigraph relation, will allow me to show some moves that are blocked by my hypothesis. Firstly and most obviously, Oliver's statement 'We cannot learn Nietzsche's lesson in reading unless we explore the relationship between the warrior and the woman'[35] is false on my hypothesis: however significant its imagery, the epigraph is dispensable from the lesson, in which we learn a practice of reading in the act of discovering more and more facets to the ascetic ideal that was treated aphoristically in section 1 of the treatise.

---

[32] Kaufmann (1974: 84).   [33] Burgard (1994: 12).
[34] Derrida (1979: 35–7). This inaugural role for Derrida is assumed by writers both pro and anti the said tradition: Burgard (1994: 3); Diethe (1996: 1).   [35] Oliver (1995: 17).

Secondly, Oliver suggests that Nietzsche repeats his question 'What do ascetic ideals mean?'

not … in order to emphasize some particular characteristic of the ascetic ideal. Rather he repeats this question in order to emphasize a particular style of reading, genealogy, which diagnoses the meaning of various cultural symptoms. The essay is as much about meaning as it is about ascetic ideals. The meaning of ascetic ideals is a pretext for a performance of reading as interpretation, reading as an art.[36]

I agree that 'the essay is as much about meaning as it is about ascetic ideals'. But is it not extreme to demote the central topic of the essay to a mere pretext? Oliver is apparently in earnest, since she calls the meaning of the ascetic ideal the essay's 'apparent topic'.[37] To me that seems a travesty of Nietzsche's achievement. He was later to say of all the Genealogy's treatises that they were 'decisive preliminary studies by a psychologist for a revaluation of all values', written so that 'in the midst of perfectly gruesome detonations, a new truth becomes visible'. The psychological truth of the Third Treatise is that 'the priests' ideal [...] was the only ideal so far'. Why? Because humanity 'would rather will even nothingness than not will' (EH, 'Genealogy of Morals'). Nietzsche claims to have enticed the reader into acknowledging an awful truth: that the real pain of suffering lies in the dread of its having no meaning. The reader is to be unsettled by the progress of this piece, into which Nietzsche transposes his struggle with the life-denying philosophy of his 'great teacher' Schopenhauer, his disillusionment with the artistic genius and father figure Wagner, his isolation and exaltation in the 'desert' where the true philosopher belongs, his vivisection of the atheism and the rigorous scholarship that are his own inheritance. On my view the treatise is about what it says it is about, the many guises and unique power of the ascetic ideal, and is at the same time the opportunity to demonstrate the art of exegesis, to show us how 'meaning' emerges from a process of potentially endless diagnostic analysis. But to rate the entire essay simply the pretext for a point concerning meaning or method risks casting Nietzsche not as a great psychologist and rhetorical strategist, but as the perpetrator of a sterile game.

The poverty of the 'standard view' lies in its starting point: a treatise and an aphorism so remote from one another in content that desperate measures

---

[36] Oliver (1993: 14).   [37] Ibid. 13.

are needed. Either we have to invent some ambitious bridging devices, or we have to decide that 'content' is not really the point after all and that the whole essay demonstrates only some methodological point about meaning or interpretation—or indeed about their supposed impossibility, as in my final quotation from Oliver:

From the very beginning of *Genealogy*, Nietzsche sets up the impossibility of reading his texts. His lesson in reading Zarathustra's aphorism in essay III becomes an example of the impossibility of reading. It is necessary to have read the earlier text, *Zarathustra*, before reading *Genealogy*, and yet the third essay of *Genealogy* supposedly teaches us how to read *Zarathustra*.[38]

This analysis fails on more than one count, according to me. On my hypothesis the Third Treatise is not a lesson in reading Zarathustra's aphorism: the lesson would be the same if the *Zarathustra* extract were not there. Hence the presence of the extract is no basis for the thought that the Third Treatise 'teaches us how to read *Zarathustra*'. But I believe Oliver also errs in overgeneralizing here: it is doubtful whether even the 'standard view' supports the claim that *Zarathustra* is incomprehensible or unreadable as a whole before we understand the *Genealogy* as a whole—if that is what is meant. Secondly, neither Nietzsche nor his reader need espouse the view that reading is impossible. Oliver is here relying on the *Genealogy*'s Preface, section 8, where Nietzsche says, 'it will [...] be a while before my writings are "readable"' and 'If this book is unintelligible to anyone and hard on the ears, the fault [...] does not necessarily lie with me. It is clear enough, presupposing, as I do, that one has first read my earlier writings,' and principally (he continues) that one has read *Zarathustra*. Nietzsche has mischievously constructed a predicament of sorts for the reader: she will need to read Nietzsche's other works before comprehending the *Genealogy* with comfort, while none of Nietzsche's other works is yet 'readable'. However, in this context (and according to my hypothesis) 'readable'—in Nietzsche's own quotation marks—means 'readable in the manner the treatise demonstrates', or 'readable in appropriately bovine, ruminatory fashion'. Nietzsche merely doubts, realistically, whether anyone is yet able to do that. So I think Oliver is over-inflating Nietzsche: to say it will be some time before his writings are readable in a certain manner is far

[38] Ibid. 35.

from saying that reading them is impossible as such, and indeed seems to exclude it.

8 Sources of Resistance?

On the hypothesis of this chapter, we have the large body of the Third Treatise functioning admirably as an illustrative commentary on its section 1, and the *Zarathustra* extract set free as an epigraph and offering a great wealth of associative material. But we have removed the need to seek arcane or stretched readings of Nietzsche's very conception of exegesis or reading, or to take him as ironically propounding its impossibility. We shall say that Nietzsche's art of exegesis is illustrated relatively straightforwardly: a clipped aphorism about the meanings of the ascetic ideal (some of its many manifestations and the psychology behind them) and the ultimate single meaning of its power[39] is unfolded into a complex treatise about the many meanings of the ascetic ideal and the ultimate single meaning of its power. And what does this arduous and possibly endless process illustrate? How to ruminate, how to slow down, how, for the patient, self-questioning, emotionally engaged reader, Nietzschean aphorisms can be found abundant in painful and exhilarating insights that their concise style hides from superficial view.

That is the news which I said might be resisted because it makes things less extreme. If I may be allowed to speculate, such potential resistance might originate from two prejudices, one of narrower, the other of wider scope. For the narrower prejudice, imagine someone who approached Nietzsche with the fixed assumption that every mention of 'reading' and 'exegesis' must have a symbolic connection with the metaphor of 'woman', and that every occurrence of 'woman' must at some level engender a

---

[39] Nietzsche shifts to this aspect of the original question in *GM* III. 23. After declining to enumerate every significance of the ascetic ideal (he'd never finish), Nietzsche speaks of 'the last and most terrible aspect that the question of the meaning of this ideal has for me. What does the very *power* of this ideal mean, the *enormity* of its power? Why has it been given room to this extent? Why has there not been better resistance?' The answer has already been given aphoristically in section 1: it is because the ideal appeased the *horror vacui* of the human will, which would rather will nothingness than not will. Humanity would rather allow its own worthlessness, self-contempt, and self-destruction to give its painful existence a meaning than acquiesce in the meaninglessness of existence. We had little hope of grasping that in its aphoristic form; sections 23–8 decipher it, preparing us for its climactic restatement at the very end.

theoretical position on language, style, and interpretation. If that were so, then perhaps, despite evidence to the contrary, the Third Treatise *must* be some kind of 'commentary' on 'wisdom as woman'. But I would ask such a reader where this 'must' would come from. Short of a repellent strain of authoritarianism, how could one think that the local interpretation of any passage in Nietzsche could be constrained in advance by such global postulates?[40]

The wider prejudice would be some a priori conviction that if Nietzsche ever undertook to illustrate the art of exegesis, then his way of going about it must issue as bizarre a challenge as possible, and imply a conception of interpretation than which none could be more radical or surprising. Such a conviction would also deserve a sceptical response, if only because the slow, cowlike chewing-over advocated by Nietzsche scarcely resembles the ironic leaps and contortions it takes to conjure a maximally radical theory of interpretation (or even the semblance of one) out of the relationship between the Third Treatise and its epigraph.

Beneath some recent Nietzsche-interpretation there seems to operate what I might call a will to extremity, or a will to perversity: a drive whose end is that Nietzsche should testify to a supposed bottomless irony and arbitrariness in all writing and an inability of meanings ever to be stable or decidable. Nietzsche sets his reader many challenges and is a pioneer in problematizing authorship and reading. But we are free, let us remind ourselves, not to view him through the filter of the late twentieth century's more extreme efforts in theorizing. Removing the presumed illustrative connection between the 'wisdom is woman' epigraph and the 'art of exegesis' may be a step towards denying the will to perversity. Nietzsche's cow need not jump over the moon.

---

[40] Here I take encouragement from Carol Diethe's refreshing work in wresting the 'Nietzsche and woman' question and its relevance to feminism away from a generation of deconstructionist theorists whose 'excitement became a new dogma in its turn', and whose dogma has now 'outstripped its usefulness'; see Diethe (1996: 1; 1994, esp. 126–7).

11

Disinterestedness and Objectivity

The ascetic ideal embodies a valuation of our actual, this-worldly life as a 'wrong path', an existence which ought to negate itself, together with the promise of redemption through the attainment of some other realm that is higher or purer than the merely human.[1] While this ideal is clearly to be found in the outlook of priests and in the ethics and metaphysics of Christianity, Nietzsche's more fundamental point is that—like the institution of punishment in the Second Treatise—this same ideal acquires new guises, new functions, new meanings through history. Hence the title of the Third Treatise is 'What do Ascetic Ideals [plural] Mean?' Nietzsche seeks to answer his leading question first by revealing unity behind the plurality: many apparently disparate phenomena can be explained as configurations of the same pattern of self-denial in the face of a projected higher value. Then the question becomes: What functions are served by all the interpretations of ourselves and the world that conform to this pattern?

As I have said, Nietzsche's route through the many manifestations of the ideal is labyrinthine and readers may struggle to discern structure in the text.[2] At the beginning of the treatise, Nietzsche asks what meaning ascetic ideals have among artists, philosophers, scholars, women, priests, saints, and 'the psychologically failed and out of sorts'. In practice four of these figures dominate the essay: artist, philosopher, priest, and scholar. Nietzsche begins in sections 2–4 with the artist he knew best, Richard Wagner, generalizing a little about artists as such; he next (section 5) makes a transition to philosophers who theorize about art and beauty, in particular Kant and Schopenhauer, then (from section 6) fastens on Schopenhauer's advocacy of an ascetic form of aesthetic experience. From here he moves

[1] See *GM* III. 11 for a clear statement of the ideal along these lines.
[2] For some remarks on the structure of *GM* III, see Ch. 10 above.

to the meaning of ascetic ideals for philosophers in general, arriving by the end of section 10 at the graphic assimilation of the philosopher to the ascetic priest who 'has functioned as the repulsive and gloomy caterpillar-form in which alone philosophy was allowed to live and in which it crept around'.

Section 11 announces that the figure of the ascetic priest is the true key to answering the treatise's guiding question about the meaning of ascetic ideals, and initiates a wide-ranging rumination on the influence of the ascetic priestly mentality on our culture, values, and philosophizing. This gives way in section 23 to the question why there has been no counter to the ascetic ideal, whereupon Nietzsche stages a dramatic revelation: that despite their emancipation from the religious world-view, today's progressive, idealistic scientists and scholars manifest through their attitude to truth the very same ideal as the ascetic priest. Sections 27 and 28 conclude the treatise with the question why the ascetic ideal in all its guises has exercised such a hold over human beings; Nietzsche responds with another monumental thesis: that this ideal has been the only way to give a meaning to our existence and the suffering it contains.

While morality elevates to the status of absolutes 'the instincts of compassion, self-denial, self-sacrifice', the aesthetic tradition valorizes a related passivity, detachment, and selflessness, and culminates in the idea of a subject whose will is blissfully suspended in a passive 'mirroring' of the world. Section 12 of the Third Treatise shows Schopenhauer's persistent presence as a subtext for the later Nietzsche:[3] although not named, he is (as not every reader seems to notice[4])quoted directly: the words 'pure, will-less, painless, timeless subject of knowledge' comprise Schopenhauer's exact formula for the subject in aesthetic experience, and it is in opposition to this that Nietzsche claims that there is '*only* a perspectival "knowing"'. In this chapter I examine Nietzsche's critique of the aesthetics of disinterestedness and his opposition to the notion of knowing as will-less objectivity, while in Chapter 12 below I look at Nietzsche's substitute conception of knowledge.

---

[3] For more on this, see Janaway (1998a, esp. 1–7, 13–36) (the latter pages overlapping somewhat with the present chapter).

[4] For an earlier analysis of *GM* III. 12 that makes its Schopenhauerian background clear, see Atwell (1981).

1 Beauty and the Philosophical Beast

Nietzsche begins his treatment of art, artists, and philosophical conceptions of the aesthetic by questioning Wagner's 'homage' to a self-denying form of chastity in his last opera, *Parsifal*, saying that it marked a strange reversal of the authentic direction towards 'spiritualization and sensualization' that characterized the composer's art and life (*GM* III. 3). Wagner lived sensually and, according to Nietzsche, would have ended more true to himself as an artist had he celebrated sensuality. 'What does it mean', Nietzsche asks, that he turned towards asceticism? (*GM* III. 2). The question of meaning here calls for a psychological insight into the function Wagner's 'turn' may have served for him as an artist and as a human being. In his ruminatory diagnosis Nietzsche combines disillusion over the particular case of Wagner with some more general thoughts about artists. First, he suggests that artists tend to want to be in reality what they depict, even though they cannot: 'a Homer would not have written an Achilles nor Goethe a Faust, if Homer had been an Achilles or if Goethe had been a Faust'.[5] The artist is merely the precondition or womb of the work, but is so close to it that he cannot resist over-identifying with it. So perhaps Wagner wanted to see himself as a self-denying ascetic. Secondly, artists always stand in need of some extra-artistic scheme of values to give them authority and protection—they are 'valets of a morality or philosophy or religion'—and Wagner used Schopenhauer's philosophy in this manner, falling first under the spell of Schopenhauer's metaphysical account of music, then exhibiting a tendency to 'speak metaphysics' as 'a kind of mouthpiece of the "in itself" of things, a telephone of the beyond', till he finally 'spoke *ascetic ideals*' (*GM* III. 5). It is hinted in this that all metaphysical theorizing has an origin in ascetic values. But we now leave artists behind, conveyed swiftly to what Nietzsche calls 'the more serious question': 'what does it mean when a real *philosopher* pays homage to the ascetic ideal?' (*GM* III. 5).

At first it is philosophers' aesthetic theorizing that preoccupies Nietzsche:

Schopenhauer used the Kantian formulation of the aesthetic problem for his own purpose—although he almost certainly did not view it with Kantian eyes. Kant intended to honor art when, among the predicates of the beautiful, he privileged

---

[5] *GM* III. 4. This effectively repeats one of Plato's arguments against poets at *Republic* 599a–600e.

and placed in the foreground those that constitute the honor of knowledge: impersonality and universal validity. [...] I wish only to underscore that Kant, like all philosophers, instead of envisaging the aesthetic problem starting from the experiences of the artist (the one who creates), thought about art and the beautiful from the viewpoint of the 'spectator' [...] If only this 'spectator' had at least been sufficiently familiar to the philosophers of the beautiful, however!—namely as a great *personal* fact and experience, as a wealth of most personal intense experiences, desires, surprises, delights in the realm of the beautiful! [...] 'The beautiful,' Kant said, 'is what pleases *without interest.*' Without interest! Compare this definition with one made by a real 'spectator' and artist—Stendhal, who in one place calls the beautiful *une promesse de bonheur* [a promise of happiness]. What is *rejected* and crossed out here, in any case, is precisely the one thing Kant emphasizes in the aesthetic condition: *le désintéressement.* Who is right, Kant or Stendhal?

(*GM* III. 6)

'Interest' here is clearly sexual, and it is worth noting that the core of Kant's notion of aesthetic judgement (or judgement of taste) is the exclusion of all *desires* from the grounds of judgement and from the causes of the pleasure on which judgement is grounded.[6] Kant's 'Analytic of the Beautiful'[7] is written from the point of view of the spectator rather than that of the active, creating artist. It gives a general theory of aesthetic judgement, according to which the judger claims universal validity for a judgement of beauty on the grounds of a disinterested, or desire-free, liking for the experience of some object. The prime theme here is not art, but beauty in general. Kant later gives an account[8] of the production of art through genius, which he calls the 'inborn productive faculty of the artist', 'a talent for producing that for which no determinate rule can be given', of which 'originality must be its primary characteristic'.[9] Genius enables the rare human being to find thought-animating aesthetic ideas in imagination and express them in perceptual form.[10] All of this is conceived of as original, non-rule-governed, and exceptional activity on the part of the artist—surely that would be a few steps in the right direction for Nietzsche? But here we touch on a traditional problem about Kant's aesthetic theory: how well do his account of pure judgements of beauty in the 'Analytic of the Beautiful' and his later account of expressive artistic genius fit together? The worry is that the

---

[6] See Kant (2000: 90–6). For an interpretation of the exclusion of desires in Kant's account, see Janaway (1997*b*).

[7] Kant (2000, §§1–22). [8] See ibid. 182–207. [9] Ibid. 186. [10] Ibid. 192–5.

theory is broken-backed, in that what is analysed as beauty does not apply itself well to the case of art.

Nietzsche's second complaint is that even on the spectator's side Kant's detachment of beauty from desire is wrong and unnatural. According to the opposed view Nietzsche associates with Stendahl, beauty concerns the perception of something in which we discern a relation to the satisfaction of desires, of which the most basic are sexual desires.[11] On Kant's behalf we could reply that this does not prevent there being a further sense to the term 'beautiful' which is amenable to an analysis in terms of disinterested pleasure. 'Beautiful' might be an ambiguous term, having a connection with desirability in common use, while lacking that connection in a slightly more specialized use. Nor is this distinctly aesthetic use really the preserve of specialists: most people would be quite ready to describe a piece of music, a tree, or a landscape as beautiful, without its being the case that they envisage the satisfaction of any particular desires by the object in question. But even supposing there are such distinct senses of beauty, Nietzsche's pressing question remains: Why has aesthetic theory been so keen to prioritize disinterestedness at the expense of other species or conceptions of beauty?

Why, again, does Kant think of the encounter with beauty in terms of impersonality and universality? Nietzsche writes of a 'wealth of most personal intense experiences, desires, surprises, delights', which get forgotten in the Kantian account of judgement. He charges Kant with faulty observation and naivety about human psychology. In fact the problem may be more of a systemic one. Kant insists that in aesthetic judgements one 'speaks with a universal voice' rather than merely reporting the occurrence of a subjectively pleasing experience. Kant need not deny the kind of 'personal' phenomenology Nietzsche describes, but must debar it from playing any role in grounding the universality of a judgement of beauty. Though Nietzsche does not make the point explicitly here, it is not difficult to see this assumption of a universal state of mind purified of personal affect and desire as another instance of the valuation of selflessness that Nietzsche is

[11] In *TI* Nietzsche says that Schopenhauer wants to see in beauty the negation of the drive to procreation—to which Nietzsche then replies, 'Someone contradicts you, and I fear it is nature' (*TI*, 'Expeditions of an Untimely Man', 22). In his book *Art* (1914) Clive Bell rejected 'beautiful' as an aesthetic term on similar grounds: 'Surely, it is not what I call an aesthetic emotion that most of us feel, generally, for natural beauty.... When an ordinary man speaks of a beautiful woman he certainly does not mean only that she moves him aesthetically ... With the man-in-the-street "beautiful" is more often than not synonymous with "desirable" ' (see Bell 1995: 102).

exposing in the *Genealogy* as a whole. Recall in particular his complaint at the start of the book about 'the prejudice that takes "moral", "unegoistic", "*désintéressé*" to be concepts of equal value'.[12]

After the brief discussion of Kant, Nietzsche reverts to his more serious target, Schopenhauer. Schopenhauer uses a notion of 'will-lessness' which is superficially similar to Kant's 'disinterestedness', but crucially different,[13] in that Schopenhauer thinks of aesthetic experience as a kind of altered state of consciousness where desire, emotion, bodily activity, and ordinary conceptual thought are all suspended, our individuality forgotten, and a peaceful release attained from the trials of the will.[14] Nietzsche first treats Schopenhauer as a psychological case study, delving into his personal affects to explain his philosophical position:

There are few things about which Schopenhauer speaks so certainly as about the effect of aesthetic contemplation: he says of it that it counteracts precisely *sexual* 'interestedness,' much like lupulin and camphor, that is; he never grew tired of glorifying *this* breaking free from the 'will' as the greatest merit and use of the aesthetic condition. [...] And could one not finally urge upon Schopenhauer himself the objection that he was very wrong in thinking himself a Kantian in this, [...] that the beautiful is pleasing to him, too, out of an 'interest', even out of the strongest of all, the most personal of all interests: that of the tortured one who breaks free from his torture?

(*GM* III. 6)

Once again a philosophical theory receives a diagnosis in terms of underlying affects. Schopenhauer, in this picture, *desires* 'will-less contemplation' because it offers the comfort of release from desires that give him pain. And Schopenhauer's own expressed thoughts on the intrusiveness of sexual desire, as a 'malevolent demon, striving to pervert, to confuse, and to overthrow everything' might be said to convict him even more strongly than Nietzsche's analysis.[15]

Nietzsche alleges that a characteristic of Schopenhauer is typical of all philosophers—they feel a rancour against sensuality and a cordiality towards the ascetic—and that all philosophy hitherto has been an expression of

---

[12] *GM* I. 2. See also *BGE* 33 for the explicit assimilation of the 'morality of self-abnegation' and 'the aesthetic of "disinterested contemplation"'.

[13] On the differences, see Janaway (1997*b*: 461–3; 2003).

[14] See Schopenhauer (1969: i. 178, 196–8).   [15] See ibid. ii. 533–4.

192 DISINTERESTEDNESS AND OBJECTIVITY

the ascetic ideal. This allegation can be interpreted as follows: Philosophers have always affirmed the life of the kind of creature they themselves are: cerebral, withdrawn, contemplative. How? By denying or suppressing their bodily and sensuous nature.

> Every animal, thus also *la bête philosophe*, instinctively strives for an optimum of favorable conditions under which it can vent its power completely and attain its maximum in the feeling of power [...] What, accordingly, does the ascetic ideal mean for a philosopher? My answer is—one will have guessed it long ago: at its sight the philosopher smiles at an optimum of the conditions for highest and boldest spirituality (*Geistigkeit*)—in this he does *not* negate 'existence', rather he affirms *his* existence and *only* his existence.
>
> (*GM* III. 7)

Part of Nietzsche's case is a simplified anecdotal picture of philosophers' lifestyles. Philosophers do not marry, apparently. They regard the livelier bodily passions as an obstacle, and retreat from commitments that impinge upon their self-absorbed mentation. All 'great fruitful inventive spirits' have lives characterized 'to a certain degree' by poverty, humility, and chastity, and gravitate to a 'desert' of solitude. Nietzsche slips into the mode of heartfelt soliloquy when describing the optimal conditions for philosophical work: 'oh it is lonely enough, believe me!' and 'I was just thinking of my most beautiful study, of the Piazza di San Marco, assuming it is spring, likewise forenoon, the time between 10 and 12' (*GM* III. 8).

Nietzsche next suggests that in earlier times philosophers took on the pose of self-castigating ascetics, mimicking the figures of 'priest, magician, soothsayer [...] religious human generally' in order to instil fear in those around them, because being a philosopher or 'contemplative' was itself an odd and vulnerable way of life ('inactive, brooding, unwarriorlike'; *GM* III. 10) and philosophers had to be able to protect themselves against a suspicious community. This reveals that the 'aloof stance of philosophers, world-negating, hostile toward life, not believing in the senses, de-sensualized', which may appear essential to being a philosopher, is in fact only a convenient outer shell or chrysalis: 'until the most recent time the *ascetic priest* has functioned as the repulsive and gloomy caterpillar-form in which alone philosophy was allowed to live and in which it crept around' (*GM* III. 10). Nietzsche completes this discussion by asking again, in the manner of the ending of the Second Treatise, whether there is enough 'freedom of the will' that the potential might one day be fulfilled for a philosopher to emerge as a fully fledged 'colorful and dangerous winged animal'.

2 The Pure Will-less Subject

In section 12 of the Third Treatise, Schopenhauer re-emerges through the unacknowledged quotation of his phrase 'pure, will-less, painless, timeless subject of knowledge'.[16] For Schopenhauer this 'pure, will-less subject' is the subject of aesthetic experience, a state of consciousness in which all our desires, interests, and feelings are suspended, and we exist merely as a subject of knowledge that mirrors the world without imposing subjective forms upon it. In particular, space, time, and causality are absent as organizing forms of our experience. We abandon ordinary empirical consciousness for a 'higher' consciousness; we perceive not the ordinary spatio-temporal world of particular material things, but universal Ideas, which Schopenhauer conceives along Platonic lines. This state of aesthetic suspension has, allegedly, two features of value: because the will is temporarily absent, we enter a state of unusual calm, in which striving, seeking, fleeing, and suffering cannot occur; and we simultaneously achieve greater objectivity than in our rule-governed empirical knowledge of the world.

Schopenhauer reasons as follows:[17]

1. Empirical consciousness of the world is always within the forms of space, time, and causality imposed by the subject.

2. The subject's intellectual imposition of space, time, and causality on experience is driven by human needs, interests, and affects (in short, intellect is governed by will).

3. The 'higher' aesthetic consciousness is a form of contemplation by the intellect quite independent of human needs, interests, and affects.

4. So the aesthetic consciousness is independent also of those subjective forms (space, time, and causality) that are necessitated by our having needs, interests, and affects.

5. So aesthetic consciousness is a more objective cognition of the world than ordinary empirical consciousness.

---

[16] See ibid. i. 179.   [17] See esp. ibid. 178–9.

Having accepted the Kantian framework of space, time, and causality as governing empirical knowledge of the world, Schopenhauer makes two radically un-Kantian moves. First, he attributes to this framework a purely instrumental necessity: experiencing causally ordered material objects in space and time is a condition of our inhabiting the world in such a way as to satisfy our desires and needs, to predict and manipulate things, ultimately to survive and reproduce, driven by the will, or indeed will to life, that is primary in human beings and explains the ordinary operation of their intellect. This leaves the way open for a second, drastic move: that when we step back from willing, the Kantian rules about experience and knowledge simply need not apply. Will-free cognition is allowed to break the rules, and is portrayed as superior because it does so.

The vision behind Schopenhauer's theory of aesthetic experience is Platonic, not Kantian. Objects of knowledge exist beyond the empirical realm, beyond mere appearance, and cognition of them is an abnormal and uncommonly uplifting state of mind. The objects of this cognition, which Schopenhauer even calls Platonic Ideas, are universals rather than particular spatio-temporal objects, and they are not subject to time, change, or causality. Schopenhauer departs from Plato in holding that these Ideas are known by a kind of perception which excludes conceptual thought and ratiocination. Reason too is demoted to an instrumental role in our survival as living creatures and cannot take us to the supposed higher realm. So what happens in aesthetic experience, according to Schopenhauer, is that we free ourselves of the will, and

we relinquish the ordinary way of considering things, and cease to follow under the guidance of the forms of the principle of sufficient reason merely their relations to one another...Thus we no longer consider the where, the when, the why, and the whither in things, but simply and solely the *what*. Further, we do not let abstract thought, the concepts of reason, take possession of our consciousness, but, instead of all this, devote the whole power of our mind to perception, sink ourselves completely therein, and let our whole consciousness be filled by the calm contemplation of the natural object.[18]

Nietzsche's term 'objectivity' and his 'eye' metaphor in *GM* III. 12 gain their energy by tapping into his predecessor's account. Schopenhauer's

---

[18] See Schopenhauer 178.

subject of aesthetic experience leaves behind empirical particulars and survives as the receptor for the eternal Ideas which are the 'adequate objectification' of the thing in itself, or the nearest approach we can make within experience to reality 'itself'. At the same time the subject loses the sense of himself or herself as an individual and becomes, in Schopenhauer's words, 'the *single* world-eye that looks out from every cognizing being'.[19] Thus, allegedly, the object is raised to the level of the universal, and the subject, by way of a loosening of the sense of his or her individuality, progresses towards an identification with the world as a whole. Aesthetic experience achieves greater objectivity than everyday understanding or scientific knowledge, in that the explanatory connections pertaining among the subject's representations—connections instrumental in attaining the goals of willing—are all dissolved. Because these connections of space, time, and causality are forms inherent in the subject, their temporary abeyance yields a cognition closer to 'what truly is', as Plato would put it.[20] The artistic genius is pre-eminent in attaining this kind of cognition, according to Schopenhauer:

the *gift of genius* is nothing but the most complete *objectivity* ... the capacity to remain in a state of pure perception, to lose oneself in perception, to remove from the service of the will the knowledge that originally existed only for this service ... the ability to leave entirely out of sight our own interest, our own willing, and our aims, and consequently to discard entirely our own personality for a time, in order to remain *pure knowing subject*, the clear eye of the world.[21]

Nietzsche contends that this Schopenhauerian objectivity is a sham for two reasons. It makes a theoretical mistake about the nature of knowledge, and it misrepresents its own motivation, concealing its own end-directedness, its own specific expression of a 'will'. In both cases, as we shall see, Nietzsche's objection adopts a quasi-Schopenhauerian position in order to counter Schopenhauer. First, as the latter part of *GM* III. 12 makes clear, in demanding the lapse of all active, interpreting powers, and hoping to leave in operation something resembling an eye that looks in

[19] Ibid. 198; my trans. of *das eine Weltauge, was aus allen erkennenden Wesen blickt.*
[20] Schopenhauer's motto for the Third Book of *The World as Will and Representation* is Plato's 'Ti to on men aei, genesin de ouk echon ... ?' ('What is that which always is, and has no coming into being?'). The same title page announces 'the Platonic idea' as 'the object of art'. For Schopenhauer's problematic conflation of Plato's Ideas and Kant's thing in itself, see Schopenhauer (1969: i. 170–8) and my discussion in Janaway (1996).   [21] Schopenhauer (1969: i. 185–6).

no particular direction and from nowhere, Schopenhauerian objectivity demands an impossibility. Such interpreting powers attach necessarily to any striving, embodied being, for whom to lack such powers would be to have no cognition at all. Secondly, the aspiration towards utter will-lessness is self-deluding, since the very act of conceiving such would-be escape from the desires and attachments of embodiment is itself the fulfilment of an end, the stilling of a pressing desire. The theory of pure painless objectivity owes its existence to a felt need within the theorizer.

Schopenhauer's notion of objectivity is a paradigmatic instance of the ascetic ideal's combined self-belittlement and self-transcendence. It presupposes that one can cease to acquiesce in one's preordained place as an individuated outlet for the world-will's self-expression, and rise above the disvalue of ordinary human existence towards a state of salvation or redemption (*Erlösung*). Although Nietzsche's critical conception of the ascetic ideal eventually subsumes almost every aspect of extant culture, Schopenhauer provides the most immediate and decisive model of the ideal—and also the most vulnerable. In Platonism or Christianity, my fallen or embodied existence stands to be redeemed through my continuing to exist as something that supposedly I truly am: a pure, timeless, immaterial essence. For Schopenhauer, by contrast, there is no immortal soul, no divine purpose, no rational essence in me or in the world. The only 'order of things' is the brute fact of existence and the blind striving for existence. The 'real self' is the will to life.[22] So the only hope is that this self will manage to gain enough knowledge, or sustain enough suffering, that it is brought to *negating itself*. Schopenhauer's conception of redemptive objectivity approaches the limit of self-destructiveness, and fulfils its paradigmatic function for Nietzsche because of this very extremity.

This may appear to take us far from the aesthetic theory in which the pure, will-less subject originates. How can that aesthetic theory lead us to the 'limit of self-destructiveness'? Why should 'objective knowledge', which requires a knowing subject for whom this state is conceived as blissful, be linked at all with an aspiration towards the extinction of the subject? Unless we can see how these ideas are connected in Schopenhauer, we stand little chance of understanding them as Nietzsche's subtext in the

---

[22] Schopenhauer ii. 606.

Genealogy. Schopenhauer's philosophy unfolds a long continuum of states which redeem what he sees as the absence of positive value in life. Aesthetic experience is at one end of the continuum, extinction at the other. The key to the unity of his thought is the thesis that value can be retrieved *to the extent that the individual embodiment of will abates*. One wills less and less, and locates significance less and less in the individual living manifestation of will one happens to be. In aesthetic experience willing abates totally but temporarily, and one ceases to be aware of oneself as individual. But similar notions of selfless objectivity apply in Schopenhauer's ethics and philosophy of religion. In describing those who have undergone the ultimate redemption which he calls the denial of the will, Schopenhauer asks us to recall his characterization of aesthetic experience and imagine the 'pure, will-less, timeless' state prolonged indefinitely.[23] Aesthetic objectivity prefigures the disintegration of one's ability to place value in the striving, egoistic, material individual one is—that disintegration which is for Schopenhauer the sole hope of cheating life of its emptiness of genuine, positive worth. This disintegration connects with his morality of compassion too: 'the identity of all beings, justice, righteousness, philanthropy, denial of the will to life, spring from *one* root ... the virtuous action is a momentary passing through the point, the permanent return to which is the denial of the will to life'.[24]

Up to a certain point on the Schopenhauerian continuum of detachment from individuality the subject of knowledge remains: it apprehends the aesthetic universals, it regards other living things as equal in value to itself. But further along this same continuum lie states which can be described as extinction. At the furthest point is the individual's death, which Schopenhauer describes as 'the great opportunity no longer to be I'.[25] But the state of 'denial of the will' occupies a point poised between objective knowing and extinction. In this state one has not died; one continues to exist, but experiences the saintly or fully resigned vision which eschews assertion of will and identification of self with any individual component of the world-whole. Philosophical analysis must stop here, for Schopenhauer, and yield to mystical utterance or silence. In the final section of his book[26] he must describe denial of the will in contradictory ways: 'Only knowledge remains; the will has vanished,' and 'such a state cannot

---

[23] See ibid. i. 390.   [24] Ibid. ii. 610.   [25] Ibid. 507.   [26] Ibid. i. 408–12.

really be called knowledge, since it no longer has the form of subject and object'. 'We have before our eyes in perfect saintliness the denial and surrender of all willing,' but this 'now appears to us as a transition into empty *nothingness*'.

The World as Will and Representation, a book that opens with 'The world', closes with the word 'nothing' (*Nichts*), and in its sublimely eloquent and unnerving final pages presents nothingness as the opposite of willing, and as 'the final goal which hovers behind all virtue and holiness'; we are naturally disposed to fear it, but must learn to embrace it, or face the lack of any consolation:

Before us there is certainly left only nothing; but that which struggles against this flowing away into nothing, namely our nature, is indeed just the will to life which we ourselves are ... That we abhor nothingness so much is simply another way of saying that we will life so much, and that we are nothing but this will ... Yet this consideration is the only one that can permanently console us, when, on the one hand, we have recognized incurable suffering and endless misery as essential to the phenomenon of the will, to the world, and on the other see the world melt away with the abolished will, and retain before us only empty nothingness.[27]

Nietzsche's expression 'willing nothingness' (*das Nichts wollen*; *GM* III. 1, 28) is a pointed misuse of Schopenhauerian terms. In Schopenhauer's language 'nothingness' and 'willing' are supposed to be mutually exclusive conditions. But Nietzsche is not fooled. Why is nothingness portrayed as the ultimate 'goal'; why is it conceived as offering 'consolation'; why is it posited as the occasion of redeeming value, to be positively welcomed as such? Because the theorist of nothingness is willing it mightily as the resolution of affective needs of his own: he wants or needs some validation to be granted to existence, to stave off folding under total despair. We see this need fulfilled when Schopenhauer announces that 'nothing else can be stated as the aim of our existence except the knowledge that it would be better for us not to exist'.[28] Life at least has the point of coming to realize its own pointlessness. Nietzsche's formula 'willing nothingness rather than not willing' gives acute expression to this feature of Schopenhauer's axiological system.[29]

---

[27] Schopenhauer 411.   [28] Ibid. ii. 605.
[29] I return to 'willing nothingness' and the ending of *GM* III in Ch. 13 below.

3 Schopenhauer as Subtext in *Genealogy* III. 12

With this wider picture in place the attentive reader will find Schopenhauerian markers in section 12 from beginning to end. The phrase 'will to
contradiction and anti-nature' is a play on words which takes another stab
at Schopenhauer's central idea of 'will to life'. The ascetic priest (and the
philosopher in his commonest guise to date) is a life form whose fundamental drive is *against* life. The ascetic character paradoxically tends towards a
kind of survival or continuation of existence, but that whose existence is fostered is the attitude of negation towards life, an anti-corporeal, anti-sensual,
anti-sexual orientation. Schopenhauer himself is the paradigm of this apparently contradictory 'will to life'—as witness the case study discussed above.
Nietzsche's mention of Vedanta philosophy in the same section is also
a signpost towards Schopenhauer, who revered this school of thought
and especially its doctrine of 'exaltation beyond our own individuality'.[30]
Schopenhauer remarks that the Upanishads—a favourite book throughout
his life—describe a state of contemplation in which 'subject and object
and all knowledge vanish'.[31] Nietzsche's phrase 'to refuse to believe in the
self, to deny one's own "reality"' reflects two aspects of Schopenhauer's
position, one descriptive, the other evaluative. Schopenhauer finds value in
the loss of one's self-identification as 'I', not only because it is a redemptive
release, but on the grounds that it realigns us with the true state of things.
To move away from regarding the 'I' as a secure primary entity is to be
relieved of an error and to come nearer to the 'realm of truth and being'.

Nietzsche then turns and affirms this apparently self-denying movement:

Finally let us, particularly as knowers, not be ungrateful toward such resolute
reversals of the familiar perspectives and valuations with which the spirit has raged
against itself all too long now, apparently wantonly and futilely: to see differently in
this way for once, to *want* to see differently, is no small discipline and preparation of
the intellect for its future 'objectivity'—the latter understood not as 'disinterested
contemplation (*interesselose Anschauung*)' (which is a non-concept and absurdity),
but rather as the capacity to have one's pro and contra *in one's power*, and to
shift them in and out: so that one knows how to make precisely the *difference* in
perspectives and affective interpretations useful for knowledge.

[30] See Schopenhauer (1969: i. 205–6, 355; ii. 639).   [31] Ibid. ii. 611 n.

And now the subtext at last breaks through to the surface and becomes quoted text:

For let us guard ourselves better from now on, gentlemen philosophers, against the dangerous old conceptual fabrication that posited a 'pure, will-less, painless, timeless subject of knowledge'; let us guard ourselves against the tentacles of such contradictory concepts as 'pure reason', 'absolute spirituality', 'knowledge in itself': here it is always demanded that we think an eye that cannot possibly be thought, an eye that must not have any direction, in which the active and interpretive forces through which seeing first becomes seeing-something are to be shut off, are to be absent; thus, what is demanded here is always an absurdity and non-concept of an eye. There is *only* a perspectival seeing, *only* a perspectival 'knowing'; and *the more* affects we allow to speak about a matter, *the more* eyes, different eyes, we know how to bring to bear on one and the same matter, that much more complete will our 'concept' of this matter, our 'objectivity' be. But to eliminate the will altogether, to disconnect the affects one and all, supposing that we were capable of this: what? would that not be to *castrate* the intellect? ...

Schopenhauer polarizes will and intellect, and likes to tell us that while the brain is the focus of the intellect, the genitals are the focus of the will.[32] Hence when Nietzsche speaks of 'castrating the intellect' he makes a direct assault on Schopenhauer's aspiration towards a will-free operation of the intellect: we must accept the intellect as essentially will-driven, rather than obstructed by, or at the mercy of, a will that is alien to it. There is an argument fairly near the surface in this final passage: (1) all knowledge is active interpretation rather than passive reception of data; (2) all active interpretation is in the service of the will; so (3) all knowledge is in the service of the will. Hence Schopenhauer's beloved will-lessness could not be a state of knowledge. But note how impeccably Schopenhauerian the assumptions of this argument are. It was Schopenhauer, following Kant, who initially insisted on premiss (1): the human intellect actively shapes the objects of knowledge. Then Schopenhauer added his own powerful idea that the intellect is an instrument of the embodied will to life: the intellect must be rooted in a living, striving entity, and the forms it imposes on experience understood as serving the functions of organic life, ultimately grounded in the requirements of survival and reproduction. So Schopenhauer himself should have reached (3) as his conclusion, and

<hr>

[32] See e.g. Schopenhauer i. 203.

indeed he did in a way: all *empirical* knowledge, all knowledge that I can reach as an ordinary individual member of the human species, is in the service of the will. But he could not rest there, impelled, as Nietzsche would say, by a drive to reject and despise the willing self, and posit a timeless, painless realm of which this self has hitherto fallen short.

Having made will to life the explanatory basis of the human intellect and its capacity for empirical knowledge and reason, Schopenhauer apparently wishes it were not so: he yearns for an older Platonic state of knowledge, which according to his own theory is not possible for the ordinary human subject. Aesthetic experiences therefore become the exception: a precious opportunity to revisit the Platonic conception of a 'purer' knowing consciousness and a 'higher' realm of objects for it to know. Why did Schopenhauer seek this will-less objectivity? Because he could treat it as redemptive in a way nothing else could be. His own intellectual activity was driven by a hidden 'will': his fear of despair, his inclination to embrace the promise that pure knowledge could, at the limit, prepare the way for the extinction of the human individual, whose cognitive enterprise and very existence were otherwise spoiled by his or her essence, the will to life.

Yet it would be wrong to speak of an outright rejection of Schopenhauer on Nietzsche's part. Nietzsche, after all, should want us to judge his 'great teacher' from the point of view of as many of our affects as we can. When he suggests that the urge to affirm the notion of selfless objectivity can be put to positive use because it reverses 'familiar perspectives and valuations', he implements his own perspectivism: using one's affects for and against to grasp an opposed philosophical system can be a source of improved 'knowing' and an occasion for gratitude. But, having now seen what Nietzsche's perspectivism is contrasted with, our task must be to examine what it positively amounts to.

12

Perspectival Knowing and the Affects

As we set out to examine Nietzsche's claim that there is only perspectival knowing, two more brief comments on Schopenhauer will put us on the right track. First, for the subject to be will-less in Schopenhauer's account is for it to lose all its affective states, since under 'willing' Schopenhauer comprehends

all desiring, striving, wishing, longing, yearning, hoping, loving, rejoicing, exulting, and the like, as well as the feeling of unwillingness or repugnance, detesting, fleeing, fearing, being angry, hating, mourning, suffering, in short, all affects and passions (*Affekte und Leidenschaften*). For these are only movements more or less weak or strong, stirrings at one moment violent and stormy, at another mild and faint, of our own will that is either checked or given its way, satisfied or unsatisfied.[1]

Secondly, Schopenhauer's position on objectivity and the affects is neither idiosyncratic nor implausible. Here, for example, he speaks for the philosophical mainstream of many centuries:

In order to see that a purely objective, and therefore correct, apprehension of things is possible only when we consider them without any personal participation in them, and thus under the complete silence of the will, let us picture to ourselves how much every affect (*Affekt*) or passion (*Leidenschaft*) obscures and falsifies knowledge, in fact how every inclination or aversion (*Neigung oder Abneigung*) twists, colours, and distorts not merely the judgement, but even the original perception of things.[2]

---

[1] Schopenhauer (1999: 10).
[2] Schopenhauer (1969: ii. 373); trans. slightly modified from Payne's to bring out the similarity to Nietzsche's vocabulary.

This view of the relation between objective knowledge and the affects amounts to orthodoxy. Yet exactly this is what Nietzsche rejects in *GM* III. 12, whose chief conclusions are delivered in the following statement:

There is *only* a perspectival seeing, *only* a perspectival 'knowing'; and *the more* affects we allow to speak about a matter, *the more* eyes, different eyes, we know how to bring to bear on one and the same matter, that much more complete will our 'concept' of this matter, our 'objectivity' be.

A passage in the same section glosses Nietzsche's new understanding of 'objectivity' as:

the capacity to have one's pro and contra *in one's power*, and to shift them in and out: so that one knows how to make precisely the *difference* in perspectives and affective interpretations useful for knowledge.

It is time then to examine the kind of 'objectivity' and the kind of 'knowledge' that Nietzsche regards as possible and desirable.

1   Seeing and Knowing

There have been many interpretations of the 'perspectivism' announced in the sentences quoted above. At one time what could be called a 'Received View'[3] proclaimed that Nietzsche's perspectivism—often regarded as central to his whole philosophy—was the radical doctrine that there can be no human knowledge that is not a falsification of reality, that all our beliefs are 'mere interpretations', and that no one set of beliefs enjoys epistemic privilege over others. Recently there have been readings that deny this position to Nietzsche and are cogent enough to dislodge the 'Received View' from its canonical status.[4] These anti-radical readings suggest that Nietzsche's position in the *Genealogy*[5] allows for some human beliefs to be true and some to be false.

---

[3] So called by Leiter (1994: 334). Leiter (p. 352 n. 2) gives a good start on a bibliographical survey of proponents of the 'Received View'.   [4] Clark (1990, ch. 5); Leiter (1994).
[5] Though perhaps not elsewhere. The influential account of Clark (1990) depends on a developmental account of Nietzsche's thinking about truth and reality, which I shall not rehearse here, save to say that Clark (see esp. p. 103) assigns the *Genealogy* to a final phase of Nietzsche's thinking in which he gives up the notion that truth is correspondence to a transcendent thing in itself, and hence can discard his former claim (expressed in the early essay 'On Truth and Lies in the Non-Moral Sense') that all accepted 'truths' are falsifications of reality.

One line of approach favoured by anti-radical readings is to examine the implications of Nietzsche's assimilation of knowing to seeing. If we understand why there can be 'only a perspectival seeing', we may perhaps grasp more easily in what sense there is and can be 'only a perspectival knowing'. It is constitutive of seeing that it is mediated by the activity of a physical organ which must be situated somewhere in spatial relation to what is seen, and which functions in numerous contingent ways that determine or constrain the way it is seen—what frequencies of light it responds to, how fast it processes the input, and so on. As Nietzsche says (*GM* III. 12), there could not be an eye that was not characterized by being at some determinate place and having some determinate mode of functioning: 'an eye that must not have any direction, in which the active and interpretive forces [...] are to be shut off, are to be absent' is absurd and impossible. In this sense all seeing is perspectival: from a specific place, by a specific type of organ.[6] But that in itself implies neither scepticism not relativism—neither that all vistas yielded up by our eyes are falsifications of reality, nor that every vista makes an equally worthwhile contribution to perception. If the analogy with seeing carries over in this respect to the case of knowing, then Nietzsche should hold that knowledge is never 'from nowhere' and always comes with some limitation or specificity owing to the condition of the knower. But, as far as the analogy goes, he need be neither a global sceptic nor an even-handed relativist about knowledge. He should happily allow that some knowledge-claims are superior to others, that some at least are true and some false. A switch of metaphors may help to bring this non-radical line of interpretation further into focus:[7] a map is always a selective representation of a terrain, showing roads but not altitudes, altitudes but not populations, populations but not mean daytime temperatures, and so on. The idea of an absolute map that excluded nothing that anyone might want to know about the terrain is absurd: but we cannot conclude from that that all maps fail to represent any terrain truly, or that no map is more accurate than another, or that no map can be out and out false or fictional.

---

[6] There are notebook entries that make a close connection between 'perspective' or 'perspectivism' and 'specificity'. See *KSA* xiii. 370–1, 373–4 (nn. 14 [184], [186] (1888), previously pub. as *WP* 567, 636).

[7] I take this straight from Leiter (1994: 356 n. 26), who attributes the idea to Frithjof Bergmann.

2 Affects as Enabling and Enhancing Knowledge

In the case of *knowing*, then, what is it that makes it necessarily perspectival? What is it about the condition of the knower that corresponds to the inbuilt constraints of specificity of place and function that shape all seeing? Nietzsche actually says rather little about this in our passage. He mentions the 'active and interpretive forces', which presumably pertain not just to the 'eye' but to that which it is a metaphor for, i.e. the knowing human mind. Nietzsche perhaps trades on the post-Kantian platitude that knowledge of a world of objects has as a condition that the human mind actively contribute organizing structures to any data it receives, so that non-selective passive reception can be no model of knowledge at all. However, Nietzsche's 'active and interpretive forces' are not very much like Kant's synthesis of intuitions under concepts of the understanding and are in some respects more akin to Schopenhauer's notion that the intellect's operations are in the service of the will. The heavy emphasis in our passage falls, not on purely cognitive Kant-style features of the mind, but on *affects*. It is the affects—the very mental states that for the philosophical orthodoxy 'twist, colour, and distort' judgement and perception—that Nietzsche portrays as enabling and expanding knowledge. These points are hammered home in the last half-page of section 12: 'To eliminate the will altogether, to disconnect the affects' would be to disable knowledge; 'To have one's pro and contra in one's power' is to make one's knowledge more 'objective'; the plurality of affects, the greatest possible difference in affective interpretations, is 'useful' for knowledge and makes it more 'complete'.

What is an affect? At times, as we have seen, Nietzsche talks simply of 'inclinations and aversions', 'pro and contra', or 'for and against'—descriptions that parallel Schopenhauer's vocabulary and his view that all affects are positive or negative stirrings of the will. It seems that for Nietzsche too all affects are at bottom inclinations or aversions of some kind. But their range is extensive. In the *Genealogy* and *Beyond Good and Evil* alone he explicitly uses the term for the following: anger, fear, love, hatred, hope, envy, revenge, lust, jealousy, irascibility, exuberance, calmness, self-satisfaction, self-humiliation, self-crucifixion, power-lust, greed, suspicion, malice, cruelty, contempt, despair, triumph, feeling of looking down on, feeling of a superior glance towards others, desire to justify oneself in the eyes of others, demand for respect, feelings of laziness, feeling of a command, and brooding over bad deeds.[8] Affects are, at the very least, ways in which we *feel*. Many specific instances are what we would call emotions, some are perhaps moods, while affects of 'commanding' or of 'looking down on' someone are not obviously describable as either moods or emotions. The class of affects is likely to include further felt states such as an instinctual like or dislike for something, a sense of unease, a faint thrill at a certain thought, and so on until we reach states for which we have no terminology:

words really exist only for *superlative* degrees of these [inner] processes and drives. [...] Anger, hatred, love, pity, desire, knowledge, joy, pain—all are names for *extreme* states: the milder, middle degrees, not to speak of the lower degrees which are continually in play, elude us, and yet it is they which weave the web of our character and destiny.

(*D* 115)

Some affects are beneath accurate apprehension by ourselves, and some are unconscious.[9] But all seem to be *feelings* of one sort or another. And if we respect the fact that Nietzsche gives such prominence to affects in his discussion of perspectival knowing, we shall have to surmise that for him the inbuilt constraint upon knowledge that makes it 'only perspectival' lies in the knowing subject's affective nature. So Nietzsche's perspectivism about knowledge must involve the two claims: (1) that *there is only knowledge that is guided or facilitated by our feelings*, and (2) that *the more different feelings we allow to guide our knowledge, the better our knowledge will be.*

Commentators have tended to miss this, or to give it little emphasis. For example, in his clearly formulated account Leiter gives the following as two constitutive claims of Nietzsche's epistemic perspectivism:

Necessarily, we know an object from a particular perspective: that is, from the standpoint of particular interests and needs (perspectivism claim) .... The more perspectives we enjoy—for example, the more interests we employ in knowing the object—the better our conception of what the object is like will be (plurality claim).[10]

—but here neither claim reflects the emphatic linkage of perspectives to affects in Nietzsche's text. Leiter sometimes includes 'affects' in his wording,

---

[8] See *BGE* 19, 23, 187, 192, 260; *GM* I. 10, 13; II. 11; III. 15, 20.
[9] See *GS* 354; Richardson (1996: 34–8).   [10] Leiter (1994: 345).

thus: 'all knowing is mediated by particular interpretive needs (interests, affects)'.[11] But since neither interests nor needs are obviously affects (nor are affects needs or interests) this inclusion leaves the central role of affects in perspectival knowing obscure. Clark also talks predominantly of 'interests', thus:

we can understand cognitive perspectives as constituted not only by beliefs, but also by those factors on the side of the subject responsible for beliefs, such as cognitive capacities and practical interests … [Nietzsche] takes cognitive capacities and interests to be rooted in practical interests, in particular, the interests in control and survival.[12]

The distinction of 'practical interests' from 'cognitive interests' and the assignment of priority to the former is promising, since it chimes well with Nietzsche's admonition not to eliminate the will altogether on pain of castrating the intellect—but again Clark does not mention the affects as such.

Perhaps such accounts arise because of a picture like this: members of the human species have practical needs to identify sources of nourishment, safety, and danger, to predict and explain the behaviour of inanimate objects, other sentient beings, and each other, to be able to live relatively harmoniously with one another, to ensure the perpetuation of their community, and so on; and the patterns of evidence-gathering, belief formation, belief-testing, and the like that structure human cognition and count as furthering knowledge depend for their existence and legitimacy on the role they play in serving such needs. What is known by any human knower is rooted in these basic practical needs, or (presumably) in other more elaborate practical needs inherent in various cultural activities, up to and including such activities as scientific investigation. Now there is no reason to doubt that Nietzsche would accept something like this. On the contrary, he is prone to say, '*Usefulness for preservation* […] is what motivates the development of the organs of knowledge […] a species seizes that much reality *in order to become master of it, to take it into service*,'[13] and he would include scientific knowledge in this view.[14] But none of this helps us to understand in any clear way why disconnecting the affects would disable knowledge or why multiplying them would enhance it.

---

[11] Ibid. 347. Affects are somewhat more prominent in Leiter's later account (2002: 272–3).
[12] Clark (1990: 133).   [13] *WLN* 258 (n. 14 [122] (1888), previously pub. as *WP* 480).
[14] See *GS* 121; *BGE* 4.

Could some account be given in which interests are, after all, affects? Suppose we equate 'interests' with desires and say that whatever someone desires is an interest of theirs. Then, assuming that 'desiring' is an affect (since Nietzsche seems to relate will and affect closely, and since desiring is an undeniable case of willing), interests would be a species of affects. To say that no knowing is free of interests would be to say that no knowing is free of affects; and to say that knowledge is enhanced by multiplying our interests would be to say that knowledge is enhanced by multiplying one kind of affects. But this train of thought has little to recommend it. Collapsing interests into desires in any simple way is notoriously questionable;[15] and the key clause 'interests are a species of affects' rings extremely oddly, the oddness stemming, I think, from an intuition that my affects are felt states of mine, while my interests are not. But, all that aside, Nietzsche says that affects as such, unqualified, enable and enhance our knowledge, and even if we turned interests into a species of affects, we still would not have explained his making this general claim.

Another thought might be that someone's affects are at least tightly related to their needs and interests. We might hypothesize that if a person has some need or interest, he or she typically experiences characteristic affects: that, for instance, someone who has a need for food will always feel the need as a pain or craving and its fulfilment as a comfort, and similarly with other needs and interests. In that case, given the claim that all knowledge is 'from the standpoint of particular interests' or 'rooted in practical interests', a would-be 'knower' without accompanying affects would be inconceivable. We might, conversely, think that every affect is felt as a response to something's acting for or against an interest, or to something's satisfying or frustrating a need: then Nietzsche's insistent denial of affect-free knowing would at least entail a denial of knowing unconnected with needs and interests. Affects may, however, lack any obvious dependence on interests or needs of the agent, or work against them. My feeling overwhelming nausea at the thought of my child's undergoing surgery is an affective response that threatens to obstruct what my child and I really need. Someone's feeling ashamed at finding another sexually attractive does not always further anyone's interests, needs, or desires, and can block them in an unhealthy way. Nietzsche himself is

---

[15] See e.g. Wiggins (1991: 5–6, 16–17).

adamant that our feelings of compassion for the weak and feelings of guilt about our natural instincts can make us ill and obstruct attainment of the 'power and splendour' of which humanity is capable. If there are affects that conflict with, or simply do not arise out of, needs and interests of the agent, then it remains unclear how we can explicate the perspectivism of *GM* III. 12 solely by invoking these needs and interests.

What, then, can Nietzsche mean when he talks of the affects enabling and enhancing knowledge? I suggest that we begin not with a generalization about all knowing, but with a specific example extremely close to home: Nietzsche's own interpretative task in the *Genealogy*, his search for knowledge about the various phenomena of morality. In earlier chapters I argued that arousing the affects is central to Nietzsche's aims as a writer, and that it deserves to be so because of the prominence of affects in his explanation of the genesis of our moral attitudes. For example, I argued that in order to further our understanding of the slave revolt in morality Nietzsche encourages us to recognize our own ambivalent inclinations and aversions—our mixed feelings for or against compassion, aggression, humility, prowess, equality, nobility—and to reconstruct the history of attitudes to 'good' and 'evil' in imaginative engagement with the feelings of both the oppressed slave and the self-defining master. I suggested that when he invites us to identify with the fears and resentment of a defenceless sheep and with the fond disdain of a natural predator, he provides a way of gaining insight into the origins of the modern notion of responsibility for action. Again, in convincing us of cruelty's role in the genesis of guilt and punishment, he seduces us into acknowledging, beneath our more obvious feelings of anger and disgust, a streak of joyfulness in seeing and making suffer. All these seem good examples of 'making the difference in perspectives and affective interpretations useful for knowledge'—knowledge of the nature of our own moral attitudes. An even more local example occurs in the first half of *GM* III. 12 itself, which invites us to feel the philosophical products of asceticism as a 'triumph', commenting that we should 'not be ungrateful toward such resolute reversals of [...] familiar perspectives and valuations'—in other words, to see things through the eyes and feelings of the ascetic is beneficial to our inquiry because it enables us to have a more complete insight into the ideal that, according to Nietzsche, dominates Christian and post-Christian culture.

A further small but significant point about Nietzsche's vocabulary might assist in reorienting our expectations about the kind of knowledge or inter-pretation Nietzsche has most immediately in mind. He talks of completing our 'objectivity' and our 'concept' of something—but of what kind of thing? Some accounts of perspectivism foreground the issue of 'knowing an object from a particular perspective',[16] which may carry the suggestion that Nietzsche's main concern is the traditional epistemological problem of knowledge of individual bodies in the external world. But it is unnecessary to read Nietzsche as referring to an *object* in this specific manner.[17] His word here is *eine Sache*, which may mean simply a *matter* or *topic* of discussion. Back in the Second Treatise (section 4) he investigated a particular *düstere Sache*, a gloomy matter, namely 'the consciousness of guilt, the entire "bad conscience"' which turned out to be an immensely complex set of psychological and cultural phenomena. Another such *düstere Sache* for him is 'reason, seriousness, mastery over the affects, this entire gloomy matter called reflection',[18] and there are similar uses of the term in the *Genealogy* to denote a topic of discussion, an area of human life under investigation.

So Nietzsche's practice in the *Genealogy* suggests the belief that our feeling shocked, embarrassed, disgusted, or attracted by some phenomenon *tells us something about* that phenomenon—that is, that feelings themselves have cog-nitive potency. If, for the time being, we consider perspectivism in restricted application only to Nietzsche's particular quest for 'knowing' about the topic of morality, we can construe it in terms of the following two claims:

> *Affective perspectivism claim*: Concerning the phenomena of morality (good–evil evaluation, guilt, responsibility, the ideal of suppressing the natural instincts, and so on) there is only perspectival knowing, i.e. only knowledge informed by our affects.
>
> *Affective plurality claim*: The more of our affects we allow ourselves to feel and bring to bear upon the phenomena of morality, the better will be our understanding of those phenomena.

---

[16] See Leiter (1994: 345).

[17] Cox (1999: 139–68) argues for the stronger claim that Nietzsche's perspectivism cannot be construed as assuming the everyday conception of objecthood, but rather undermines that notion.

[18] *GM* II. 3. Other instances in the *Genealogy*: punishment is the *Sache*, or topic of discussion, in *GM* II. 13; the hatred of rule and hierarchy that dominates science is a *schlechte Sache*, a bad thing (*GM* II. 12); human history itself would have been a *dumme Sache*, a stupid thing, without the spirit that the powerless introduced into it (*GM* I. 7).

Such a construal has the advantage of fitting the method of writing about morality that we have seen Nietzsche use throughout the *Genealogy*. And the otherwise rather obscure notion of 'shifting one's pro and contra in and out' seems an appropriate description of the activity Nietzsche expects of his own more alert and sensitive readers.

But, it will be objected, Nietzsche is putting forward a general theory of knowledge; and how plausible a general theory would it be to maintain that there is never affect-free knowledge of any kind, and never any cognitive advantage in minimizing the affects? We could try to deflect this objection by treating the generalizing talk as merely a dramatic overstatement on Nietzsche's part. The notion that we have in *GM* III. 12 a 'general theory of knowledge' is perhaps somewhat inflated. It is not encouraging that Nietzsche places 'knowing' (as well as 'objectivity' and 'concept') in quotation marks; and the whole section does not, in all honesty, read as if its first purpose is to make some authoritative contribution to epistemology. On the other hand, there is evidence elsewhere that he does indeed regard all claims to knowledge as necessarily driven, guided, coloured, filtered, by deep and often unacknowledged dispositions of feeling: for instance, his claim that philosophers all arrive at their theories by sifting some 'fervent wish that [...] they defend [...] with rationalizations after the fact' (*BGE* 5). Furthermore, the injunction to stop believing in non-perspectival knowing is delivered explicitly to philosophers who have theorized about knowledge in general. Schopenhauer is the only philosopher quoted directly, but Nietzsche alludes to other conceptions of knowledge in phrases that sound more or less rationalist, Kantian, or Hegelian ('pure reason', 'absolute spirituality', 'knowledge in itself')—theoretical conceptions of knowledge that supposedly go wrong because they attempt to exclude the affects from knowing in a general way. It would be natural for him to mean his counter-claim also as a general one.

So we are faced with two strikingly controversial general claims: (1) that it is impossible for there to be any knowing that is free of all affects, and (2) that multiplying different affects always improves knowing. The first claim on its own could in principle be given a relatively innocuous reading, parallel to 'An environment free of all bacteria is impossible' or 'A train service free of all delays is impossible'. In other words, we might think we had to deal merely with the thought that knowing with absolute impartiality and absence of emotion is an unrealizable ideal. But that reading would remain implicitly wedded to the orthodoxy that feelings are a kind of 'dirt' in the machine of cognition, an imperfection or interference, albeit one we can be realistic enough to tolerate. It seems clear that this is not Nietzsche's position. For him, feelings make knowledge *possible*. They are not ineliminable occupational hazards for the knower, but constitutively necessary conditions of the knower's knowing anything at all. We may recall that he decries the would-be pure, will-less subject of knowledge as a 'contradiction', 'absurdity', and 'non-concept'—something strictly impossible, not just practically unrealizable. This strong reading of the first claim is also borne out by the fact of Nietzsche's making the second claim, that multiplying different affects always improves knowing. For if affects were merely an impurity that had to be tolerated in the quest for knowledge, the right policy would still lie in seeking to diminish them, rather than in calling for their augmentation in both number and variety.

If Nietzsche is making these two claims, how is he to account for knowledge that does aspire towards affective neutrality, such as scientific knowledge and the kind of impersonal dialectic championed by philosophy (as classically conceived)? Science and impersonal dialectic can certainly no longer be singled out as privileged paradigms of knowledge for Nietzsche; but now they threaten either to be quite aberrant forms of knowledge, or not to be forms of knowledge at all—unless Nietzsche can somehow convince us that such forms of knowledge, when properly understood, are not affect-free. In fact, Nietzsche's second perspectivist claim—that multiplying the affects enhances knowledge—can stand even if scientific investigation has to be construed as a form of knowledge purged of all affects. For he can hold that knowing something *only* scientifically gives us a poorer understanding of it than knowing it through a variety of psychological, imaginative, rhetorical means—affect-arousing means—in addition to those of science. Once again his own shift from philological *Wissenschaft* to the manner of writing displayed in the *Genealogy* bears out the intelligibility of such a claim for Nietzsche. It is beyond question that Nietzsche regards the *Genealogy* as providing greater knowledge about morality than any combination of the traditional *Wissenschaften* could have attained unaided.

3 Who Interprets?

Nietzsche's other general claim—that there is no form of knowing that is not affective—looks harder to sustain. We are prompted to seek some theoretical ground for Nietzsche's refusal in principle to allow affect-free knowledge. At this point it will help to consider who or what is the knower, the subject of knowledge, for Nietzsche. The readings of perspectivism discussed so far have tended towards the implicit assumption of what we might call 'a commonsense conception of human knowing' in which 'the subject of perspectivism is simply the ordinary, individual, human … knower'.[19] But faced with the questions 'Who knows?', 'Who thinks?', 'Who interprets?' Nietzsche's official position is that there is no such subject as ordinarily conceived. He repeatedly urges that we should be suspicious towards the concept of a subject or 'I'. The I is 'just an assumption or opinion, to put it mildly', it has 'become a fairy tale, a fiction, a play on words', and enjoys 'a merely apparent existence'. Instead we are to think of 'soul as subject-multiplicity', and view the self as a plurality of sub-personal elements in competitive interaction with one another, elements that, as we have seen, are will-like in character (' "under-wills" or under-souls').[20]

Nietzsche commonly calls such elements 'drives'. In the case of a philosopher, for example, *who he is* is equivalent to 'what order of rank the innermost drives of his nature' stand in, and thinking itself is 'only a relation between these drives' (*BGE* 6, 36). But it is evident that drives are closely related to affects, for he also says that the social construction that is the self is built out of 'drives and affects' (*BGE* 12), and talks elsewhere of 'our drives and their for and against'.[21] We may wonder whether drives and affects are even properly distinguishable kinds.[22] It would be foolhardy to expect consistent terminological rigour here, but unless the recurrent

---

[19] Cox (1999: 120). Cox goes on to provide a convincing argument that Nietzsche's perspectivism must be read in the light of his rejection of the unitary subject. My discussion has benefited from this account and from Richardson's discussion of perspectivism's dependence on Nietzsche's 'power ontology' (Richardson 1996: 35–9).

[20] See *BGE* 12, 16, 17, 19, 34, 54; *TI*, 'Reason in Philosophy', 5; 'The Four Great Errors', 3.

[21] *WLN* 139 (n. 7 [60] (1886–7), previously pub. as *WP* 481). Here 'our needs' stands in apposition to 'our drives and their for and against'. I argued above against interpreting the perspectivism of *GM* III. 12 primarily in terms of an agent's needs and interests. But it may be that for Nietzsche all affects relate to the 'needs' and 'interests' of sub-personal drives.

[22] As suggested by Cox (1999: 126–7): 'The disposition that composes [subjects] is itself made up of microdispositions—what Nietzsche variously calls "drives" (*Triebe*), "desires" (*Begierden*), "instincts"

expression 'drives and affects' is to be taken as merely pleonastic, we might hypothesize that a drive is a relatively stable tendency to active behaviour of some kind, while an affect, put very roughly, is what it feels like when a drive is active inside oneself. Affects, as we have seen, are glossed as inclinations and aversions or fors and againsts. An affect would then be a positive or negative feeling that occurs in response to the success or failure of a particular drive in its striving, or in response to the confluence of the activities of more than one drive within oneself. In *Human, All Too Human* Nietzsche already thought that 'a drive to something or away from something divorced from a feeling one is desiring the beneficial or avoiding the harmful, a drive without some kind of knowing evaluation of the worth of its objective, does not exist in man'.[23] And in a late notebook entry he asks, 'Can we assume a *striving for power* without a sensation of pleasure and unpleasure, i.e. without a feeling of the increase and diminution of power?'[24]

Given the claim that this plurality of will-like striving components held in tension is what I am, it makes sense prima facie to hold that if I am to *know* anything, it must be through some activity of the drives that compose me and the feelings essentially involved in their activity. There is, officially, nothing else available to do the knowing. Thus in further notebook entries Nietzsche writes: 'It is our needs *which interpret the world*: our drives and their for and against. Every drive is a kind of lust for domination, each has its perspective'; and '*Who interprets?*—Our affects.'[25] Earlier we discussed the picture of 'life as will to power' found in the *Genealogy* and *Beyond Good and Evil*, the idea that the entire organic world, the human organism included, contains active processes in which one part of nature overcomes and presses an interpretation upon another. I claimed that Nietzsche was likely to have meant such a view with some degree of literalness—and that claim is strengthened by our present interpretation of the perspectival nature of knowing. Out of the inner tension and competition among striving and feeling dispositions, constantly interpreting and seeking to become master over whatever they encounter, come thinking, meaning, and valuing. It

---

(*Instinkte*), "powers" (*Mächte*), "forces" (*Kräfte*), "impulses" (*Reize, Impulse*), "passions" (*Leidenschaften*), "feelings" (*Gefühlen*), "affects" (*Affekte*), pathos (*Pathos*), and so on.'

[23]   *HA* I. 32. See also Richardson (1996: 37).

[24]   *WLN* 248 (n. 14 [82] (1888), previously pub. as part of *WP* 689).

[25]   *WLN* 139, 96 (nn. 7 [60] (1886–7), [2] 90 (1885–6), previously pub. as *WP* 481, 254).

would seem that, given Nietzsche's view of the self, knowing would likewise have to be some aggregate of the multiple affective interpretations that occur within the one human being.

Now to return to the question of why and whether affect-free knowledge is impossible for Nietzsche. In *Beyond Good and Evil* he concedes that there is a rare type of 'knower' who indulges in a 'pure' form of knowing:

> with scholars, the truly scientific people [...] there might really be something like a drive for knowledge, some independent little clockwork mechanism that, once well wound, ticks bravely away *without* essentially involving the rest of the scholar's drives.
>
> (*BGE* 6)

But because the self is composed of drives and affects, such 'pure' pursuit of knowledge is an exception, a sort of harmless sideshow. And besides, not even this kind of genuinely impersonal investigation—into philology, fungus, or chemistry—is 'pure' in its motivation, Nietzsche adds; rather it is instrumental towards the attainment of more material goals, earning a living, supporting a family, and so on. With *philosophy*, by contrast, 'there is absolutely nothing impersonal':

> I do not believe that a 'drive for knowledge' is the father of philosophy, but rather that another drive, here as elsewhere, used knowledge (and mis-knowledge!) merely as a tool. But anyone who looks at people's basic drives [...] will find that they all practiced philosophy at some point,—and that every single one of them would be only too pleased to present *itself* as the ultimate purpose of existence and as rightful *master* of all the other drives. Because every drive craves mastery, and *this* leads it to try philosophising.
>
> (*BGE* 6)

Nietzsche tends to regard genuine philosophers as thinkers with some original grand vision of the world and a distinct set of values that is expressive of their character. They may picture themselves as emotionally neutral, disinterested seekers after truth, and may indeed succeed in suppressing many of their feelings, but their self-image is false. 'My suppressing my feelings' can be redescribed as one sub-personal drive gaining ascendancy over another—'our intellect is only the blind instrument of *another drive* which is a *rival* of the drive whose vehemence is tormenting us' (*D* 109). And, as we saw in the case study of Schopenhauer above, the *theory* of will-less, affect-free objectivity and the pure selfless eye of knowledge is itself driven by affects: fear, discomfort, yearning for safety and rest.

So the slogan 'There is only perspectival knowing' is, as slogans tend to be, an oversimplification of Nietzsche's views. He regards it as possible, in exceptional cases, to pursue knowledge in disconnection from the sum of one's affects and drives, but this type of 'little clockwork mechanism' cannot be the basis of a general theory of knowing, nor an accurate guide to the nature of knowing subjects. The 'subject of knowing' is a composite of drives and affects that are the real loci of interpretations. One can *conceive* oneself as an affect-free knower—hence the appearance of philosophers hitherto in that 'caterpillar-form' of the ascetic priest—but this is to portray oneself falsely. The suppression of feelings is attainable to a degree, but is itself an enterprise driven by further sub-personal attractions and repulsions; and the very idea of the pure subject of knowledge is something we invent not primarily for theoretical reasons, but because of the exigencies of deep-seated affects.

4 Some Problems

Construed in this manner, Nietzsche's conception of perspectival knowledge still faces some hard questions. (1) What makes an aggregate of the activities of someone's drives a case of *knowing*, as opposed to a case of something else? Can the activity of the multiple drives and affects give rise to interpretations that are capable of meeting even the minimum requirement for knowledge, that of being true? (2) If each of the sub-personal elements of the self (whatever they are called) wants mastery, strives, interprets, and grasps something of reality, is not each of them just a miniature subject? Far from abandoning the subject-conception inherited from the philosophical tradition, have we not simply denied it application at the level of the individual human being and smuggled it back into our description of the sub-personal community of drives? (3) How in Nietzsche's conception can one be said 'to have one's pro and contra *in one's power*, and to shift them in out'? How can we 'make [...] the difference in perspectives and affective interpretations useful for knowledge'? How can we 'bring to bear' our many affects on one and the same matter, and 'allow [them] to speak' about it? What, in short, must the self be, in order to perform such operations?

And finally, (4) can Nietzsche, with his apparently eliminativist conception of the self, explain how the philosopher's conception of the self-conscious subject or 'I', erroneous or not, could even have come about?

A minimal requirement for any recognizable conception of knowledge is that there be a distinction between true and false representations, and hence between what represents and what is represented. If the drives and affects are all there is to the self, and the self is to do anything called 'knowing', then drives and affects must be capable of representing something outside themselves. Nietzsche appears to think that this can be achieved through a notion of *willing* (or striving) combined with one of *resistance* (or obstruction). He thinks of will to power as expressing itself towards resistances, and illustrates the process with the model of the protoplasm sending out pseudopodia and feeling around for something it might assimilate into itself. A sub-personal drive likewise comes up against something other than itself, which it feels as a resistance to its own activity. It either overcomes the resistance or is overcome by it, giving rise to affects of (roughly) gratification, frustration, exhaustion, or reinvigoration—feelings of increase or diminution in power.[26] But with this notion of registering the other through resistance and active appropriation there seems no room for veridical versus non-veridical representation of the other. As John Richardson puts it, the 'viewpoint' of each locus of willing is not a conscious one, is not separable from its 'doing' or activity, and is 'not chiefly theoretical (in aiming at "facts")'.[27] Furthermore:

we mustn't think that these perspectives aim basically at truth, at mirroring the world. It's not that the drive takes a theorizing view aimed to see how the world truly is, as a step before applying that neutral information back to its practical ends. It views the world from its interests.[28]

If there is no self besides what arises from antagonistic and hierarchical relations between such drives, it is unclear how Nietzsche will arrive at an account of knowledge on the part of human beings—or at least unclear how he will sustain the possibility of both true and false beliefs on the part of the knower, in the manner that initially seemed to be accommodated by his eye metaphor.

---

[26] See *WLN* 264–5 (n. 14 [174] (1888), previously pub. as *WP* 702 and 703). Poellner (2001: 101–2) is also useful here.

[27] Richardson (1996: 37).   [28] Ibid. 37.

It may be that Nietzsche believes there is no ultimate mystery concerning how true and false beliefs arise out of the activity of more primitive drives, because he thinks of 'interpretation' as a single type of phenomenon exemplified at every level of complexity from the protoplasm to the human agent. This calls up our second problem, the threat of miniature subjects, or homunculi. As I noted above in discussing the will to power, it is unclear how Nietzsche wishes his intentionalistic descriptions of the sub-personal to be taken. In practice he never shakes off the terminology of willing and representing. Although the 'under-wills' are not to be conceived as *consciously* willing or *consciously* representing,[29] we must at least envisage a likeness in kind between the activity of the lower-level components of the multiple self and the states conventionally ascribed to subjects, such as believing, desiring, and feeling emotions. But Nietzsche does little to enlighten us further on the nature of that likeness.

Our passage from *GM* III. 12 suggests that for 'knowing' to occur, a mere multiplicity of affect-interpretations will indeed not suffice. There must also be those operations upon affects, or upon interpretations, which Nietzsche calls 'having them in one's power', 'shifting them in and out', and so on. This then prompts our question (3): What must the self be for these operations to occur? Perhaps some kind of controlling subject? In similar passages in *Beyond Good and Evil* and *Human, All Too Human* Nietzsche speaks blatantly of free agency with respect to one's affects:

To freely have or not have your affects, your pros and cons, to condescend to them for a few hours; to *seat* yourself on them as you would on a horse or often as you would on an ass:—since you need to know how to use their stupidity as well as you know how to use their fire.[30]

You shall become master over yourself [...] You shall get control over your For and Against and learn how to display first one and then the other in accordance with your higher goal.[31]

It seems clear that there must be some kind of self-conscious unity for the notion of controlling affects and bringing them to bear on one and the same

---

[29] See Richardson 36–7.

[30] *BGE* 284; trans. modified from Norman's. Norman has 'your stupidity' and 'your fire' for *ihre Dummheit* and *ihr Feuer*, but the correct translation of *ihre* and *ihr* must be 'their'.

[31] *HA* I, Preface, 6 (pub. 1886). 'For and Against' translates *Für und Wider*, rendered elsewhere as 'pro and con'.

subject matter to make sense. I have to be aware that affects *A* and *B*, each of which may 'speak' interchangeably about the same subject matter, are both *mine*. I have to be that which feels both affects, regards itself as feeling them both, and takes some attitude towards its subject matter in the light now of this affect, and now of that. I suggested in an earlier discussion that Nietzsche's revaluative project is conceived as a task for a self-conscious and potentially autonomous subject to carry out; it seems right to view his suggestion of 'having one's affects within one's control' and manipulating them 'in accordance with a higher goal' as part of that same overall project. In using the fullness of our affective responsiveness to the world, we come to occupy ourselves, as it were, in a more complete and healthy way, to fulfil our potential as cognizers. But if the way in which we are to reach this healthier cognitive state is by rethinking what we are and by conscious identification with as many of our affects as possible, we must arguably be unified self-conscious subjects, subjects of 'I'-thoughts. So we cannot simply be a multiplicity of drives and affects, as Nietzsche's official position proclaims.

An alternative, Kantian position would allow for self-conscious unity within experience without reawakening any of the metaphysical notions that Nietzsche repudiates—the self or 'I' as non-empirical, unchanging essence, as thinking substance, as something ontologically primary and irreducible, as cause of thinking. Kant makes the transcendental claim that it is a condition of there being experience at all that it is that of a self-conscious 'I'. But, for Kant, no metaphysical conclusions can be drawn from the holding of this condition; hence his criticisms of rational psychology in the 'Paralogisms of Pure Reason': how this 'I' is realized ontologically is left entirely open by the transcendental claim.[32] If he espoused this Kantian position, Nietzsche could hold that at the level of physiological description there are drives and affects in various sorts of relations, and, compatibly with this, that for there to be the operations of 'controlling' and 'shifting in and out' in regard to the affects, there must be a subject that conceives itself as a single self-conscious 'I'.[33] His eliminativist treatment of the self

---

[32] See Kant (1998, 'Transcendental Deduction of the Categories' and 'Paralogisms of Pure Reason').

[33] Even Schopenhauer's more simplistic position could be of some help to Nietzsche here: that we 'find ourselves as' the (unified) subject from our own point of view, while from an objective, third-person standpoint we are nothing but organic functions expressive of will to life (see Schopenhauer 1969: i. 5; ii. 272–8).

could then be seen as directed primarily against traditional metaphysical conceptions, and his denial of *any* subject or 'I' regarded as a polemical overstatement.[34]

Given that he eschews this Kantian route, however, Nietzsche's alternative approach towards explaining the (apparent) unity of self-consciousness is the solely naturalistic one of positing integration of the multiple drives under one dominant drive. An example of this can be found in *Daybreak* 109, where Nietzsche gives a penetrating account of ways in which one might 'combat the vehemence of a drive'—Nietzsche gives no specific illustration, but we might imagine someone struggling with overpowering sexual urges or addictive cravings. The discussion concludes thus:

> *that* one *desires* to combat the vehemence of a drive at all, however, does not stand within our own power [...] in this entire procedure our intellect is only the blind instrument of *another drive* which is a *rival* of the desire whose vehemence is tormenting us [...] while 'we' believe we are complaining about the vehemence of a drive, at bottom it is one drive *which is complaining about another*; that is to say: for us to become aware that we are suffering from the *vehemence* of a drive presupposes the existence of another equally vehement or even more vehement drive, and that a *struggle* is in prospect in which our intellect is going to have to take sides.
>
> (*D* 109)

A single drive can empower itself by subordinating many other drives to its own activity, and Nietzsche sees organization by a dominant drive as giving unity to one's character and actions. That I will to resist my addictive cravings is not 'up to me', is not the resolve of an 'I' that is external to the complex of drives and affects, but is itself the activity of a strong drive within me. There is no controlling self that determines *ex nihilo* what my ends, purposes, and values are. Fair enough. But I have to be, in my own self-conception, a sufficiently unified self that *I* can 'take sides' between the various drives that (though I did not originally will them) I find within myself. Likewise, it is not just that each of the affects I find within myself has a goal of its own, but rather that *I* have a goal in pursuit of which I can flexibly use the affects I feel. When Nietzsche is thinking of his ideal, creatively evaluating, perspectivally knowing individual, he freely imbues

---

[34] See Gardner (forthcoming).

this individual with the status of a unified, self-conscious, autonomous subject, in a way that fails to mesh comfortably with his eliminativist description of what the individual amounts to 'in reality'.[35]

If it were just that Nietzsche's ideal, value-creating, perspective-wielding 'new philosopher' presupposes the vocabulary of the unified self which his theoretical descriptions deny, the problem could be finessed by saying that Nietzsche sets us a daunting task: out of the base raw material of warring, organic strivings, which is all humanity has the right to assume itself to be, to create something whole, something with form, goal, and concentrated mastery—a recognizable Nietzschean task. The gap between the given and the goal would accord at least with the enormity and rarity of the achievement Nietzsche invokes. But our question (4) shows that this is not the end of the problem. For how could we come to think of ourselves erroneously in the manner of the philosophical tradition, as simple substances, self-transparent rational thinkers, pure subjects of knowledge, radically free, neutral subjects of choice, and so on? How did we get to regard ourselves at as unitary selves at all, erroneously or not? As Sebastian Gardner succinctly puts it,

How, except in the perspective of an I, of something that takes itself to have unity of the self's sort, can a conception of unity sufficient to account for the fiction of the I be formed? (As it might be put: How can the 'idea' of the I *occur* to a unit of will to power or composite thereof—or to anything *less* than an I?)[36]

In other words, if we were not already unitary, self-conscious selves, how could we have imagined that we were? This raises the prospect that Nietzsche's eliminativist picture of the self may be out of step not only with his re-evaluative project, but also with his diagnosis of the origins of our metaphysical errors. If only a unified self can make these metaphysical errors, and only a unified self can have the goals and perspectival adaptability that lead to healthier knowing and valuing, then, though we can learn not to think of ourselves as pure metaphysical subjects, Nietzsche's philosophy as a whole demands that we do not regard ourselves *only* as complex hierarchies of drives and affects.

---

[35] This 'lack of fit' argument is developed persuasively by Gardner (forthcoming), to which I am indebted.

[36] Gardner (forthcoming). Some while ago I expressed the problem similarly: 'Can a collection of sub-personal drives fabricate a unitary self that comes to regard those drives as its own? Or must there be a presupposed unitary self as author of the fiction?' (Janaway 1989: 355).

In various ways, then, Nietzsche appears to require a unified self of a kind that his official position would deny. It is hard to find a resolution to this predicament. But some of Nietzsche's remarks—that human beings are a combination of 'creature' and 'creator' in a way that is difficult to comprehend (*BGE* 225), and that there is no need to follow clumsy naturalists in abandoning the hypothesis of 'the soul' (*BGE* 12)—show him alive to a central tension in his view of the self, and even keen to cultivate our awareness of that tension. His perspectivism is perhaps another case in point: in support of the view that our interpretations are saturated and constituted by a plurality of feelings he dissolves the self into a multiplicity of affects and drives. But his aims of improving our capacity for knowing and skilfully using our affects demand more of a self than that: he needs his enquirer to be an active and sufficiently unified self that can represent its subject matter truly, that rides on top of the inner multiplicity, and that can self-consciously adopt attitudes towards it.

13

The Ascetic Ideal, Meaning, and Truth

In this chapter I address three of Nietzsche's themes in the Third Treatise: the role of the ascetic priest in the creation of values; the persistence of the ascetic ideal in the overvaluation of truth by modern scientists and scholars; and the claim that the ascetic ideal gains its power by giving a meaning to suffering and hence to human existence.

1 The Ascetic Priest

The clearest single statement of the significance of the ascetic priest in the Third Treatise is probably the following:

The idea we are fighting about here is the *valuation* of our life on the part of the ascetic priest: he relates our life (together with that to which it belongs: 'nature', 'world', the entire sphere of becoming and of transitoriness) to an entirely different kind of existence which it opposes and excludes, *unless*, perhaps, it were to turn against itself, *to negate itself*: in this case, the case of an ascetic life, life is held to be a bridge for that other existence. The ascetic treats life as a wrong path that one must finally retrace back to the point where it begins; or as an error that one refutes through deeds.

(*GM* III. 11)

Nietzsche comments in section 11 of the treatise that we can begin to tackle the question of ascetic ideals seriously once we have the ascetic priest in sight. A complex analysis of the role of this powerful agent in the transformation of values unfolds through sections 11–22—something Nietzsche regarded as an important achievement, to judge by his retrospective comment in *Ecce Homo* that the Third Treatise answers the question 'whence the ascetic ideal, the priests' ideal, derives its tremendous *power*', and his final overall verdict that 'This book contains the first psychology of the priest' (*EH*, 'Genealogy of Morals').

Commentators have pointed out that Nietzsche's treatment of the ascetic priest is marked by ambivalences both descriptive and affective. For Henry Staten the ascetic priest is 'the figure who emerges as the real protagonist of Nietzsche's tale, a protagonist who is neither merely hero nor merely villain, neither merely noble nor merely slave'.[1] The affective or evaluative (hero–villain) ambivalence towards the priestly figure is persistent but relatively unproblematic. We have seen that Nietzsche consistently laments the loss of vitality and self-affirmation, the waning of healthy, plural instincts that results from valuing selflessness, but is liable at the same time to admire certain successful transformations of values for their creativity, their imposition of new forms upon the material of humanity, in short their discharge of power and attainment of mastery. In the case of the ascetic priest the element of admiration is at its most intense, because the priest is a threefold embodiment of will to power. He successfully overturns the prevailing tendency to value the simpler warrior-like virtues and creates new conceptions of the good, achieves command over the weak to whom his priestly interpretations minister, and (most impressively) gains mastery over himself. All three aspects are reflected here:

Dominion over ones who suffer is his realm, it is to this that his instinct directs him, in this he has his most characteristic art, his mastery, his kind of happiness. He must be sick himself [...] but he must also be strong, lord over himself more than over others, with his will to power intact, so that he has the confidence and the fear of the sick, so that for them he can be a foothold, resistance, support, compulsion, disciplinarian, tyrant, god. He is to defend them, his herd—against whom? Against the healthy, no doubt, also against envying the healthy; he must by nature oppose *and hold in contempt* all coarse, tempestuous, unbridled, hard, violent–predatory health and powerfulness.

(*GM* III. 15)

The ascetic life is characterized by 'an unsatiated instinct and power-will that would like to become lord not over something living but rather over life itself, over its deepest, strongest, most fundamental preconditions'

---

[1] Staten (1990: 47–8). Ridley (1998: 45–50, 61) addresses the same ambivalences.

(*GM* III. 11). In unleashing such powerful counter-forces the priest makes an unparalleled achievement of the kind Nietzsche admires, yet the values created in the process are those of life-denial which Nietzsche decries as a decline into sickness. This ambivalence, far from being a defect in Nietzsche's position, is close to being its central point.[2] He refers to the ascetic life as a 'self-contradiction', as 'life *against* life', an 'incarnate will to contradiction and anti-nature', 'an attempt [...] to use energy to stop up the source of the energy'.[3] But such a conflicted phenomenon is eminently possible on his account:

> the ascetic ideal springs from the protective and healing instincts of a degenerating life that seeks with every means to hold its ground and is fighting for its existence [...] This ascetic priest, this seeming enemy of life, this *negating one*—precisely he belongs to the very great *conserving* and yes-*creating* forces of life.

(GM III. 13)

In describing the ascetic priest as both noble and slave, however, Nietzsche appears not just ambivalent, but more genuinely inconsistent. In the First Treatise he discusses the priestly class in sections 6 and 7,[4] but dwells little on their role, no doubt simplifying matters because his eye is fixed on the slave as psychological type. He portrays the priestly class as aristocratic, talking of the 'priestly-noble manner of valuation' as something that 'can branch off from the knightly-aristocratic and then develop into its opposite' (*GM* I. 7). Yet a few lines further on Nietzsche describes the priest as the 'most powerless' of enemies, governed by a thirst for revenge and the deepest of hatreds that grows out of his powerlessness — a profile that coincides with that of the oppressed slave and lacks any hint of nobility.[5] As Aaron Ridley writes, 'Nietzsche unquestionably finds it difficult to keep the priest in his place—as a noble whose mode of evaluation is the "opposite" of the knights' and who is yet no slave.'[6] The motivation for thrusting the priest into the slavish mould in the First Treatise may be that

---

[2] Ridley (1998: 61) says, 'It is extremely hard for Nietzsche to maintain a stable attitude to the priest.' On my view he is not trying to maintain a stable attitude, but consistently manifesting an ambivalence that he wishes to thematize.   [3] *GM* III. 11, 12, 13.

[4] *GM* I. 16 also reiterates the description of the Jews as the 'priestly people of *ressentiment*'.

[5] Nor is this problem confined to *GM* I. Ridley points out that in *GM* III. 15 the priestly psychology is above hatred and 'holds in contempt [...] more readily than it hates', while yet in *GM* III. 11 the priest is once again ruled by a '*ressentiment* without equal'—though this time against life itself rather than a more powerful human adversary. (See Ridley 1998: 45, 49.)

[6] Ridley (1998: 49).

Nietzsche is assimilating the Jewish people to slaves who revolt against their masters. If an entire people is enslaved or oppressed, their characteristic psychology may be reactive and revenge-driven throughout all strata from priestly leaders downwards, so that the whole people, governed by priests and directed unanimously towards revenge against an alien oppressor, can be described both as 'priestly' and as a 'people of *ressentiment*'. But this contributes nothing to an analysis of the priest's distinctive role and psychological formation.

'Nobility' and 'slavishness' appear to be concepts of greater complexity than Nietzsche's breakneck pace in the First Treatise can easily accommodate. At the outset the nobles are defined by their being de facto powerful in relation to another, subservient class. But Nietzsche is most interested in their psychology: how they regard themselves and others, how they conceive values, how they respect, despise, and find fulfilment. The prototype noble enjoys a status of social power that is naturally accompanied by a noble psychology. But the priestly class, while enjoying noble social status and power externally, diverge psychologically from their 'knightly-aristocratic' colleagues. Nietzsche makes clear in a number of places that even the least reflective of ancient aristocracies employ religion as a means of symbolizing and enhancing their power.[7] In the process of interpreting the world-order and explaining to the nobles what is of value in themselves, religion gives to the priests the distinct role of skilled interpreters. Priests can remain psychologically noble to the extent that they define their own worth in active self-affirmation rather than in reactive opposition to an oppressor—hence they are slaves neither socially nor psychologically. But being physically inactive, weak, and non-aggressive, it is natural for them to place value in passivity, meekness, and bodily abstinence. They are no less *powerful* for that: their strength lies in intellectual inventiveness, in the ability to interpret, conceptualize, mediate, and persuade, and for Nietzsche interpretation is consistently an instance of mastery and control, an instance of will to power.[8] So by inventing an ambitious conceptual scheme in which their own characteristics are explained as the most valuable, while the spontaneous natural instincts, robust action, and bodily existence become an aberration from states of true being and value, they attain their own spiritualized form of mastery. It

---

[7] See esp. *GM* II. 23; also II. 7, 19.   [8] Recall *GM* II. 12.

is because these valued characteristics are shared by the necessarily passive slaves that Nietzsche can, without genuine contradiction, portray the priest as a noble self-affirmer whose value system is slavish and denying of the natural self.

In the Third Treatise there is a parallel and similarly non-contradictory description, partially quoted above, of the ascetic priest as a physician who shares the sickness of his patients, while being strong and lord over himself.[9] The active work of the priest presupposes a condition for which the weak require a remedy. This condition consists in their suffering itself, the inability to ward off suffering, and a resultant feeling of listlessness (*Unlustgefühl*), also called the listlessness of depression (*Depressions-Unlust*).[10] In an intricate and centrifugal discussion, peppered with historical references, Nietzsche tells how the priest administers palliative care by instigating new feelings in the weak and by teaching them to reinterpret their existing inescapable feelings. The discussion is prefaced by a headline statement:

> If one wanted to sum up the value of the priestly mode of existence in the shortest formula one would have to say straight away: the priest *changes the direction* of *ressentiment*. For every sufferer instinctively seeks a cause for his suffering [...] 'I am suffering: for this someone must be to blame'—thus every diseased sheep thinks. But his shepherd, the ascetic priest, says to him: 'That's right, my sheep! someone must be to blame for it: but you yourself are this someone, you alone are to blame for it—*you alone are to blame for yourself*!' ... This is bold enough, false enough: but one thing at least has been achieved by it, in this way, as noted, the direction of the *ressentiment* has been—changed.
>
> (*GM* III. 15)

Nietzsche divides the means used to combat listlessness—all of which merely alleviate symptoms, leaving the causes of suffering and depression untouched—into two kinds: the 'innocent' and the 'guilty'. The 'innocent' means are as follows: (1) 'Hypnotization' or 'general muffling of the feeling of life' through avoidance of 'whatever stirs up affect'—an abstention from

---

[9] In *GM* III. 15. Nietzsche there says of the priest, 'He must be sick himself, he must be related to the sick and short-changed from the ground up in order to understand them'. Ridley (1998: 50) takes the phrase 'be related to the sick' as Nietzsche's retraction of 'be sick'—'and in this retraction the difference that makes all the difference is acknowledged.... The priest's relation to the "sick" ... is not one of identity.' I have sought to argue rather that the priest's being genuinely sick is not in contradiction with his achieving self-mastery and being in a sense genuinely strong.

[10] See *GM* III. 17, 20.

all willing and emotional excitement that anaesthetizes and suppresses the susceptibility to pain and amounts to another form of 'un-selfing' (*GM* III. 17, 18, 19). (2) Diversion through constant 'mechanical activity' or work, so that consciousness has no room left over to be filled with suffering (*GM* III. 18). (3) 'Prescription of a *small joy* that is easily accessible and can be made a regular practice', the sole example of which mentioned is the pleasure of giving joy to others, which induces towards them a measure of felt superiority, so that 'by prescribing "love of one's neighbour" the ascetic priest is basically prescribing an arousal of the strongest, most life-affirming drive [...]—the will to power' (*GM* III. 18). (4) Herd formation, in which 'the individual's vexation with himself is drowned out by his pleasure in the prospering of the community' (*GM* III. 19). 'Out of a longing to shake off the dull listlessness and the feeling of weakness, all the sick, the diseased strive instinctively for a herd organization: the priest intuits this instinct and fosters it' (*GM* III. 18). These 'innocent' means, abstinence, devotion to work, love of one's neighbour, loyal membership of the flock—all recognizable as practices that might be advocated by priests—function by masking, deadening, or distracting from the underlying suffering of depression that afflicts the weak and sickly.

But Nietzsche finds more interesting the so-called 'guilty' means (*GM* III. 19) that work by provoking an *excess* of emotion, an excess that frees the human being

from everything that is small and small-minded in listlessness, dullness, being out of sorts [...] Basically all great affects have the capacity to do so, assuming that they discharge themselves suddenly: anger, fear, lust, revenge, hope, triumph, despair, cruelty; and indeed the ascetic priest has unhesitatingly taken into his service the *whole* pack of wild dogs in man and unleashed first this one, then that one, always for the same purpose, to waken man out of slow sadness, to put to flight, at least for a time, his dull pain, his lingering misery, always under a religious interpretation and 'justification'.

(*GM* III. 20)

For all the length of the list here, the single outstanding emotion that serves this liberating function is the feeling of *guilt*. Nietzsche now interweaves his account of the ascetic priest with that of guilt from the Second Treatise, and resumes the heightened tone of free-flowing outrage that was so expressive in the earlier 'guilt before God' passage. Here is an extract from *GM* III. 20:

everywhere that *wanting*-to-misunderstand-suffering made into life's meaning, the reinterpretation of suffering into feelings of guilt, fear, and punishment; everywhere the whip, the hair-shirt, the starving body, contrition; everywhere the sinner breaking himself on the cruel wheels of a restless, diseased–lascivious conscience; everywhere mute torment, extreme fear, the agony of a tortured heart, the cramps of an unknown happiness, the cry for 'redemption'. [...] This old great magician in the battle with listlessness, the ascetic priest—he had obviously been victorious, *his* kingdom had come: people no longer protested *against* pain, they *thirsted* after pain; '*more* pain! *more* pain!' thus cried the longing of his disciples and initiates for centuries.

We learned in the Second Treatise that human beings came to interpret their sufferings as punishment, and invented an entire world-order of 'higher values' in order that suffering might be comprehended as something perpetually deserved. Now we see how that same transformative process requires a particular kind of agent, someone who intimately grasps the value of self-denial before absolute values that are 'not of *this* world',[11] but who, from a position of social dominance, can claim authority for the vision of the world that makes suffering deserved, and can prescribe the pain of guilt feelings as an alleviation of the dull sense of pointlessness felt by suffering humanity.

The priest empowers the weak by enabling them to find the highest truth and the highest value in their very sufferings, and expresses his own power in effecting such a highly charged transformation. What then is wrong with all this? Simply that the priest's 'cure' for depression makes the sick sicker. Nietzsche calls the ascetic ideal the '*true doom* in the history of European health', ahead of alcohol poisoning and syphilis (*GM* III. 21). Under the guise of 'improving' humanity, the ascetic ideal has, according to him, succeeded in weakening us into a neurotic self-destructiveness and physiological oversensitivity.

2 Faith in the Value of Truth

The last quarter of the Third Treatise contains a startling reversal. In section 23 Nietzsche asks where is the ideal that stands in opposition to

---

[11] Cf. *GM* III. 20, where Nietzsche quotes 'My kingdom is not of *this* world' from John 18: 36.

the ascetic ideal. 'But I am told it is *not* lacking,' he replies: has not a new ideal already arrived and replaced the old? '[O]ur entire modern *science* (*Wissenschaft*) is said to be witness to this—this modern science, which [...] clearly believes in itself alone, clearly possesses the courage to itself, the will to itself and has so far got along well enough without God, the beyond, and virtues that negate.' It can look as though science and other modern academic pursuits have escaped the ascetic ideal. (*Wissenschaft* is not merely 'science' but covers, for instance, Nietzsche's erstwhile discipline of classical philology.) Practitioners of *Wissenschaft* enjoy autonomy from religious world-views, and are apparently not beholden to the kind of ascetic values Nietzsche has traced through their moral, priestly, and philosophical manifestations. But Nietzsche does not accept that *Wissenschaft* provides a counter-ideal. The majority of modern scientists and scholars can be discounted because their work gives no evidence that they pursue any ideal at all: they are nothing more than blinkered labourers or hacks, earning their living by pursuing their own tiny corner of research and dulling themselves into a state where they pose no questions about the value or direction of their lives: 'the competence of our best scholars, their mindless diligence, their heads smoking day and night [...]—how often all this has its true sense in preventing something from becoming visible to oneself! Science as a means of self-anaesthetization: *are you acquainted with that?*' (*GM* III. 23). There are exceptions, though, namely 'the last idealists [...] among scholars and philosophers today', who indeed pursue a single, high-minded ideal—they are the 'unbelieving ones', rigorous, atheistic, naturalistic thinkers who on principle shun 'higher' values and transcendent entities and avoid smuggling moral judgements into their description of the world:

These negating and aloof ones of today, these who are unconditional on one point—the claim to intellectual cleanliness—these hard, strict, abstinent, heroic spirits who constitute the honor of our age, all these pale atheists, anti-Christians, immoralists, nihilists, these skeptics, ephectics, *hectics* of the spirit [...] these last idealists of knowledge in whom alone the intellectual conscience today dwells and has become flesh—in fact they believe themselves to be as detached as possible from the ascetic ideal, these 'free, *very* free spirits'; and yet [...] this ideal is precisely *their* ideal as well, they themselves represent it today, and perhaps they alone [...] These are by no means *free* spirits: *for they still believe in truth.*

(*GM* III. 24)

The inclusion of these unbelieving investigators within the ascetic ideal is the great surprise of the Third Treatise, and perhaps of the whole book, since we would expect Nietzsche to place himself in this very category of anti-Christian immoralists, but outside the class of things 'ruined' by the ascetic ideal (*GM* III. 23).

First, what does Nietzsche mean by 'believing in truth', and what would be the alternative?[12] One thing he does not mean in this passage is that we should or might cease to believe in the existence or possibility of truth. Aside from problems about the internal consistency of his doubting the existence of truth while himself seeking truths in the *Genealogy*, the fact is that Nietzsche simply says nothing of this sort in his discussion of truth in the Third Treatise. When he states that modern atheistic, immoralist thinkers 'still believe in (or have faith in) truth', he is not suggesting that in seeking truth they are pursuing chimeras and that nothing could ever count as discovering truths.[13] He is charging them with *valuing* truth in a certain way.[14] They have 'an unconditional will to truth', and a 'belief in a *metaphysical* value, a value *in itself of truth*', in truth posited 'as being, as God, as highest authority'. They perpetrate an 'overestimation of truth (more correctly [...] belief in the *in*assessability, *un*criticizability of truth)'. And it is precisely here that Nietzsche's challenge engages: 'The value of truth is for once to be experimentally *called into question*.' The complaint is that truth may have been valued *more highly* than it deserves and that it has been held sacrosanct, i.e. of such value that the question about its value *cannot even be raised*. So there are in principle two steps involved in the critique that Nietzsche encourages here. One is to acknowledge truth as something that can be put in the dock for an assessment of its value, positive or negative; the other is to mount the prosecution case: that truth really fails to have the unconditional positive value it has been accorded.

But should we even allow the case to come to court? It might be thought that there is something perverse or even incoherent in wanting to stage an assessment of the value of truth. Considering truth as a property of beliefs, the very idea of a belief seems to incorporate that of its aiming at truth. Truth is what we want out of our beliefs, and essentially so: an attitude of wanting, trying, or hoping to acquire false beliefs would be a

---

[12] For an excellent discussion of the same issues, see May (1999, chs. 8 and 9).
[13] See Clark (1990: 181–3).   [14] See *GM* III. 24 and 25 for the ensuing quotations.

non-starter. However, there are other possible interpretations of 'calling the value of truth into question', which focus on the unconditional nature of the valuation. Here are some senses in which truth might be assumed to be unconditionally valuable:

(1) The value of our holding particular beliefs is to be assessed exclusively on one dimension, that of their truth–falsity.

(2) It is without exception better for human beings to hold true beliefs about themselves and the world rather than to entertain false representations of them.

These principles would be called into question by the truth of, respectively:

(1*a*) Our holding particular beliefs may be assessed for its value in enabling and enhancing other aspects of life, a value that can pertain despite the falsity of the beliefs held.

(2*a*) It might at times be better, or at least as good, for human beings to entertain false representations of themselves and the world rather than to have true beliefs about them.

We can find Nietzsche offering critiques of the unconditional value of truth on both these grounds. Thus he comments elsewhere (GS 121) that 'the conditions of life might include error' and that 'life [is] not an argument'—i.e. that the beliefs without which we would be unable to survive are not *eo ipso* proved true. In similar vein:

> We do not consider the falsity of a judgment as itself an objection to a judgment [...] The question is how far the judgement promotes and preserves life, how well it preserves, and perhaps even cultivates, the type. And we are fundamentally inclined to claim that the falsest judgements [...] are the most indispensable to us [...]—that a renunciation of false judgements would be a renunciation of life, a negation of life. To acknowledge untruth as a condition of life: that clearly means resisting the usual value feelings in a dangerous manner.
>
> (BGE 4)

Nietzsche's examples of false judgements here are synthetic judgements a priori, 'the fictions of logic', and 'numbers'. We could not live without carving up the world of our experience into causes and effects, measurable quantities, reidentifiable substances as opposed to properties, and so on. To ask in what sense these categorizations are false raises difficult questions for

Nietzsche interpreters.[15] The immediate question, however, is not whether such beliefs, or all beliefs, are false, but whether being true or false is the sole criterion of value for beliefs. And it is clear that the passage just cited commits Nietzsche to a denial of 1, and to support for 1a—beliefs or judgements can be valuable 'for life' and for the various purposes of human beings, *despite* their being false; the truth or falsity of beliefs can matter less than what the holding of beliefs allows us to achieve. (Note too that this is antithetical to pragmatism about truth. Being useful or life-promoting does not constitute being true; the two are quite distinct properties of beliefs or judgements.[16])

Another common thought in Nietzsche is that there is value in deliberately created fictions, false pictures that are valuable to us not despite, but *in virtue* of, their falsity. An example is the well-known aphorism 'Truth is ugly: *we possess art* lest we perish of the truth'.[17] In the Third Treatise, Nietzsche states that 'art, in which precisely the *lie* hallows itself, in which the *will to deception* has good conscience on its side, is much more fundamentally opposed to the ascetic ideal than is science' (*GM* III. 25). On the same broad theme one might also cite several passages in *The Gay Science*:

if we convalescents still need art, it is *another kind* of art—a mocking, light, fleeting, divinely untroubled, divinely artificial art [...] we have grown sick of this bad taste, this will to truth, to 'truth at any price', this youthful madness in the love of truth [...] today we consider it a matter of decency not to wish to see everything naked, to be present everywhere, to understand and 'know' everything.

(GS, Preface, 4)

Had we not approved of the arts and invented this type of cult of the untrue, the insight into general untruth and mendacity that is now given us by science—the insight into delusion and error as a condition of cognitive and sensate existence—

---

[15] Such judgements would count as false if we were entitled to the assumption that there exists a 'true world' beyond our experience, and that it lacks the structure and organization with which we invest 'this world' of ours, the empirical world. Clark (1990) argues that Nietzsche tended to make this assumption early in his career and finally, at least in *TI*, abandoned it (see *TI*, 'How the True World Finally Became a Fable'). Others have pointed out that passages claiming that every judgement is a falsification persist throughout Nietzsche's writings alongside passages that passionately urge the need to strive for truth. For a clear recent discussion, see Anderson (2005: 185–92).

[16] This in response to the suggestion by Danto that 'Nietzsche ... advanced a pragmatic criterion of truth: p is true and q is false if p works and q does not' (Danto 1965: 72). I suppose that this line no longer enjoys currency, despite Nehamas's statement that 'no other view has won more adherents over the last thirty years' (Nehamas 1998: 242 n. 50).

[17] KSA xiii. 500 (n. 16 [40] (1888), previously pub. as *WP* 822).

would be utterly unbearable. *Honesty* would lead to nausea and suicide. But now our honesty has a counterforce that helps us avoid such consequences: art, as the *good* will to appearance.

(*GS* 107)

And it is not only the practice of art as such that Nietzsche values in this manner, but a creative attitude towards the world and ourselves that we can extrapolate from art:

What means do we have for making things beautiful, attractive, and desirable when they are not? And in themselves I think they never are! Here we have something to learn [...] from artists, who are really constantly out to invent new artistic *tours de force* of this kind. To distance oneself from things until there is much in them that one no longer sees and much that the eye must add *in order to see them at all*, or to see things around a corner and as if they were cut out and extracted from their context, or to place them so that each partially distorts the view one has of the others and allows only perspectival glimpses, or to look at them through coloured glass or in the light of the sunset, or to give them a surface and skin that is not fully transparent: all this we should learn from artists.

(*GS* 299)

To 'give style' to one's character—a great and rare art! It is practised by those who survey all the strengths and weaknesses that their nature has to offer and then fit them into an artistic plan until each appears as art and reason and even weaknesses delight the eye. [...] For one thing is needful: that a human being should *attain* satisfaction with himself—be it through this or that poetry or art; only then is a human being at all tolerable to behold!

(*GS* 290)

The consistent claim of this strand in Nietzsche's thought, which can be traced all the way back to *The Birth of Tragedy*,[18] is that to value truth at the expense of artistic fiction-making and beautification is to render our existence unsatisfying or unbearable. But there is a threat of contradiction lurking here. What is unbearable without artistic beautification? Is it the unvarnished truth about the way things are 'in themselves'? Or is it 'the insight into delusion and error as a condition of cognitive and sensate existence'? Do we need artistic invention to mask a hideous reality we would otherwise confront, or to escape from the horror of knowing that

---

[18] See esp. *BT* 3, 9.

whenever we seek truth we shall be systematically deluded? It is unclear to what extent Nietzsche resolves this tension. Yet in a way the two opposing risks are instances of the same predicament: that of discovering too much truth. Either we discover the truth that the world is nasty, uncaring, and destructive; or we discover the truth that what we are doomed to consider as the truth about the world is forever an illusion. Both outcomes give rise to a pessimism or disillusionment, one over the world's value for us, the other over our own epistemic impotence.

The central idea either way is that the acquisition of truth needs to be tempered—on pain of despair—by the artistic fashioning of beautiful fictions. But now we seem to have moved from considering merely the value of our holding true beliefs, to assessing the contribution that the *pursuit* of truth makes to a life as a whole. If we take *Wissenschaft* as a type of truth-seeking activity, project, or form of life, then a further claim about the unconditional value of truth comes forward for scrutiny:

(3) The pursuit of truths is the single pre-eminently valuable activity for human beings.

The previous discussion should already have cast some doubt over (3), however. For if, like Nietzsche, one holds (1a) and (2a), it is hard to see what grounds there could be for believing (3), rather than

(3a) Other human activities may be more valuable than, or at least of comparable value with, the pursuit of truths.

If we should be at least as concerned with the life-enhancing qualities of our actual beliefs as with their truth, and if creating satisfying fictions is at least as valuable as arriving at true beliefs, then we ought at least to devote some of our energies to artistic fiction-making, and some to shielding a bedrock of beneficial beliefs from too much scrutiny. (The over-examined life is not worth living?) And then there can be no plausible defence of the claim that a life devoted single-mindedly to the pursuit of truths is a life of uniquely superlative or self-sufficient worth.

It is, I suppose, unclear whether there are scientific idealists and anti-Christian immoralists who would subscribe to propositions (1)–(3) and who have neglected to put them under cross-examination. But let us suppose that there are or have been such people: still the question remains why their taking such a stance constitutes their being *exponents of the ascetic ideal*. One part of the answer is that the priestly ideal and the scientific truth-ideal have parity of structure. The priest believes in a realm of higher, divine value, the truth-idealist in the unconditional value of the pursuit and attainment of true beliefs. The priestly ideal holds human life to be a 'wrong path', a worthless existence, and an obstacle that needs to be negated if redemption is to be achieved. The truth-ideal regards the pursuit of true beliefs not as a means to our valuing life but as an end in itself, and deems the sacrifice of other ends and satisfactions that are extraneous to the pursuit of truth as worthwhile and necessary.

But Nietzsche regards the life of disciplined learning not merely as analogous to priestly asceticism but as literally an ascetic life. The unconditional belief in truth obligates a kind of professional abstinence in philosophers:

that stoicism of the intellect that finally forbids itself a 'no' just as strictly as a 'yes'; that *wanting* to halt before the factual, the *factum brutum* [...] that renunciation of all interpretation (of doing violence, pressing into orderly form, abridging, omitting, padding, fabricating, falsifying and whatever else belongs to the *essence* of all interpreting)—broadly speaking, this expresses asceticism of virtue as forcefully as does any negation of sensuality (it is basically only a *modus* of this negation).

(*GM* III. 24)

Negation of sensuality per se is also present in the life of enquiry, for while the priestly ideal labels the multiple instincts and feelings of the natural human being as pernicious, the truth-ideal calls for an attitude that is impersonal, emotionally cold and detached—'a certain *impoverishment of life* is a presupposition here as well as there—the affects become cool, the tempo slowed, dialectic in place of instinct, *seriousness* impressed on faces and gestures' (*GM* III. 25). In this image of enquiry, the goal of attaining truth is unrealizable unless the enquirer can suppress the natural self, that multiplicity of drives and affects that for Nietzsche are the genuine agents of interpretation and knowledge. In this way the unconditional valuation of truth emerges as a genuine version of the ascetic ideal. We posit something external, namely truth, as highest value, and persecute ourselves for our failure to reach up to it. We set up truth 'as God, as highest authority' and in the perpetual pursuit of it still practise a form of self-denial, a truncating of the personality, but one that gives life a point and direction.

It is noteworthy that Nietzsche appears to implicate himself in this very ideal. Just as he personalized his account of the philosopher's need for solitude and self-discipline earlier in the treatise, he now views this 'commendable philosophers' abstinence' from within, from 'too close a proximity perhaps' (*GM* III. 24). And in later works he continues to paint an ascetic picture of his own mode of enquiry:

Truth has had to be fought for every step of the way, almost everything else dear to our hearts, on which our love and our trust in life depend, has had to be sacrificed to it. Greatness of soul is needed for it: the service of truth is the hardest service.

(*A* 50)

Philosophy, as I have so far understood and lived it, means living voluntarily among ice and high mountains [...] How much truth does a spirit *endure*, how much truth does it *dare*? More and more that became for me the real measure of value. [...] Every attainment, every step forward in knowledge, *follows* from courage, hardness against oneself, from cleanliness in relation to oneself.

(*EH*, Preface, 3)

Does Nietzsche then situate his own project within the ascetic ideal he is criticizing? If so, there is no contradiction. It is coherent for Nietzsche to call into question the most advanced methods of enquiry that he has needed to carry him up to a certain point—to kick away the ladder. Enquirers who idealize truth and subordinate their lives to it are the sole contemporary guardians of 'the intellectual conscience' (*GM* III. 24) and Nietzsche is one of them, but what distinguishes him is his realization that their form of enquiry must undermine itself: 'what meaning would *our* entire being have if not this, that in us this will to truth has come to a consciousness of itself *as a problem*?' (*GM* III. 27).

So the scientific truth-ideal is analogous in structure to the ideal of the ascetic priest, and is psychologically parallel in demanding abstinence and detachment from the rest of life. But the assimilation does not rest there, for Nietzsche alleges that the truth-ideal has right at its heart a genuinely *moral* imperative: to be truthful. To be truthful is to tell the truth honestly and fully as one sees it. If holding true beliefs is a potential good, being truthful is a distinct good, and, as Nietzsche alleges in an elegant extended argument in *The Gay Science*, a good *of a distinct kind*. The argument is as follows:[19]

(1) In science truth is valued unconditionally.
(2) The unconditional valuation of truth is *either* the will not to let oneself be deceived (not to hold false beliefs) *or* the will not to deceive, including the will not to deceive oneself.
(3) A prohibition on holding false beliefs could be grounded only in prudential considerations concerning harm and utility.
(4) But in advance of experience it cannot be decided whether holding true beliefs is more advantageous in human existence than holding false beliefs.
(5) So an unconditional valuation of the holding of true beliefs has no grounds.
(6) So the unconditional valuation of truth is the prohibition of deceit, including deceit of oneself.
(7) The unconditional prohibition of deceit is a moral prohibition.
(8) Therefore, the unconditional valuation of truth in science is a moral valuation.

This argument helps us to see why Nietzsche states in the Third Treatise that science never creates values, but must look to a value-ideal from outside itself, and that science is not just similar to the ascetic ideal, but is its latest and purest 'forward-driving force' (*GM* III. 25). Science has the shape it does because it follows a *moral* imperative, whose genesis is in the Christian virtue of truthfulness.

At the close of his discourse on the will to truth, Nietzsche assumes his most minatory prophetic voice and locates himself mid-way through an inexorable process in which Christian values will 'overcome themselves':

All great things perish through themselves, through an act of self-cancellation [...] In this manner Christianity *as dogma* perished of its own morality; in this manner Christianity *as morality* must now also perish—we stand at the threshold of *this* event. Now that Christian truthfulness has drawn one conclusion after the other, in the end it draws its *strongest conclusion*, its conclusion *against* itself; this occurs, however, when it poses the question '*what does all will to truth mean?*' [...] It is from the will to truth's becoming conscious of itself that from now on [...] morality will

---

[19] *GS* 344, a passage to which Nietzsche refers his readers twice in *GM* III. 24.

gradually *perish*: that great spectacle in a hundred acts that is reserved for Europe's next two centuries, the most terrible, most questionable, and perhaps also most hopeful of all spectacles.

(*GM* III. 27)

The continuing questioning of the origins and meanings of morality—Nietzsche's own project—is driven by truthfulness. Without this imperative urging the investigator to complete honesty, however painful and difficult, we would not have been able to reveal the nature of morality and undermine our trust in it. But without the prior dominance of morality itself we would not have had the requisite drive to discover the truth at all costs. Only because our values have been and still remain moral ones can the drive to truth be strong enough to question our values. So we find Nietzsche acknowledging not only that he is included in the ascetic truth-ideal,[20] but that his own formation through the core values of morality itself is a prerequisite of his ability to call the value of moral values into question. Indeed Nietzsche appears here as the instrument of a process that morality is inflicting upon itself.

3 Giving Meaning to Suffering

If religion, morality, philosophy, academic learning, and science have all been re-formations of the same basic ascetic material, driven throughout by a need to devalue ourselves, to diminish our own particular, transient, and vulnerable existence by comparison with some superior and unconditionally valuable entity or state, the question arises: Why? Nietzsche's answer is, in short, that the ascetic ideal enables our existence to be meaningful. The first and last sections of the Third Treatise rehearse the telling formula:

the human will [...] *needs a goal*— and it would rather will *nothingness* than *not* will [...] man was *rescued* by [the ascetic ideal], he had a *meaning* [...] now he could *will* something [...] And, to say again at the end what I said at the beginning: man would much rather will *nothingness* than *not* will.

What then are 'not willing' and 'willing nothingness'? 'Not willing' means, I suggest, becoming goal-less and ceasing to be able to give 'meaning'

---

[20] He says, 'we knowers today, we godless ones and anti-metaphysicians' are included in the ascetic ideal, but who can this mean but himself, since he knows no friends? (See *GM* III. 24, 27.)

to existence. 'Willing nothingness', on the other hand, means the great nihilistic self-negation that Nietzsche explains as

> hatred of the human, still more of the animal, still more of the material, this abhorrence of the senses, of reason itself, this fear of happiness and of beauty, this longing away from all appearance, change, becoming, death, wish, longing itself [...] an aversion to life, a rebellion against the most fundamental presuppositions of life.
>
> (*GM* III. 28)

Why on earth would this be a preferred stance for human beings to occupy? Nietzsche's diagnosis is that by making diverse forms of self-hatred constitutive of our most fundamental conceptions of self, world, and value, we have successfully shielded ourselves from a threatening tide of arbitrariness and pointlessness. We have attained meaning for our suffering, yet done so at the expense of worsening our sufferings:

> [Man] *suffered* from the problem of his meaning. He suffered otherwise as well, he was for the most part a *diseased* animal: but the suffering itself was *not* his problem, rather that the answer was missing to the scream of his question: '*to what end* suffering?' Man, the bravest animal and the one most accustomed to suffering, does *not* negate suffering in itself: he *wants* it, he even seeks it out, provided one shows him a *meaning* for it, a *to-this-end* of suffering. The meaninglessness of suffering, not the suffering itself, was the curse that thus far lay stretched out over humanity—*and the ascetic ideal offered it a meaning*! Thus far it has been the only meaning; any meaning is better than no meaning at all; in every respect the ascetic ideal has been the '*faute de mieux*' *par excellence* there has been thus far. In it suffering was *interpreted*; the enormous emptiness seemed filled; the door fell shut to all suicidal nihilism. The interpretation—there is no doubt—brought new suffering with it, deeper, more inward, more poisonous, gnawing more at life: it brought all suffering under the perspective of *guilt*.[21]

On the basis of this passage one can argue that the final message of the book is deeply humane and liberating. Thus Arthur Danto reads Nietzsche's insight as: 'Suffering really is meaningless, there is no point to it, and the amount of suffering caused by *giving* it a meaning chills the blood to contemplate.'[22] We erect conceptual constructions such as religions, moralities, metaphysical systems, because we feel a need to *interpret* the

---

[21] *GM* III. 28; cf. II. 7 on meaninglessness of suffering.   [22] Danto (1988: 24).

plain and simple first-order sufferings of which life is full. We say, for example: 'We deserve to suffer, because our existence is an affront or transgression against some higher order'; or 'We can be sure that suffering is ultimately tolerable because it would not come to us unless it were meant in fulfilment of some greater purpose'. But such interpretation of the fact of suffering torments us with a new more sophisticated level of suffering. This pattern has indeed been exemplified more than once in the *Genealogy*, in the picture of the self-torture wrought through conceiving ourselves as guilty before God, and in the ascetic priest's ability to reverse the direction of *ressentiment*. For Danto, Nietzsche's diagnosis is that, in satisfying this need to impose meaning on suffering, we have become sick, and that is surely right, given Nietzsche's extensive laments over the 'insane pathetic beast man' and the 'true doom of European health'. Danto claims further that Nietzsche's therapeutic aim is to free us altogether from this need to give suffering a meaning. According to Danto, 'it goes against [our] instinct to believe, what is essentially the most liberating thought imaginable, that life is without meaning', but Nietzsche is urging us to believe just this, to release ourselves from 'meanings which truncate the lives they are supposed to redeem'[23] and to undergo a 're-education and redirection' of the will, 'its return to the goals of simply normal life'.

This reading has a strong appeal. It seems a fitting culmination of Niet-zsche's anti-Christian, anti-metaphysical polemic and an exemplification of the rancour-free tragic wisdom he advocates, facing the harsh and prob-lematic aspects of life with an attitude of joy, without asking that they be redeemed by higher meanings or purposes.[24] And yet there are some questions to pose of Danto's reading. First, do Nietzsche's parting words in the *Genealogy* leave us with the genuine *possibility* of the human will's finding no significance in human suffering, of the will's having no overall direction and leaving existence imbued with no meaning, unable to answer the question *wozu Mensch überhaupt?*—'to what end man at all?' *Could* the human will be so radically altered that it would in future tolerate such a vacuum? Secondly, would Nietzsche really find this a *desirable* outcome? After all, his Second Treatise ended in a climactic evocation of the task of the human of the future, who 'makes the will free again, [and] gives back

---

[23] Ibid. 25, 27.
[24] See *TI*, 'What I Owe to the Ancients', 5. I follow Ridley's conception of tragic wisdom; see Ridley (1997: 23–4).

to the earth its goal and to man his hope'. The human of the future is to redeem humanity precisely from the same will to nothingness—a task beyond Nietzsche, but delegated to his greater literary offspring Zarathustra (*GM* II. 24, 25). In that passage the godless anti-metaphysician is not one who teaches the need to abandon the search for meaning in favour of wanting 'simply normal life', rather one who is strong enough to create new meaning and direction on an ambitious scale. Danto's vision of human beings freed of yearnings for overarching and redemptive meanings is attractive. But the thought of our pursuing nothing but healthily ordinary goals is arguably closer to Nietzsche's notion of 'not willing' than it is to his dream of restoring a goal and a hope to humanity and the whole planet. What would differentiate Danto's human beings from Zarathustra's 'last man', who 'will no longer shoot the arrow of his longing beyond man'?[25] One way to escape from truncating meanings is to eschew all meanings, one way to evade the ascetic ideal is to have no ideals at all, but I am not convinced that it is the way Nietzsche prefers.

Where, then, is the arrow of Nietzsche's longing directed? The close of the *Genealogy* is not explicit on this point, and the book in some ways ends as enigmatically as it began. But his claim that the ascetic ideal is dominant 'for want of anything better' (*faute de mieux*) must surely provoke us to find a more positive alternative, an attitude to one's existence that keeps the will alive without the self-destruction of willing nothingness. In earlier writings Nietzsche locates the antithesis of self-hatred in an 'ideal of the most high-spirited, vital, world-affirming individual' who wants 'what was and what is [...] *just as it was and is* through all eternity' (*BGE* 56), in clear reference to the doctrine of eternal recurrence that was Zarathustra's teaching.[26] He also talks of people becoming 'human beings who are new, unique, incomparable, who give themselves laws, who create themselves!' (*GS* 335) and proclaims that 'one thing is needful: that a human being should *attain* satisfaction with himself—be it through this or that poetry or art' (*GS* 290).

Because he has these goals of aesthetic self-satisfaction and complete self-affirmation I suggest that Nietzsche is not against giving meaning to suffering, but in favour of it. I assume that 'giving meaning' means making

---

[25] Z I, 'Zarathustra's Prologue', 5; trans. Kaufmann.

[26] See Z III, 'On the Vision and the Riddle', 'The Convalescent', 'The Seven Seals', and IV, 'The Drunken Song'; also *GS* 341.

sense to oneself of the existence of something, and that 'giving meaning to suffering' means making sense to oneself of the suffering that occurs in one's life. Nietzsche's notion of giving meaning to suffering must differ crucially from the ascetic ideal in making a sense of suffering that is affirmative of self. But it differs in other ways too. The ascetic ideal generalizes about all human suffering and teaches us to make sense of it within a ready-made metaphysical picture: all human suffering is to be redeemed because of the place of humanity in a universal world-order of values. Nietzsche's ideal differs in that for him the sense we can make of our suffering is *creatively achieved* rather than given, and *personal* rather than universal. Rather than offering a blanket response of *Mitleid* to those who suffer in any way, Nietzsche calls upon us to recognize

the entire economy of my soul and the balance effected by 'misfortune', the breaking open of new springs and needs, the healing of old wounds, the shedding of entire periods of the past [...] that there is a personal necessity of misfortune; that terrors, deprivations, impoverishments, midnights, adventures, risks, and blunders are as necessary for me and you as their opposites; indeed to express myself mystically, that the path to one's own heaven always leads through the voluptuousness of one's own hell.

(GS 338)

Some relatively commonplace reflections support Nietzsche here. People who suffer intensely through illness, betrayal, and isolation (all known to Nietzsche himself) sometimes embrace these misfortunes as an integral component of their lives, as part of what made them who they are, as things that they would go through again if they had to relive their lives—and this affirmativeness is often experienced by others as unintelligible. The sense to be made of such misfortunes cannot be known to any of us in advance and is an individual task in relation to the particularities of each life.

The goals of self-affirmation and aesthetic self-satisfaction that emerge as candidates to counter the ascetic ideal tend in different directions. The ascetic ideal inclines us to despise and feel guilty about large areas of the natural self and its doings, and to wish we were other than we are. In the counter-ideal of self-affirmation Nietzsche imagines this attitude reversed into a positive willing towards the whole self. But if one wants everything about oneself to be as it *is* and everything about one's past experiences and actions to be as it *was*, one wants, implicitly, to affirm the full *truth* concerning oneself without pretence, distortion, omission, or obfuscation, to look life in the face and 'own' it all, terror and tedium included. On the other hand, the ascetic ideal also has at its core the unconditional valuation of truthfulness, and to escape this valuation one would have to pursue the goal of creative *falsifying*—distortion, artifice, stylization—in regard to oneself. In this light aesthetic self-satisfaction looks to be a distinct goal from that of total self-affirmation. If Nietzsche proposes more than one counter-ideal, that in itself should come as no surprise. After all, the more affects we bring to bear upon the interpretation of ourselves the better we shall understand ourselves, and to insist on there being only 'one way' would be to risk perpetrating a new monistic 'deification' rather in the manner of the ascetic ideal itself. But whether self-affirmation and aesthetic self-satisfaction are indeed distinct goals, and whether, if distinct, they are compatible, are among the questions I shall pursue in the final chapter.

14

Beyond Selflessness

In reading Nietzsche's *Genealogy* one encounters an incomparable voice that has permeated many of the cultural dialogues of our age, a mind of great depth and ingenuity, and a literary masterpiece whose power, subtlety, wit, and attention to psychological detail repay almost endless close reading. Nietzsche is that rare philosophical writer to whom one can return again and again, as to a great piece of music, for the sheer fulfilment of hearing the same phrases, yet confident of finding fresh nuances and experiencing new shocks of realization. And maybe this is achievement enough. But in this book I have sought to examine what hypotheses about our moral values Nietzsche puts forward as true in the *Genealogy*, what beliefs and feelings he would have us question and revise, what transformation of values he hopes to foster, and what range of means he adopts towards those ends. I shall close by concentrating on just two broad questions: (1) What attitude or attitudes towards morality might we be persuaded to hold if Nietzsche's writing does its job? (2) What alternative evaluative stances does Nietzsche offer us to replace morality as we call it into question or contemplate the prospect of its gradually perishing?

1 Questions of Persuasion

For most people, I suspect, reading Nietzsche's *Genealogy* does not bring about a radical change in their first-order practical values, not even if they read him closely, repeatedly, and with devotion. Which of us would be influenced to send our children to a school where they were taught that all human beings are not equal? Who would be even slightly tempted to support legislation that rated some people's right to existence a thousandfold (or even twofold) higher than others'? How many would prefer the treatment of the elderly and infirm to be rid of all compassion, or turn to disparaging their colleagues for their selfless contributions to the common good? If we are the kind of reader Nietzsche expected, we will have entered with a bedrock of moral attitudes of broadly Judaeo-Christian character, and though we might happily sneer at the slavishness, reactiveness, and self-torturing sickness he portrays in morality's adherents (and though we may do so even knowing ourselves to be included as targets), reading Nietzsche does not generally remove all or any of those attitudes from us.

This in itself is not a fatal objection to Nietzsche, for a number of reasons that we have encountered above. When Nietzsche predicts that his works will fall largely on deaf ears, it is precisely because morality is, just as he says, so thoroughly embedded in the psyche and culture of the post-Christian West. He views the coming task of changing, reversing, or experimentally questioning our values as one to be undertaken by a few remarkable human beings of great strength and health, while for the remaining masses morality continues to be an appropriate set of values. And because he regards the undermining of morality as a process that morality will inflict upon itself from within, through a hundred acts over two centuries, he cannot expect his own writings to change anyone's values overnight, rather to awaken a clearer consciousness of an inexorable process of decline at the slower-moving level of a whole culture.

However, reading Nietzsche with any degree of sympathy should incline us to regard as fairly convincing a certain picture of the *nature* of moral values, and to the extent that we are convinced here we may be led to question our attitude towards those values we find ourselves continuing to have. Nietzsche persuades us that morality's various tenets and constitutive attitudes are historical constructions, to which there have been (and may still be) genuine alternatives. Placing high value upon compassion, guilt, and the suppression of our more aggressively expansive instincts, believing everyone's well-being to be of equal kind and importance, expecting everyone to be a subject of rational free choice capable of acting similarly and blameable for failure to do so—these are not absolute, eternal, or compulsory attitudes for human beings to hold, but attitudes invented and perpetuated to fulfil a host of functions and needs. It is hard to dismiss this general claim, even if one does not subscribe to every aspect of Nietzsche's master–slave story, his profile of the ascetic priest, or his account of the moralization of bad conscience. The moral attitudes that we now take for granted as *the* values, as the 'values in themselves', were brought into existence and sustained through enormous cultural ingenuity by specific types of human beings, standing in specific power-relations to others, and governed by specific internal drives both innate and learned.

Still, one can argue, the fact that moral values are not *the* values *überhaupt* does not exclude their being the best ones for us to have. That they are a historical construct does not show that their construction was in any way a bad thing, nor does the manner of their construction, whatever its details, decide whether it is good for us to continue having them as ours. To think otherwise is to risk committing the often discussed 'genetic fallacy'. So we might at the very least consider that the historical shifts Nietzsche locates constituted clear progress beyond what went before. This latter thought, as we have seen, is one Nietzsche himself agrees with in some respects. The creation and elaboration of Judaeo-Christian values, centred around the promotion of selflessness, brought about the development of man as an 'interesting' animal with a proper history, gave rise to an inner life, expressed an unparalleled form-creating will on the part of humanity, brought forth cultural products of the highest order, and enabled us to value truthfulness, the very instrument Nietzsche uses in his project of revaluation. However, none of this negates his central charge that morality has caused us to be ill, self-conflicted, self-hating, and deluded in ways that are ugly and unnecessary for us. Morality has fostered weak and reactive tendencies in humans, elevated self-punishment to a supreme good, taught us to loathe and fear large parts of the psyche, inclined us to conform to the lowest common denominator, discouraged creativity and fullness of life, systematically deceived us about the true nature of ourselves, and subordinated the human to spurious 'absolutes' and 'beyonds' posited primarily for the gratification of blaming ourselves over our constitutional inability to live up to them. If there is such a thing as progress in values, in Nietzsche's eyes we have not come nearly as far as we might, and only if morality withers away is there hope of our going further.

One obvious way to counter this Nietzschean diagnosis is to seek reasons for regarding morality in a positive light. Counter-arguments of this kind might be of different strengths: (1) acknowledge the detriments of morality that Nietzsche alleges, but locate distinct advantages that outweigh them; or (2) dismiss the Nietzschean diagnosis as a lurid overstatement, and proceed to show how morality is unambiguously progressive relative to other systems of value; or (3) argue that morality is an indispensable system of value to which, come what may, none can be conceived as superior. Reading Nietzsche should convince most people that the last of these is a case of overambition powered by some questionable drives. But to pursue any of these lines one must follow Nietzsche's chief demand and put forward some criteria for assessing *the value of* our having moral values. One question that then arises is whether there is available any plausible criterion of assessment that does not already presuppose the values of morality itself. For example, someone might claim that morality is the system of values that best serves the interests of humanity. But then those conceptions of humanity's best interests that show morality in a strong light tend to be those that Nietzsche has argued to be part of the very same historical construct. For example, morality might be said to benefit the greatest number of people by its potential to protect them from some degree of suffering they might otherwise be exposed to. But, when we have read the *Genealogy*, we may be persuaded that many of the constituent assumptions here—that suffering is something in principle lamentable about life, that well-being consists chiefly in the absence of suffering, that the well-being of all humans matters equally, that values are preferable the greater the number they benefit—are all part of the same elaborate, contingent body of ideas and attitudes that is morality. If so, these assumptions cannot be accepted as external, non-moral criteria by which to judge morality's value as one system of values in contrast with others.

Another kind of external criterion that we might think to establish independently of morality is that of answering to the best account of human nature. But there are certain conceptions of the human agent that Nietzsche argues, plausibly, to be themselves already moralized, and to mask what would reveal itself to any psychologist scrupulous enough to remove specifically moral categories from his or her descriptive repertoire.[1] For example, someone might think of evaluating morality vis-à-vis other systems of values on the grounds that it recognizes that agents are all alike in being, or at least in being ideally capable of being, motivated by rational ends that transcend their contingent characters and circumstances, and that it assigns praise and blame primarily on the assumption of a

---

[1] See Williams (1994, esp. 239–40).

human capacity for neutral free choice. Nietzsche's claim is that if we persist in holding to such familiar metaphysical conceptions of free agency, subjecthood, and pure rational motivation, we do so because we have a prior affective attachment to moral evaluation, an attachment itself arising from the need to reconcile various negative affects with an inbuilt drive towards discharging strength. In that case, such metaphysical conceptions cannot be used as an independent yardstick by which the moral mode of evaluation is to be defended against competing modes. Similarly again, character traits that morality approves and tends to foster in its adherents, such as compassion, humility, and the various nuanced forms of selflessness to which Nietzsche draws attention, can be appealed to as important virtues or basic goods only *within* the framework of morality itself.

To the extent that we have become thoroughly moralized beings, our intuitions and instincts as well as our theories will be predisposed to favour morality. This is not to say that we cannot justify morality, or some aspects of it, to ourselves. But the *Genealogy* encourages us to think that there is an alternative: that we could in principle escape from these predispositions, and that, if we could arrive at a place where our attachment to morality was suspended and where we might choose it or not as our system of values, some of us at least might find other values more worthy of our allegiance. The enormous challenge of finding an evaluative space outside morality itself is continually apparent to Nietzsche, as witness his evocations of the discomfort and danger, the 'seasickness' and 'dizziness' that his kind of enquirer should be expected to feel before the 'immense new vista' opened up by his works.[2] Nietzsche is clear that such a revaluation demands a wholesale suspension of theory, intuition, and accustomed emotional polarities. It may be that we would find this revaluation ultimately an undesirable or unbearable prospect, or one impossible for us to accomplish. But to have raised the question of its possibility at all is already a powerful and original achievement. And supposing we do not or cannot accomplish such a revaluation, what will be the explanation? Can we acquit ourselves of Nietzsche's allegation that our inability to see past morality is owed to our being imprisoned in inherited affects and having weak and self-conflicting configurations of drives? Reading Nietzsche corrodes our confidence that we will really be able to justify our allegiance to morality in any sense other

---

[2] See esp. *GM*, Preface, 6; and *BGE* 23.

than that of admitting that, given who we are, we are simply unable to give it up.

If Nietzsche persuades, he does so by first luring the reader into that space where conviction in moral values is suspended. Even if we subsequently 'relapse' into moral judgement-making, this experience of suspension allows a practice of self-scrutiny to set in. Nietzsche is hailed by wide consensus as a 'master of suspicion'[3] of equal stature with Marx and Freud: he has taught us not to trust our ingrained assumptions about value, selfhood, history, and philosophy, and given us an unparalleled exhibition of the kind of psychological probing that can unsettle them. This very art of self-suspicion is arguably among Nietzsche's greatest gifts to philosophy, if not the greatest. He reminds philosophers of what, in his view, they should already know—that the greater truthfulness (*Wahrhaftigkeit*) might reside not in the positions they solemnly support with argument, but in 'every little question-mark you put after your special slogans and favorite doctrines (and occasionally after yourselves)' (*BGE* 25). His critique of morality produces not so much a body of doctrine held up for us to believe, as a sharp and versatile working tool that can detach us from accustomed attitudes, enabling us to grasp the psychology and history that underlie them, and to assess their potential worth to us in the present and future.

By his own lights Nietzsche will not have succeeded solely by virtue of convincing readers of the truth of certain propositions about the phenomena of morality. Rather he seeks to enable us in the end, through 'thinking differently', to 'feel differently'. The *Genealogy*, as I have read it, aims for a psychology that is both explanatory and potentially therapeutic. Nietzsche's rhetorical practice throughout indicates at least an implicit awareness that the 'calling into question' of moral values will succeed only if he arouses our affects and enables us to scrutinize them. The situation is perhaps broadly analogous to that concerning the effectiveness of psychoanalysis as described by Freud:

There is an outdated idea…that a patient's sufferings result from a kind of ignorance, and that if only this ignorance could be overcome by effective communi-cation (about the causal links between the illness and the patient's life, about his childhood experience, etc.), a recovery must follow. But the illness is not located

---

[3] The much used phrase comes from Ricœur (1969: 149–50).

in the ignorance itself, but in the foundation of ignorance, the *inner resistances* that are the cause of the ignorance and continue to sustain it …. Explaining what the patient does not know, because he has repressed it, is only one of the steps necessary in preparation for therapy …. However … psychoanalysis cannot manage without such an explanation.[4]

Where then is the 'illness' from which Nietzsche seeks recovery? It lies in the fact that, in the process of self-interpretation of which morality is symptomatic, we disown the vast bulk of what truly composes the self. There is a fundamental pressure within us towards discharging strength and mastering resistances (the 'will of life', 'instinct for freedom', or 'will to power'[5]). When direct discharge of strength upon external objects is frustrated by physical or social impotence, or by the rules of civilized living, this pressure does not cease, but is channelled into higher level activities, into reinterpretations of the suffering to which one is subjected: we interpret those who are strong and self-expressive as culpably evil for failure to refrain from inflicting harm, or we interpret ourselves as perpetually deserving of suffering because we possess instincts that infringe against and alienate us from things we regard as having 'higher' value. Impelled in these interpretations by the affects and drives of what remains our real self, we thus attain a kind of mastery that makes our existence bearable and meaningful, but in the process do violence to ourselves by treating large parts of our natures as alien and hateful. And for Nietzsche these very parts, the drives, the affects, the tendencies to expansion, overcoming, and release of strength are the essence of life. We have fallen into a fundamental conflict here: punishing others and then ourselves for having the very instinctive drives that all the while are governing our interpretative activity, and becoming a kind of creature that can carry on living only by adopting a stance that is life-denying.

Now none of these processes of self-interpretation could have succeeded in enhancing feelings of power unless the real mechanisms that give rise to them were hidden from the interpreters. So, although Nietzsche neither theorizes repression in anything like the Freudian manner nor even has a distinct term for it, something of the kind must be present in his overall psychology. For instance, when he explains the invention of the notion of evil and its passive contrary, moral goodness, as caused by the *ressentiment*

---

[4] Freud (2002: 7).   [5] Cf. *BGE* 259; *GM* II. 17, 18.

that the weak felt in reaction to a conflict between their drives towards dominance and their actual inability to offer retaliation when harmed, it is clear that the inventors of morality cannot present their activity to themselves in these terms. They must believe in the evaluative categories they use. They claim to have no underlying aggression and feel no hatred or *ressentiment*, and are glad to be blessed with the virtue of non-retaliation. They must sustain a false image of themselves that denies the operation of their drives.

Nietzsche expects his thoroughly moralized audience to be captive to the same false image, which must somehow be shattered before we can even entertain the prospect of alternative values. As I have suggested in earlier chapters, bypassing rational judgement and impersonal argument to address us personally at the level of our habitual affective attitudes enables Nietzsche to make the (according to him) true foundation of our moral values vividly apparent, and allows us to experience the connectedness of our evaluations to those of the characters whose affective structure is exposed in the genealogical exercise. This process, I have argued, has the potential to put us in touch with the complexity and ambivalence that characterizes us at the level of drives, and opens the possibility of our suspending and evaluating the appropriateness of our habitual responses. In short, Nietzsche stimulates dormant affects in order to educate us about their explanatory role and lead us to suspend, question, and eventually transform our ways of feeling and valuing. He admittedly never states in so many words that he has devised such a method of persuasion or influence, nor that he is putting it into operation in the *Genealogy*. But I argue that this reading makes Nietzsche's rhetorical practice highly appropriate to his aims, and that it is supported by his insistence, in his more methodological moments, on a personal, emotional approach to enquiry and on allowing as many affects as possible to speak while keeping them in one's control.

2 Alternative Values

Although the *Genealogy*, being a polemic, is greatly more forthcoming about what it opposes than about what should or might replace what it opposes, Nietzsche is concerned that there be superior values to those he has called into question. Such superior values will have to be compatible with Nietzsche's descriptive psychology, and free of the structural self-hatred, self-denial, and inner conflict he has diagnosed as the sickness of morality. Like Plato before him, Nietzsche redescribes the structure of the psyche, finding in it greater complexity than hitherto suspected, uses his redescription to delineate which human beings are, or might be, the most psychologically healthy, and treats this kind of inner health as the standard for what would be the best way to live.

The *Genealogy* gives us principally a negative outline into which any new, superior mode of evaluation would have to fit:

1. It would not be adopted through passive reception from past cultural tradition, but created by agents themselves, and fitted to their own strengths of character.
2. It would not seek to found its values upon beliefs in anything supernatural or non-empirical.
3. It would not take it as given that human beings are essentially rational, psychologically unified, or self-transparent subjects.
4. It would not base value judgements of people on an assumption of their having absolute freedom to act.
5. It would not be motivated in reactive fashion by a drive to label and control others.
6. It would not expect a single criterion of value to apply across all human beings and all human actions.
7. It would not regard any of the human drives and instincts as intrinsically worthy of suppression or eradication.
8. It would not make the assumption that suffering is absolutely bad for human beings.
9. It would not evaluate people or actions in terms of the opposition between egoism and selflessness.

The majority of Nietzsche's gestures towards the kind of evaluative outlook that would satisfy this complex negative specification lie outside the polemical *Genealogy*. They tend to unite around the goal of attaining a maximally positive attitude towards oneself as an individual, considered as standing apart from others.[6] Having no otherworldly characteristics and no

---

[6] Christine Swanton seems right to say that for Nietzsche 'self-love is not resultant on recognizing oneself as *equal* or superior to others in worth, merit, humanity, rationality, or whatever, for it is not derived from comparisons with others. Rather, the activities of a person with self-love are

otherworldly aspirations, Nietzsche's individual would ideally find positive value in that totality of empirical acts, states, and drives that composes him- or herself. But this kind of positive attitude, which in general we might call self-love, has two principal manifestations, which deserve separate consideration: they are *self-affirmation*, or saying yes to one's life in its entirety and in every detail; and aesthetic (or quasi-aesthetic) *self-satisfaction*, the shaping of one's character so that every part of it contributes to a meaningful whole in the manner of a work of art. Our next task is to consider what such attitudes to self can really consist in.

3 Self-Affirmation: The Demon's Test

The classic text for Nietzsche's conception of self-affirmation is this section from *The Gay Science*:

The heaviest weight.—What if some day or night a demon were to steal into your loneliest loneliness and say to you: 'This life as you now live it and have lived it you will have to live once again and innumerable times again; and there will be nothing new in it, but every pain and every joy and every thought and sigh and everything unspeakably small or great in your life must return to you, all in the same succession and sequence—even this spider and this moonlight between the trees, and even this moment and I myself. The eternal hourglass of existence is turned over again and again, and you with it, speck of dust!' Would you not throw yourself down and gnash your teeth and curse the demon who spoke thus? Or have you once experienced a tremendous moment when you would have answered him: 'You are a god, and never have I heard anything more divine.' If this thought gained power over you, as you are it would transform and possibly crush you; the question in each and every thing 'Do you want this again and

expressive of a solid bonding with herself, devoid of self-contempt' (Swanton 2003: 135–6). On the other hand, Nietzsche consistently advocates the 'pathos of distance' (see *BGE* 257; *GM* I. 2, III. 14; *TI*, 'Expeditions of an Untimely Man', 37; *A* 43, 57): the 'enhancement' of humanity demands social conditions in which the few of higher caste and quality can unashamedly look down upon the rest. Only in such conditions, Nietzsche claims, did the nobles of *GM* I gain the right to consider themselves 'good'; and only in such conditions can one aspire to 'reverence towards oneself' and to 'expansions of distance within the soul'. Thus it may be—though Nietzsche gives no thought to this when discussing affirming one's entire life or giving style to one's character (*GS* 341, 290)—that his ideals of self-affirmation and self-satisfaction could be realized only in a society that fosters caste-like distinctions. But, even if that is so, it need not be the case that one affirms or is satisfied with oneself *on the grounds that* one is superior to others. It is rather that one's superiority to others is expressed in one's ability for self-affirmation and self-satisfaction.

innumerable times again?' would lie on your actions as the heaviest weight! Or how well disposed would you have to become to yourself and to life *to long for nothing more fervently* than for this ultimate eternal confirmation and seal?

(GS 341)

Here I shall not discuss the notorious notion of eternal return (or recurrence) per se, nor even the question whether the thought of eternal return is, in the way Nietzsche believes, a good test of the degree of one's self-affirmation.[7] My aim is simply to clarify the attitude of self-affirmation itself, the state of 'being well disposed to oneself and to life' that Nietzsche proposes can be tested by this thought. However, I agree in two respects with a broad understanding of the eternal recurrence favoured by Maudemarie Clark and Alexander Nehamas among others:[8] (1) that the truth of the cosmological proposition that every event recurs eternally is not required for Nietzsche's purposes in this passage (or in any of his published references to the idea of eternal recurrence); (2) that the function of imagining the reaction one would have, if one were to entertain the idea of eternal recurrence, is that of testing one's attitude to one's actual life.[9]

As we read 'The Heaviest Weight' we are apt to focus on the extreme polarity of possible reactions Nietzsche canvasses: despair versus elation. But it is worth noting that these reactions are imagined in two distinct instantiations. In the first instance Nietzsche envisages someone struck all at once in a vulnerable and disoriented moment by the scenario of infinite repetition, which is announced so as to carry an air of authoritativeness, but comes into no intelligible connection with their overall rational

[7] There are various conceivable positions here. One might hold (1) that the test of facing up to the thought of eternal return is essential to Nietzsche's conception of self-affirmation; or (2) that, even though affirmation is characterizable without recourse to eternal return, confronting the thought of eternal return would be one way genuinely to test the degree of such affirmation. On the other hand, one might claim (3) that the eternal return scenario is not a coherent thought-experiment and/or is a prospect one should remain indifferent to, and hence that it would not provide any good or worthwhile test of affirmation; or most negatively (4) that Nietzsche's trespassing on the ground of eternal return at all spoils and interferes with his conception of affirmation. All these positions are compatible with my claim in the text that Nietzsche has an intelligible conception of *self-affirmation* that might somehow be tested. Both negative challenges (3) and (4) are found in Ridley (1997). The more or less standard objection (3) is found, for example, in Simmel (1986); Danto (1965); Soll (1973); Nehamas (1985); Clark (1990). For a fuller list—and a defence of the coherence and significance of eternal recurrence—see Loeb (2006). [8] Clark (1990: 245–86); Nehamas (1985, esp. 150–1).

[9] As Nehamas puts it, 'what [Nietzsche] is interested in is the attitude one must have toward oneself in order to react with joy and not despair to the possibility the demon raises' (Nehamas 1985: 151); and, as Clark puts it, 'A joyful reaction would indicate a fully affirmative attitude towards one's (presumably, nonrecurring) life' (Clark 1990: 251).

understanding of the world.[10] The imagined reactions to the demon's scenario are immediate affective responses: an 'Oh yes!' or an 'Oh no!' With this kind of reaction it is not relevant whether the scenario to which one reacts makes sense on critical scrutiny, or whether one has good reason to react in any particular way to it. It is more that, suddenly taken off one's guard, one evinces one's true feelings—perhaps in the way that an unexpected quickening of the pulse or sinking of the stomach upon meeting an acquaintance purely by chance might uncover a depth of feeling towards that person that was as yet inaccessible to oneself. In the last two sentences of the section, however, Nietzsche is talking about a different instance: a huge transformation in one's life, a long-sustained attitude of joy or despair towards oneself. He asks: Would it be crushingly burdensome or fervently desirable if 'this thought gained power over you'? 'This thought' (*jener Gedanke*, more literally *that* thought, or *the previous* thought) must refer back to what the demon first said: 'This life as you now live it and have lived it you will have to live once again and innumerable times again.' The thought's gaining power over you suggests a persistent reliving of the imagined scenario of repetition, but also a prioritizing of the relived experience, its becoming vital to confront the thought as constantly as one can.[11]

The least obvious point in the passage is, arguably, in its last sentence. Something is *longed for* as an 'ultimate eternal confirmation and seal', but what? Is the object of my longing (1) *that my life repeat itself* again and innumerable times again? Or (2) *that I keep confronting the question* whether I would want each and every thing again eternally? Or (3) *that I should react with joy* every time the question comes to me? I suggest that both (2) and (3) must come into play to make the 'longing' intelligible. The character addressed in this passage is portrayed as desiring to have something *confirmed*, and it is quite mysterious how (1) on its own could be a confirmation of anything at all. On the other hand, *my being apprised of* the fact that I would in all cases want my life again and again would provide me with strong

---

[10] See Clark (1990: 251).

[11] If the thought of eternal return is itself an incoherent thought, as many allege (see n. 7 above), then its use as a test in a moment of vulnerable confusion may be defensible. But it is much less appealing to envisage that I should make it a matter of lifelong policy to keep on confronting myself with a thought and never reflect on its coherence, or that I should realize its incoherence and carry on regardless with the attempt to test myself against it.

evidence of my being well disposed to life and self in high degree. (2) and (3) coalesce, in fact, into one complex object of longing: I long *to confront myself repeatedly with the demon's scenario* and, whatever life may bring me, *always to react to it with joy.*

Bernd Magnus has offered a particular reading of Nietzsche's proposed affirmative attitude to life, and has raised a serious objection against it. For Magnus, Nietzsche's affirmative person must 'love each moment *simpliciter*', rather than '[view] each moment holistically ... as a necessary blemish in ... the scenario of her total life'.[12] On this reading, Nietzsche thinks of an affirmation of *each* moment, experience, or action *for its own sake.* And Magnus takes this to mean that you should 'have just the same attitude towards the cataloged moments of your greatest anguish that you [are] asked to imagine of your most cherished sexual ecstasy'.[13] If this is the right reading, then Nietzsche is open to the objection Magnus makes: that the thought of loving each moment unconditionally for its own sake, no matter whether it be sublimest ecstasy or deepest trauma, manifests an attitude impossible for any human being to adopt. The objection is, put simply, that you can't always want what you get. That would be 'a self-consuming human impossibility',[14] something that no human being would be able to sustain as a psychological attitude. The thought of affirming each and every moment of one's life with equal vehemence is, as Magnus says, truly 'abysmal':[15] in trying to imagine someone capable of standing outside the ordinary ebb and flow of positive and negative to which we are all subject, we encounter an outlook so lofty and vertiginous as to be inhuman.

I would like to propose an alternative reading, the key to which is to distinguish pro- and con-attitudes of different orders. Numerous events in any life will be undergone, remembered, or anticipated with a negative first-order attitude; but that is compatible with a second-order attitude of acceptance, affirmation, or positive evaluation towards one's having had these negative experiences. If in some course of events one is, say,

---

[12] Magnus (1988a: 171).   [13] Ibid. 172.

[14] Ibid. We might wonder if there is also a conceptual impossibility here, whether on pain of contradiction one could not affirm in the same manner both what is deeply distressing and what amounts to a positive or fulfilling experience.

[15] This is Nietzsche's own word (*abgründlich*) for the thought, but taken with a negative connotation by Magnus. See *Z*, 'Of the Vision and the Riddle'; *EH*, 'Why I Am So Wise', 3 (though the latter passage is not translated by Kaufmann—see *KSA* vi. 268).

humiliated, one's experience is as such unwelcome, painful, and so on: obviously it could not be exactly a humiliation that one underwent, unless one's primary or first-order attitude were set against, rather than for, the course of events. But instead of asking fruitlessly whether you can undergo humiliation as something positive, Nietzsche poses a different question: Would you be well enough disposed to want your life again, where that (second-order) wanting would embrace among its objects the particular hateful and excruciating humiliation from which you suffered? Facing this question is intelligible, indeed humanly possible. Answering yes to the whole of one's life in this way is scarcely easy for all human beings, but that is no objection for Nietzsche, who is searching for an extremely demanding ideal and looking to discriminate the rare few from the herd.

Nietzsche could imagine an alternative, counterfactual life without his crippling illnesses and disastrous personal involvements, without his sister's espousing the anti-Semitism (or the particular anti-Semite) that he detested, without a future in which he collapsed into a wretched final decade of insanity. On the reading canvassed by Magnus, he must aspire towards wanting each of these misfortunes for its own sake, in just the way he wanted the exhilarations of mountain air, the fulfilments of writing, or the rare peace of an untroubled sleep. On my reading, this is unnecessary. Nietzsche could, if he were strong enough,[16] wholly affirm his life while discriminating those of its contents that are against his will, negative, suffered, from those to which he has a first-order pro-attitude. Indeed he must make this discrimination: it is necessitated by the way he sometimes talks of affirmation. Consider the 'affirmation of life even in its strangest and sternest problems' in the final section of *Twilight of the Idols*,[17] and the associated conception of the tragic outlook as 'an intellectual predilection for what is hard, terrible, evil, problematic in existence, arising from well-being, overflowing health, the *abundance* of existence'.[18] If one is full enough and healthy enough to affirm what is hard, terrible, and problematic *as* hard, terrible, and problematic, then one must affirm it as something *suffered*.

---

[16] As Loeb (2005: 74) points out, Nietzsche confesses that he would not be able to fulfil the ideal he sets up: 'as we know from his notes, letters, and published works, Nietzsche does not regard himself as strong or healthy enough to affirm his life's eternal recurrence: "I do not want life *again*. How have I borne it? Creating. What has made me endure the sight? the vision of the *Übermensch* who *affirms* life. I have tried to affirm it *myself*—alas!" (*KSA* 10:4[81]).'

[17] *TI*, 'What I Owe to the Ancients', 5. Nietzsche also quotes this passage again in *EH*, 'The Birth of Tragedy', 3.   [18] *BT*, 'Attempt at a Self-Criticism', 1.

So the question for Nietzsche is whether second-order affirmation can stretch to embrace everything to which one's first-order response is negative. Magnus says that 'each of us would affirm the eternal recurrence of our lives only selectively'; 'Who among us', he asks, 'would not prefer some other possible life and world, no matter how content we may be with our present lot? ... no matter how content I may be with my life I can always imagine a better one.'[19] But note that there are two distinct points here. The latter assertion is likely to be correct for most human beings: they can usually imagine a better life. But this does not answer the first question Magnus poses, whether any of us would *prefer* some other possible life and world. For it could be that someone able to *imagine* a better life nevertheless *affirms* and *loves* nothing other than his or her actual life. I argue that this is what Nietzsche has in mind—that one could be strong enough to love everything about one's single, actual life, not *wanting* or *wishing for* anything that is merely imagined, or imaginable, however good that might have been.

In general there is no logical difficulty about being able to imagine a better X, but preferring the X one actually has. I can imagine a better car than mine, but that is not incompatible with my fervently wanting to keep my car in preference to others. Cognizance of some defect does not necessitate detachment of preference. We can identify a kind of preference for something *because it is mine*, in the sense not of property ownership, but of affective belonging, a weaker analogue of attaching to something that one loves. And in the case of love proper, many of us can probably *imagine* a friend or a parent or a lover being better—lacking certain faults as a person—without thereby being constrained to *wish* that we had as friend, parent, or lover someone who lacked these faults. I can be attached to things in a quite basic and intelligible way because they are my own, intimately a part of my personal world.

Nietzsche's affirmative ideal is to 'own' oneself without remainder: to be so intimately attached to everything about oneself—for no other reason than its simply being oneself—that no imagined possibilities are wished for in preference to the actuality. 'One must learn to love oneself with a sound and healthy love, so that one may endure it with oneself and not go roaming about' (Z III, 'Of the Spirit of Gravity', 2). The Nietzschean

---

[19] Magnus (1988a: 170, 172).

self-affirmer is a deliberate counter to the total life-denier idealized by Schopenhauer,[20] but unlike his or her antipode Nietzsche's ideal is not someone possessed of a 'correct' recipe for life who sets him- or herself a priori to affirm just whatever happens. Nietzschean affirmation responds to 'the question in each and every thing "Do you want *this*?" '—each part of one's actual individual life as it unfolds is the potential occasion of a renewed test. So the object of fervent longing—that ultimate confirmation and seal—is systematically elusive. At any point, right up until its end, life could become too difficult to affirm. But what is important for Nietzsche is not whether one ever reaches a point of absolute certainty concerning one's well-disposedness to oneself, rather that one *longs for* such a confirmation, aspires towards an ideal of self-affirmation in which one is able to affirm all of the particular parts of one's life until these affirmations amount to an affirmation of it all. This ideal is—I have argued—humanly possible, coherent to imagine, and a genuine alternative to the self-denial Nietzsche has argued to lie at the heart of our moral evaluations.

4 Facing or Fashioning?

There also occur passages in Nietzsche[21] where the ideal human being is a kind of artist, someone who shapes, edits, or fixes up the details of his or her life and character in pursuit of 'satisfaction with himself—be it through this or that poetry or art' (GS 290) or someone like Goethe of whom one can say, 'he disciplined himself to a whole, he *created* himself' (TI, 'Expeditions of an Untimely Man', 49). The most extended and probably most discussed example of creative self-formation occurs in the passage in *The Gay Science* 290 concerning 'giving style to one's character', in which a complex metaphor assigns multiple roles to the self: there are the natural

---

[20] As suggested, for example, in BGE 56.

[21] We have already seen Nietzsche advocate the application to life of artistic activities such as 'distancing oneself from things until there is much in them that one no longer sees', 'seeing things around a corner and as if they were cut out and extracted from their context', 'placing things so that each partially distorts the view one has of the others and allows only perspectival glimpses' (GS 299). Elsewhere he speaks of '*creating* something out of oneself that the other can behold with pleasure: a beautiful, restful, self-enclosed garden perhaps' (D 174) and advises that 'One can dispose of one's drives like a gardener and, though few know it, cultivate the shoots of anger, pity, curiosity, vanity as productively as a beautiful fruit tree on a trellis; one can do it with the good or bad taste of a gardener' (D 560).

strengths and weaknesses of character that are present as a given to be worked upon (the raw material), the form-giving agent (the artist) who creates beauty out of this material, the finished product itself (the art work), and the locus of a satisfaction felt in contemplation of the product (the spectator).[22]

Here Nietzsche's conception of self-satisfaction is dynamic: he emphasizes the *transition* from raw material to beautiful form, the *work* that this requires, the *achievement* of satisfaction by one's own exertions. And it is consonant with Nietzsche's frequent linkage of art with falsehood, deception, lying, and so on (all done with a good conscience)[23] that the 'artistic' activities involved in the transformative achievement embody various ways of falsifying oneself. Thus:

a great and rare art! It is practised by those who survey all the strengths and weaknesses that their nature has to offer and then fit them into an artistic plan until each appears as art and reason and even weaknesses delight the eye. Here a great mass of second nature has been added; there a piece of first nature removed—both times through long practice and daily work at it. Here the ugly that could not be removed is concealed; there it is reinterpreted into sublimity. Much that is vague and resisted shaping has been saved and employed for distant views—it is supposed to beckon towards the remote and immense. In the end, when the work is complete, it becomes clear how it was the force of a single taste that ruled and shaped everything great and small [...] one thing is needful: that a human being should *attain* satisfaction with himself—be it through this or that poetry or art.

(*GS* 290)

In the ideal of self-affirmation (or so we assumed above) things were different: the acceptance of the whole *truth* of one's life—what was and is—was to be embraced without flinching, without escape or erasure. But now the self-satisfaction to be attained through artistry consists in actively making one's character pleasing by falsifying it. We seem once more to have struck upon a deep vein of ambivalence towards truth in Nietzsche. The ultimate test of being well disposed to oneself is to confront the whole truth and love it; but the one thing needful is to modify and dissimulate so as to find oneself satisfying and beautiful. How to address this tension, or apparent tension?

---

[22] *BGE* 225 attributes a similar complexity to the self: 'in humans there is material, fragments, abundance, clay, dirt, nonsense, chaos; but in humans there is also creator, maker, hammer-hardness, spectator-divinity and seventh day'.   [23] See *GM* III. 25; *GS* 107, 299.

First, one might argue that self-affirmation and aesthetic self-satisfaction do not after all exclude or oppose one another. Perhaps one is encompassed in the other. What is 'this life' whose recurrence the demon offers me as inviting affirmation or horrified recoil? One could read it as my actively created life-narrative, the self I tell myself I am and have been. From one point of view—one that can seem eminently Nietzschean ('there are no facts, only interpretations'[24])—this is all the self I can have anyway. On this reading, I am asked to affirm my life under a construction in which it makes greatest sense to me, to construe it as, and thereby create it as, a whole in which I can take satisfaction. The 'tremendous moment' of self-affirmation would be one in which my narrative self-interpretation made the most complete sense to me as an artistic unity. Such a view is suggested by Alexander Nehamas, who elucidates the 'giving style' passage with the words:

The value of everything depends on its contribution to a whole of which it can be seen as a part … But what is it to affirm the whole of which all these features and events *have been made* parts? [my emphasis] The answer is provided by the thought of the eternal recurrence … the thought that if one were to live over again, one would want the very life one has already had, exactly the same down to its tiniest detail, and nothing else.[25]

This can be taken to imply that the life wanted again in its tiniest detail is a whole to which one has *artificially given* stylistic unity. However, we may doubt whether the constituent ideas in this picture can fit together so comfortably.

First, the presentation of the eternal return, with its invitation to affirm isolated momentary experiences such as that of the moonlight, the trees, and the spider, evokes not so much a crafted unity where every part makes sense in the whole, but rather a joyful acceptance of a different sort of wholeness: a total set of experiences whose connectedness amounts solely to their all being mine. Secondly, the eternal return scenario and the related notion of loving fate—'My formula for greatness in a human being is *amor fati* [love of fate]: that one wants nothing to be different, not forward, not backward, not in all eternity. Not merely bear what is necessary, still less

---

[24] See *WLN* 139 (n. 7 [60] (1886–7), previously pub. as *WP* 481).
[25] Nehamas (1998: 142). For Nehamas's fullest account of these issues, see Nehamas (1985, chs. 5 and 6).

conceal it [...] but *love* it'[26]—both emphasize confrontation with something that we might dare to call a real self, the necessary aspect of what one is and was, the unchangeability of one's life. And thirdly, in his frequent naturalistic mode Nietzsche is clear that what constitutes the individual is a composite of hierarchically related drives. That is what I *am*, whether I like or not, indeed whether I know it or not, for 'However far a man may go in self-knowledge, nothing [...] can be more incomplete than his image of the totality of *drives* which constitute his being' (*D* 119). The arrangement of drives that is myself is not typically conceived as something I have made into a whole, but rather is conceived as a unity (or in many cases a disunity) that has organized itself. What I must love if I am to affirm myself is the insuperable necessity of this unchosen self, and the one unalterable life-trajectory I follow through having it or being it.

A second way to address the tension between confronting the truth and fashioning the self is to collapse it in the other direction, on the grounds that self-fashioning *presupposes* truthfulness about oneself. The process of 'giving style to one's character' begins with something called 'surveying all the strengths and weaknesses that one's nature has to offer'. This implies not only that there is a 'pre-artistic' self, a raw material waiting to be given form, but that, in order to highlight or disguise the elements in one's character appropriately, one has to have apprehended a great deal (in principle everything) about one's nature, knowing it accurately enough to grasp whether some particular part is a strength or a weakness, attractive or ugly, and, if ugly, whether it will respond best to removal, concealment, or viewing from a distance. On this reading, 'giving style to one's character' rides on the back of truthfulness. It is a kind of fulfilling game of pretence with the truth always in view, a response to the challenge of giving a pleasing aspect to something one already accepts as unchangeable. What may seem dubious and even repellent in this interpretation, however, is the degree of 'doublethink' it appears to demand of the person who attains self-satisfaction. I have to be fully apprised of my weakness and ugliness of character, while simultaneously revelling in a patent dissimulation in which I appear as something beautiful to behold.

A third approach is to acknowledge that truthful affirmation and artistic style-giving are distinct ideals pulling in opposite directions, but to hold

---

[26] *EH*, 'Why I Am So Clever', 10.

that this very tension is a strength of Nietzsche's position. Recalling his treatment of the ascetic ideal, one should expect Nietzsche not to assign unconditional value to being truthful. But why insist on his flipping over into an unconditional valuation of untruthfulness? A more Nietzschean position is that there is no 'one way' to value oneself: facing the truth about oneself has value in the quest for a positive meaning to individual existence, but so too does the fictionalizing or falsifying of self that can be learned from artists. The same duality accords well with Nietzsche's perspectivism: it is fitting that one should, as it were, have in one's power both one's ability to confront oneself full-on and one's artistry in falsifying oneself, and be able to shift them in and out.

Finally, we may suggest an approach that distinguishes the ideals of truthful self-affirmation and artistic self-satisfaction but unites them into a more harmonious and noble strategy. Nietzsche writes in *Beyond Good and Evil* that someone's strength of spirit could be measured by 'how much of the "truth" he could withstand—or, to put it more clearly, to what extent he *needs* it to be thinned out, veiled over, sweetened up, dumbed down, and lied about' (*BGE* 39). Aaron Ridley offers the following reading:

every character needs sooner or later to deceive itself, and Nietzschean truthfulness can only ever be taken so far, no matter how much strength of spirit one has. And if this is right, the last role of truthfulness is truthfully to surrender to the necessity of deceiving oneself, having stood firm against one's heart's desire to capitulate sooner. Style, on this reading, is not so much a matter of opportunistic self-exculpation as the (honest) last resort of a soul that can face no more. ('As an aesthetic phenomenon existence is still *bearable* for us' [*GS* 107].)[27]

Both the capacity to withstand unveiled, unsweetened truth and the art of giving a unified style to one's character are signs of strength for Nietzsche.[28] The strong character faces as much truth as is bearable, but, inevitably failing to some degree, uses his or her artistry as a self-interpreter to reshape the truth into something pleasing. So, as Ridley says, we should not think of the stylizing and deceiving ideal as a licence to concoct some wholesale gratifying fiction about oneself. Seen in this way, the wholeness of self-affirmation and the wholeness of self-styling are both manifestations of the same high ideal of intellectual conscience.

---

[27] Ridley (1998: 140).
[28] Compare *BGE* 39's 'strength of spirit' and *GS* 290's 'strong and domineering natures'.

5 Question Marks after Ourselves

A theme that has arisen at various points in this book is Nietzsche's critique of philosophical and scholarly enquiry itself. The *Genealogy* begins with the notion that 'we knowers' are estranged from ourselves because we have not sought to know ourselves, and ends with an invitation to remove a mainstay of traditional knowledge-gathering: the unconditional valuation of holding, telling, and pursuing the truth. Nietzsche has a radical message for philosophers and 'scientific' investigators: your conception of your own activity is at fault because you picture yourselves falsely. There is no primary drive towards knowledge and truth. We philosophers are composed of many affects and drives, and the notion of a rational self or knowing subject engaged in a self-validating exercise of pure dialectical truth-seeking is as much an insidious illusion as the notion of a realm of timeless objects waiting to be discovered. Disinterested, detached knowing is a fiction, but a persistently tempting one that we must struggle to guard ourselves against.

However, we should not think of these diagnostic warnings to philosophers as merely some extra, peripheral theme of the *Genealogy*, quite separate from its central attack on moral values. In the Third Treatise atheistic truth-seeking disciplines are revealed as the purest manifestation of the ascetic ideal, and Nietzsche seeks to show how our aspirations to *philosophical* versions of selflessness, our ambitions towards disinterestedness—freedom from affect, impersonality, universality, the single perspectiveless truth, the project of pure enquiry—all stem from deep-seated valuations that are of a piece with morality itself. That philosophers pursue the truth for its own sake, that they succeed in speaking with a universal voice freed from the influence of non-rational drives and prejudices, that pure impersonal dialectic will reliably reach an answer to the question how best to live—these are self-serving distortions. The metaphors of universality, impersonality, and purity with which they have liked to portray themselves also arise out of the valuations peculiar to morality, and philosophy in turn can function as a source of rationalizations with which morality defends itself. Along with the values of morality, philosophers need to put themselves in question. If they understood how enquiry is beholden to valuations, and valuations to affects and drives, if they enquired more into themselves and made their many affects 'useful for knowledge' instead of trying to evade them, they might be less estranged from themselves and not detach knowledge from 'life'.

I have tried to suggest that Nietzsche's persistent refusal to write conventional philosophy is more than a superficial stylistic idiosyncrasy. For him it makes a crucial difference to one's success *as a thinker* whether one is personally involved in one's subject matter, whether one is capable of occupying many differing perspectives and identifying with diverse affects, whether one's deepest and most unflattering feelings are allowed a voice in one's campaign to understand oneself and try to live better. It is in pursuit of his aims of redescribing and reorienting the individual human soul, or the souls of some possible human individuals, that Nietzsche employs the manifold resources of his rhetoric, his subtle and unsubtle provocations, his confessions, autobiographical excursions, self-analysis, self-invention, and all kinds of literary artistry. My guess is that most people who admire Nietzsche and wish to study him at any length feel themselves in some way personally addressed and uplifted by his writings, have their imaginations captivated by his poetic images, are stunned and/or delighted by his barbed critiques, and feel they are gaining insights that are hard to state precisely outside the medium of his words. The characteristic experience, I suspect, is less that of being ensnared by brilliant rhetoric into formulating better philosophical propositions for an essay or journal article, more that of a persistent challenging and expanding of what it is to address philosophical issues.

So reading Nietzsche's *Genealogy* might lead us to reflect creatively on the modes of enquiry that will best fit us to improve our self-understanding and explore how we might live. If Nietzsche's picture of the psyche and his accounts of the genealogy of our moral and intellectual values are even worth entertaining as true hypotheses, then philosophers should not take it for granted that by being philosophers they are somehow in possession of a complete method for conducting ethical enquiry. It is not a matter of whether to imitate Nietzsche's style, a worthless dead-end which Nietzsche rightly discourages and makes virtually impossible; nor of a fruitless attempt to abandon the methods of reason altogether—after all, Nietzsche's own examples of things for which it is worth living on earth are 'virtue, art, music, dance, reason, intellect', and the admired wholeness of a Goethe embraces 'reason, sensuality, feeling, will'.[29] The real questions concern the intellectual endeavour to learn what to value in life: Is dialectical argument ever self-sufficient in this endeavour? Could we ever discover truly universal values? Must each investigator of values be prepared to disclose and reflect upon his or her intensely personal and deep-lying affects? Is there any really worthwhile divide between psychology and philosophy, or between philosophy and imaginative literature? Philosophers may be tempted to view Nietzsche as only a philosopher, someone concerned to propound and argue for theories about the nature of values, minds, and truths. But this is to ignore the many ways in which, page by page, he puts existing philosophy's efficacy and integrity severely to the test.

[29] *BGE* 188; *TI*, 'Expeditions of an Untimely Man', 49.

Bibliography

Works by Nietzsche

German Texts

Kritische Studienausgabe, ed. Giorgio Colli and Mazzino Montinari, 15 vols (Munich: Deutscher Taschenbuch Verlag and Walter de Gruyter, 1988).

Sämtliche Briefe. Studienausgabe, ed. Giorgio Colli and Mazzino Montinari, 8 vols (Munich: Deutscher Taschenbuch Verlag and Walter de Gruyter, 1986).

Translations

Note: *indicates a translation from which I quote unless otherwise stated. On occasion I have departed from these translations, either adopting parts of other published translations or supplying my own. Such instances are always noted.

The Anti-Christ, trans. R. J. Hollingdale (with *Twilight of the Idols*) (Harmondsworth: Penguin, 1968).*

Beyond Good and Evil, ed. Rolf-Peter Horstmann and Judith Norman, trans. Judith Norman (Cambridge: Cambridge University Press, 2002).*

Beyond Good and Evil, trans. Walter Kaufmann (New York: Vintage Books, 1966).

The Birth of Tragedy, ed. Michael Tanner, trans. Shaun Whiteside (Harmondsworth: Penguin, 1990).*

Daybreak, ed. Maudemarie Clark and Brian Leiter, trans. R. J. Hollingdale (Cambridge: Cambridge University Press, 1997).*

Ecce Homo, ed. and trans. Walter Kaufmann (with *On the Genealogy of Morals*) (New York: Vintage Books, 1967).*

The Gay Science, ed. Bernard Williams, trans. Josefine Nauckhoff and Adrian del Caro (Cambridge: Cambridge University Press, 2001).*

Human, All Too Human, trans. R. J. Hollingdale (Cambridge: Cambridge University Press, 1986).*

Nietzsche contra Wagner, in *The Anti-Christ, Ecce Homo, Twilight of the Idols, and Other Writings*, ed. Aaron Ridley, trans. Judith Norman (Cambridge: Cambridge University Press, 2005).

On the Genealogy of Morality, trans. Maudemarie Clark and Alan J. Swensen (Indianapolis: Hackett, 1998).*

On the Genealogy of Morality, ed. Keith Ansell Pearson, trans. Carol Diethe (Cambridge: Cambridge University Press, 1994).

On the Genealogy of Morals, ed. Walter Kaufmann, trans. Walter Kaufmann and R. J. Hollingdale (with *Ecce Homo*) (New York: Vintage Books, 1967).

On the Genealogy of Morals, trans. Douglas Smith (Oxford: Oxford University Press, 1996).

Thus Spoke Zarathustra, trans. R. J. Hollingdale (Harmondsworth: Penguin, 1969).*

Thus Spoke Zarathustra, trans. Walter Kaufmann, in *The Portable Nietzsche*, ed. Kaufmann (New York: Viking, 1954).

Twilight of the Idols, trans. R. J. Hollingdale (with *The Anti-Christ*) (Harmondsworth: Penguin, 1968).*

Untimely Meditations, trans. R. J. Hollingdale (Cambridge: Cambridge University Press, 1983).

The Will to Power, ed. Walter Kaufmann, trans. Walter Kaufmann and R. J. Hollingdale (New York: Vintage Books, 1968).*

Writings from the Late Notebooks, ed. Rüdiger Bittner, trans. Kate Sturge (Cambridge: Cambridge University Press, 2003).*

Other Works

ANDERSON, R. LANIER (2005), 'Nietzsche on Truth, Illusion, and Redemption', *European Journal of Philosophy*, 13: 185–225.

ANSELL PEARSON, KEITH (ed.) (2006), *A Companion to Nietzsche* (Oxford: Blackwell).

—— and LARGE, DUNCAN (eds) (2006), *The Nietzsche Reader* (Oxford: Blackwell).

ATWELL, JOHN E. (1981), 'Nietzsche's Perspectivism', *Southern Journal of Philosophy*, 19: 157–70.

—— (1995), *Schopenhauer on the Character of the World: The Metaphysics of Will* (Berkeley: University of California Press).

BARNES, JONATHAN (2001), *Early Greek Philosophy* (Harmondsworth: Penguin).

BARTHES, ROLAND (1977), 'The Death of the Author', trans. Stephen Heath, in Barthes, *Image Music Text* (London: Fontana), 142–8.

BELL, CLIVE (1995), 'The Aesthetic Hypothesis', in Alex Neill and Aaron Ridley (eds), *The Philosophy of Art: Readings Ancient and Modern* (Boston: McGraw-Hill), 98–110.

BURGARD, PETER (ed.) (1994), *Nietzsche and the Feminine* (Charlottesville: University of Virginia Press).

CALDWELL, RICHARD S. (1987), *Hesiod's Theogony* (Cambridge, Mass.: Focus Information Group).

CARD, CLAUDIA FALCONER (1998), 'Rectification and Remainders', in Edward Craig (ed.), *The Routledge Encyclopedia of Philosophy*, viii (New York: Routledge).

CARROLL, NOËL (2001), *Beyond Aesthetics: Philosophical Essays* (Cambridge: Cambridge University Press).

CARTWRIGHT, DAVID (1988), 'Schopenhauer's Compassion and Nietzsche's Pity', *Schopenhauer-Jahrbuch*, 69: 557–67.

CLARK, MAUDEMARIE (1990), *Nietzsche on Truth and Philosophy* (Cambridge: Cambridge University Press, 1990).

—— (1994), 'Nietzsche's Immoralism and the Concept of Morality', in Schacht (1994: 15–34).

—— (1997), 'From the Nietzsche Archive: Concerning the Aphorism Explicated in *Genealogy* III', *Journal of the History of Philosophy*, 35: 611–14.

—— (2001), 'On the Rejection of Morality: Bernard Williams's Debt to Nietzsche', in Richard Schacht (ed.), *Nietzsche's Post-Moralism: Essays on Nietzsche's Prelude to Philosophy's Future* (Cambridge: Cambridge University Press), 100–21.

—— and SWENSEN, ALAN J. (1998), *Friedrich Nietzsche: On the Genealogy of Morality*, trans. with introd. and notes (Indianapolis: Hackett).

CONWAY, DANIEL (2001), '*Wir Erkennenden*: Self-Referentiality in the Preface to *Zur Genealogie der Moral*', *Journal of Nietzsche Studies*, 22: 116–32.

COX, CHRISTOPH (1999), *Nietzsche: Naturalism and Interpretation* (Berkeley: University of California Press).

DANTO, ARTHUR C. (1965), *Nietzsche as Philosopher* (New York: Columbia University Press).

—— (1988), 'Some Remarks on *The Genealogy of Morals*', in Solomon and Higgins (1988: 13–28).

DENNETT, DANIEL (1995), *Darwin's Dangerous Idea: Evolution and the Meanings of Life* (New York: Simon and Schuster).

DERRIDA, JACQUES (1979), *Spurs: Nietzsche's Styles/Éperons: Les Styles de Nietzsche* (Chicago: University of Chicago Press).

DIETHE, CAROL (1994), 'review of Paul Patton (ed.), *Nietzsche, Feminism and Political Theory*', *Journal of Nietzsche Studies*, 8: 123–7.

—— (1996), *Nietzsche's Women: Beyond the Whip* (Berlin: Walter de Gruyter).

DONNELLAN, BRENDAN (1982), 'Friedrich Nietzsche and Paul Rée: Cooperation and Conflict', *Journal of the History of Ideas*, 43: 595–612.

DÜHRING, EUGEN (1865), *Der Werth des Lebens. Eine philosophische Betrachtung* (Breslau: Eduard Trewendt).

Foot, Philippa (1973), 'Nietzsche: The Revaluation of Values', in Solomon (1973: 156–68).

—— (2001), *Natural Goodness* (Oxford: Clarendon Press).

Foucault, Michel (1986), 'What Is an Author?', in Paul Rabinow (ed.), *The Foucault Reader* (Harmondsworth: Penguin), 101–20.

Freud, Sigmund (2002), 'On "Wild" Psychoanalysis', in Freud, *Wild Analysis* (London: Penguin Books), 3–9.

Gardner, Sebastian (forthcoming), 'Nietzsche, the Self, and the Disunity of Philosophical Reason', in Ken Gemes and Simon May (eds), *Nietzsche on Freedom and Autonomy* (Oxford: Oxford University Press).

Gemes, Ken (2001), 'Nietzsche's Critique of Truth', in Richardson and Leiter (2001: 40–58).

—— (2006a), 'Nietzsche on Free Will, Autonomy, and the Sovereign Individual', *Proceedings of the Aristotelian Society*, suppl. vol., 80: 321–38.

—— (2006b), ' "We Remain of Necessity Strangers to Ourselves": The Key Message of Nietzsche's *Genealogy*', in Christa Davis Acampora (ed.), *Nietzsche's On the Genealogy of Morals: Critical Essays* (Lanham, Md.: Rowman and Littlefield), 191–208.

Geuss, Raymond (2001), 'Nietzsche and Genealogy', in Richardson and Leiter (2001: 322–40).

Gibbard, Alan (1990), *Wise Choices, Apt Feelings: A Theory of Normative Judgement* (Oxford: Clarendon Press).

Gilman, Sander (ed.) (1987), *Conversations with Nietzsche: A Life in the Words of his Contemporaries* (Oxford: Oxford University Press).

Hamlyn, D. W. (1988), 'Eternal Justice', *Schopenhauer-Jahrbuch*, 69: 281–8.

Havas, Randall (1995), *Nietzsche's Genealogy: Nihilism and the Will to Knowledge* (Ithaca, NY: Cornell University Press).

—— (2000), 'Nietzsche's Idealism', *Journal of Nietzsche Studies*, 20: 90–9.

James, William (1967), 'The Will to Believe', in J. McDermott (ed.), *The Writings of William James* (Chicago: University of Chicago Press), 717–35.

Janaway, Christopher (1989), *Self and World in Schopenhauer's Philosophy* (Oxford: Clarendon Press).

—— (1996), 'Knowledge and Tranquility: Schopenhauer on the Value of Art', in Dale Jacquette (ed.), *Schopenhauer, Philosophy and the Arts* (Cambridge: Cambridge University Press), 39–61.

—— (1997a), 'Nietzsche's Illustration of the Art of Exegesis', *European Journal of Philosophy*, 5: 251–68.

—— (1997b), 'Kant's Aesthetics and the "Empty Cognitive Stock" ', *Philosophical Quarterly*, 47: 459–76.

——(ed.) (1998*a*), *Willing and Nothingness: Schopenhauer as Nietzsche's Educator* (Oxford: Oxford University Press).

——(1998*b*), 'Schopenhauer as Nietzsche's Educator', in Janaway (1998*a*: 13–36).

——(1999), 'Will and Nature', in Janaway (ed.), *The Cambridge Companion to Schopenhauer* (Cambridge: Cambridge University Press), 138–70.

——(2003), 'Disinterestedness and Objectivity: Nietzsche on Schopenhauer and Kant', *Studia Kantiana*, 4: 27–42.

——(2006), 'Naturalism and Genealogy', in Ansell Pearson (2006: 337–52).

KAHN, CHARLES (1979), *The Art and Thought of Heraclitus* (Cambridge: Cambridge University Press).

KANT, IMMANUEL (1998), *Critique of Pure Reason*, trans. Paul Guyer and Allen W. Wood (Cambridge: Cambridge University Press).

——(2000), *Critique of the Power of Judgement*, trans. Paul Guyer and Eric Matthews (Cambridge: Cambridge University Press).

KAUFMANN, WALTER (1974), *Nietzsche: Philosopher, Psychologist, Antichrist*, 4th edn (Princeton: Princeton University Press).

LAMARQUE, PETER (1990), 'The Death of the Author: An Analytical Autopsy', *British Journal of Aesthetics*, 40: 319–31.

LEITER, BRIAN (1994), 'Perspectivism in Nietzsche's *Genealogy of Morals*', in Schacht (1994: 334–57).

——(1998), 'The Paradox of Fatalism and Self-Creation in Nietzsche', in Janaway (1998*a*: 217–55).

——(2002), *Nietzsche on Morality* (London: Routledge).

LOEB, PAUL S. (2005), 'Finding the *Übermensch* in Nietzsche's *Genealogy of Morality*', *Journal of Nietzsche Studies*, 30: 70–101.

——(2006), 'Identity and Eternal Recurrence', in Ansell Pearson (2006: 171–88).

MAGNUS, BERND (1988*a*), 'Deification of the Commonplace: *Twilight of the Idols*', in Solomon and Higgins (1988: 152–81).

——(1988*b*), 'The Use and Abuse of *The Will to Power*', in Solomon and Higgins (1998: 218–35).

——MILEUR, J.-P., and STEWART, S. (1994), 'Reading Ascetic Reading: Toward the *Genealogy of Morals* and the Path Back to the World', in Schacht (1994: 376–426).

MANN, THOMAS (1959), 'Nietzsche's Philosophy in the Light of Recent History', trans. R. and C. Winston, in Mann, *Last Essays* (London: Secker and Warburg), 141–77.

MARSDEN, JILL (2006), 'Nietzsche and the Art of the Aphorism', in Ansell Pearson (2006: 22–37).

MAY, SIMON (1999), *Nietzsche's Ethics and his 'War on Morality'* (Oxford: Clarendon Press).

MONTINARI, MAZZINO (1982), 'Nietzsches Nachlaß von 1885 bis 1888 oder Textkritik und Wille zur Macht', in Montinari, *Nietzsche Lesen* (Berlin: Walter de Gruyter, 1982), 92–119.

MOORE, GREGORY (2002), *Nietzsche, Biology and Metaphor* (Cambridge: Cambridge University Press).

NEHAMAS, ALEXANDER (1985), *Nietzsche: Life as Literature* (Cambridge, Mass.: Harvard University Press).

—— (1998), *The Art of Living: Socratic Reflections from Plato to Foucault* (Berkeley: University of California Press).

OLIVER, KELLY (1993), 'A Dagger through the Heart: The Ethics of Reading Nietzsche's *On the Genealogy of Morals*', *International Studies in Philosophy*, 25: 13–28.

—— (1994), 'Nietzsche's Abjection', in Burgard (1994: 53–67).

—— (1995), *Womanizing Nietzsche: Philosophy's Relation to the 'Feminine'* (New York: Routledge).

OWEN, DAVID (2003) , 'Nietzsche, Re-evaluation and the Turn to Genealogy', *European Journal of Philosophy*, 11: 249–72.

—— and RIDLEY, AARON (2003), 'On Fate', *International Studies in Philosophy*, 35: 63–78.

PFEIFFER, ERNST (1970), *Friedrich Nietzsche Paul Rée Lou von Salomé. Die Dokumente ihrer Begegnung* (Frankfurt am Main: Insel Verlag).

PLATO (1992), *Republic*, trans. G. M. A. Grube, rev. C. D. C. Reeve (Indianapolis: Hackett).

PLOTNITSKY, A. (1994), 'The Medusa's Ears: The Question of Nietzsche, the Question of Gender, and Transformations of Theory', in Burgard (1994: 230–53).

POELLNER, PETER (1995), *Nietzsche and Metaphysics* (Oxford: Clarendon Press).

—— (2001), 'Perspectival Truth', in Richardson and Leiter (2001: 85–117).

RAWLS, JOHN (1971), *A Theory of Justice* (Cambridge, Mass.: Harvard University Press).

RÉE, PAUL (1877), *Der Ursprung der moralischen Empfindungen* (Chemnitz: Ernst Schmeitzner).

—— (1885), *Die Entstehung des Gewissens* (Berlin: Carl Duncker).

—— (2003), *Basic Writings*, ed. and trans. Robin Small (Urbana: University of Illinois Press).

REGINSTER, BERNARD (2000a), 'Nietzsche on Selflessness and the Value of Altruism', *History of Philosophy Quarterly*, 17: 177–200.

—— (2000b), 'Nietzsche's "Revaluation" of Altruism', *Nietzsche-Studien*, Jubiläumsband, 29: 199–219.

—— (2006), *The Affirmation of Life: Nietzsche on Overcoming Nihilism* (Cambridge, Mass.: Harvard University Press).

RICHARDSON, JOHN (1996), *Nietzsche's System* (New York: Oxford University Press).

—— (2002), 'Nietzsche contra Darwin', *Philosophy and Phenomenological Research*, 65: 537–75.

—— (2004), *Nietzsche's New Darwinism* (New York: Oxford University Press).

—— and LEITER, BRIAN (eds) (2001), *Nietzsche* (Oxford: Oxford University Press).

RICŒUR, PAUL (1969), *Le Conflit des interprétations* (Paris: Seuil).

RIDLEY, AARON (1997), 'Nietzsche's Greatest Weight', *Journal of Nietzsche Studies*, 14: 19–25.

—— (1998), *Nietzsche's Conscience* (Ithaca, NY: Cornell University Press).

—— (2000), 'Ancillary Thoughts on an Ancillary Test', *Journal of Nietzsche Studies*, 20: 100–8.

—— (2005a), 'Nietzsche and the Re-evaluation of Values', *Proceedings of the Aristotelian Society*, 105: 171–91.

—— (2005b), 'Guilt before God, or God before Guilt? The Second Essay of Nietzsche's *Genealogy*', *Journal of Nietzsche Studies*, 29: 35–45.

RISSE, MATHIAS (2001), 'The Second Treatise in *On the Genealogy of Morality*: Nietzsche on the Origin of the Bad Conscience', *European Journal of Philosophy*, 9: 55–81.

—— (2005), 'On God and Guilt: A Reply to Aaron Ridley', *Journal of Nietzsche Studies*, 29: 46–53.

SALAQUARDA, JÖRG (1996), 'Nietzsche and the Judaeo-Christian Tradition', in Bernd Magnus and Kathleen Higgins (eds), *The Cambridge Companion to Nietzsche* (Cambridge: Cambridge University Press), 90–118.

SANTANIELLO, WEAVER (1997), 'A Post-Holocaust Re-examination of Nietzsche and the Jews', in Jacob Golomb (ed.), *Nietzsche and Jewish Culture* (London: Routledge), 21–54.

SCHACHT, RICHARD (1983), *Nietzsche* (London: Routledge and Kegan Paul, 1983).

—— (ed.) (1994), *Nietzsche, Genealogy, Morality* (Berkeley: University of California Press).

SCHEIER, CLAUS-ARTUR (1994), 'The Rationale of Nietzsche's *Genealogy of Morals*', in Schacht (1994: 449–59).

SCHOPENHAUER, ARTHUR (1969), *The World as Will and Representation*, trans. E. F. J. Payne, 2 vols (New York: Dover).

SCHOPENHAUER, ARTHUR (1974), *Parerga and Paralipomena*, trans. E. F. J. Payne, 2 vols (Oxford: Clarendon Press).

—— (1977), *Werke in zehn Bänden*, ed. Arthur Hübscher, 10 vols (Zurich: Diogenes Verlag).

—— (1988), *Manuscript Remains*, i: *Early Manuscripts*, ed. Arthur Hübscher, trans. E. F. J. Payne (Oxford: Berg).

—— (1995), *On the Basis of Morality*, trans. E. F. J. Payne (Providence, RI: Berghahn Books).

—— (1999), *Prize Essay on the Freedom of the Will*, trans. E. F. J. Payne, ed. Günter Zöller (Cambridge: Cambridge University Press).

SILK, M. S., and STERN, J. P. (1981), *Nietzsche on Tragedy* (Cambridge: Cambridge University Press).

SIMMEL, GEORG (1986), *Schopenhauer and Nietzsche*, trans. Helmut Loiskandl, Deena Weinstein, and Michael Weinstein (Amherst: University of Massachusetts Press).

SMALL, ROBIN (2001), *Nietzsche in Context* (Aldershot: Ashgate).

—— (2003), 'Translator's Introduction', in Rée (2003, pp. xi–liii).

—— (2005), *Nietzsche and Rée: A Star Friendship* (Oxford: Clarendon Press).

SOLL, IVAN (1973), 'Reflections on Recurrence: A Re-examination of Nietzsche's Doctrine, *Die Ewige Wiederkehr des Gleichen*', in Solomon (1973: 339–42).

—— (1994), 'Nietzsche on Cruelty, Asceticism, and the Failure of Hedonism', in Schacht (1994: 168–92).

SOLOMON, ROBERT C. (ed.) (1973), *Nietzsche: A Collection of Critical Essays* (Garden City, NY: Doubleday).

—— and HIGGINS, KATHLEEN M. (eds) (1988), *Reading Nietzsche* (Oxford: Oxford University Press).

STATEN, HENRY (1990), *Nietzsche's Voice* (Ithaca, NY: Cornell University Press).

SWANTON, CHRISTINE (2003), *Virtue Ethics: A Pluralistic View* (Oxford: Oxford University Press).

TANNER, MICHAEL (1994), *Nietzsche* (Oxford: Oxford University Press).

THATCHER, DAVID S. (1989), 'Zur Genealogie der Moral: Some Textual Annotations', *Nietzsche-Studien*, 18: 587–99.

THIELE, LESLIE PAUL (1990), *Friedrich Nietzsche and the Politics of the Soul* (Princeton: Princeton University Press).

VENTURELLI, ALDO (1986), 'Asketismus und Wille zur Macht. Nietzsches Auseinandersetzung mit Eugen Dühring', *Nietzsche-Studien*, 15: 107–39.

VON TEVENAR, GUDRUN (2001), 'Pity and Compassion', Ph.D. thesis, University of London.

——(2007), 'Nietzsche's Objections to Pity and Compassion', in Gudrun von Tevenar (ed.), *Nietzsche and Ethics* (Oxford: Peter Lang AG), 265–81.

WAGNER, COSIMA (1978), *Diaries*, i: *1869–1977* (London: Collins).

WHITE, ALAN (1990), *Within Nietzsche's Labyrinth* (New York: Routledge).

WIGGINS, DAVID (1991), *Needs, Values, Truth*, 2nd edn (Oxford: Blackwell).

WILCOX, JOHN (1997), 'What Aphorism Does Nietzsche Explicate in *Genealogy of Morals*, Essay III?', *Journal of the History of Philosophy*, 35: 593–610.

——(1999), 'That Exegesis of an Aphorism in *Genealogy* III: Reflections on the Scholarship', *Nietzsche-Studien*, 27: 448–62.

WILLIAMS, BERNARD (1985), *Ethics and the Limits of Philosophy* (London: Fontana).

——(1993), *Shame and Necessity* (Berkeley: University of California Press).

——(1994), 'Nietzsche's Minimalist Moral Psychology', in Schacht (1994: 237–47).

——(2001), 'Introduction', in Nietzsche, *The Gay Science*, ed. Bernard Williams, trans. Josefine Nauckhoff, with poems trans. Adrian del Caro (Cambridge: Cambridge University Press), pp. vii–xxii.

YOUNG, JULIAN (1987), *Willing and Unwilling: A Study in the Philosophy of Arthur Schopenhauer* (Dordrecht: Martinus Nijhoff).

YOVEL, YIRMIYAHU (1994), 'Nietzsche, the Jews, and Ressentiment', in Schacht (1994: 214–36).

Index